COUP

COUP

The Day the Democrats Ousted Their Governor,

Put Republican Lamar Alexander in Office Early,

and Stopped a Pardon Scandal

by Keel Hunt

Vanderbilt University Press

Nashville

© 2013 by Vanderbilt University Press
Nashville, Tennessee 37235
All rights reserved
First printing 2013

This book is printed on acid-free paper.
Manufactured in the United States of America

Photo credits: All photos courtesy of Senator Lamar
Alexander; Sandy Campbell; Hal Hardin; Mike McWherter
and Ned McWherter, Weakley County Library, Dresden,
Tennessee; the Nashville Public Library, Nashville
Room, Special Collections—*Nashville Banner* Archives;
Tennessee Technological University *Eagle* yearbook, 1956;
the *Tennessean* Photo Library and John L. Seigenthaler,
Chairman Emeritus; and David Wilder.

Library of Congress Cataloging-in-Publication Data on file
LC control number 2012038290
LC classification F440.H86 2013
Dewey class number 976.8'05—dc23

ISBN 978-0-8265-1932-0 (cloth)
ISBN 978-0-8265-1934-4 (ebook)

What is most important of this grand experiment, the United States? Not the election of the first president, but the election of its second president. The peaceful transition of power is what will separate this country from every other country in the world.
—George Washington

For Marsha,

who gave me Shannon and Zach,

who gave us Olivia and Henry

CONTENTS

FOREWORD

The date: May 19, 1790. The New England sky, from Maine south
to New Jersey's border, gradually darkened and by noon was
like midnight—blanketed with a menacing ceiling of swirling,
low-hanging, black clouds. The sun, through the thick overcast,
appeared blood red. Rivers ran silted with a flakey, pitch-like
sediment.

People in the streets panicked. Many, fearful that the end of
the world was at hand, left their work to rush home to loved ones.
Others fell to their knees in prayer. In the Connecticut legislature,
there was near bedlam. Members cried out for immediate
adjournment. In the midst of it, Colonel Abraham Davenport
stood, demanding silence.

"I am against adjournment," he shouted, and the tumult died.
"The day of judgment," he declared "is either approaching—or it
is not."

"If it is," he said, "I choose to be found here, doing my duty."
He called for lighted candles, and the business of the government
went forward.

AS I READ AND REREAD the manuscript of *Coup*, by Keel Hunt, I was reminded, more than once, of the anecdote about Colonel Davenport, often
recited by John F. Kennedy during his 1960 presidential campaign. The
point of the future president's story was that in times of crisis, leaders must
stand with vision and courage against the clamor of the crowd.

It was 189 years and a thousand miles from that day in Hartford to a dark
day in Tennessee history when leaders in the state legislature faced a different sort of crisis, but one requiring the same vision and courage exemplified
by Colonel Davenport so long before.

The date: January 17, 1979, a morning when the weather was markedly
unlike that frantic day the New Englanders' world went black. (For a time it
was believed that an eclipse of the sun was responsible for that "dark day" in
Connecticut. More recently scientists have argued that a massive forest fire
in Canada was the cause of the furor.) The sun, this morning in Nashville,
peeked briefly from an overcast sky, then vanished as chilled rain began to
fall. All the while, the Cumberland River ran its choppy, brindle flow, un-
colored by the dusting of snow that fell about nightfall.

Tennesseans hoped the weather would warm by Saturday, when Lamar Alexander, a Republican, was scheduled to be sworn in as the state's forty-fifth governor, succeeding Ray Blanton, a Democrat.

Then, suddenly, at mid-morning on that damp, brisk Wednesday, a cloud of political corruption, invisible but palpable, enveloped the state capitol, threatening to spoil Alexander's carefully arranged inaugural plans.

For state officials at the highest level, it was a single, hellish "dark day" that must have seemed endless until, finally, it climaxed with what Keel Hunt calls the "coup." Honey Alexander, within hours of being Tennessee's first lady, remembers it as "the worst day of my life."

The individual stories of those government officials involved in the coup—each account unique, but all of them intersecting—were scattered like disconnected pieces of a jigsaw puzzle on the table of history until the author conceived this book. Perhaps because it happened so quickly, and without major disagreement, protest, or dissent, this truly historic moment has been buried in the public mind. In unearthing the drama in gripping detail, Keel Hunt assures that the "dark day" will be remembered as a bright one in which conflicted politicians came together in the public interest.

For weeks before that day, there had been a flow of news reports and political rumors about dishonesty at the core of the incumbent Blanton administration. Journalists had been referring to it as the pay-for-pardons scandal, in which cash changed hands to win executive clemency for convicts, some of them murderers and rapists.

In December, there had been the shocking spectacle of the governor's legal counsel and two other close Blanton aides caught in an FBI sting linked to the corruption. There had been video-taped evidence that marked money had been paid to Blanton's legal counsel in return for the release of a notorious criminal. Federal agents arrested the governor's lawyer in his office in the capitol building, after finding some of the marked bills in his pocket.

Then on Monday night, January 15, five days before the scheduled end of his term, Blanton publicly acknowledged that he had, indeed, signed pardons and clemency documents that would free fifty-two inmates, some of them sentenced to long terms for violent crimes.

The governor denied that he had taken cash for clemency and claimed he had acted because a court had found prison conditions overcrowded. (After his term ended, Blanton eventually went to prison but not for selling prison pardons. He was convicted for accepting money from a businessman for whom he had approved liquor store licenses.) Although the public had no hint of it, the FBI had evidence that thirteen more convicted criminals were to be released immediately. Nor was it known that additional documents had been prepared for Blanton's signature for the release of at least twenty-eight more convicts before Saturday.

A sense of frustration and disgust gripped the leadership of the Tennessee legislature. Ned McWherter, the house speaker, felt it. So did John Wilder, the lieutenant governor, who presided over the Senate. As public angst grew with each daily news report of the venality, McWherter and Wilder felt paralyzed and powerless. They were close to Blanton, their fellow West Tennessean and fellow Democrat, but distressed by his conduct.

The state constitution was plain. The governor had the sole power to pardon. The constitution stated clearly that the only way to remove a governor for malfeasance was by impeachment—a tedious process that could take weeks, perhaps months. Bill Leech, the state attorney general, also a Democrat, whose job it was to officially advise the legislature on legal matters, felt the same sense of disillusionment and impotency.

Some six blocks away from the capitol, Hal Hardin, the US attorney, had every reason to share the sentiments of Leech, Wilder, and McWherter. Almost four years earlier, Hardin had been the first state judge Governor Blanton had appointed to the bench. Now, having left his judicial post, he was the chief federal law enforcement officer in Middle Tennessee, appointed by the president of the United States. He had direct access to the FBI's intelligence.

With each passing minute that morning, Hardin lived with the fear that still other violent criminals would be loosed on the streets. Like McWherter, Wilder, and Leech, Hardin was a Democrat. Like them, he considered the governor's prison pardon binge a betrayal of public trust. Unlike them, Hardin was a *federal* employee, with no authority, jurisdiction, or business stopping the actions of the state's governor. Still, Hardin knew, as the other Democrats in office knew, that what was happening was wrong—criminally, morally, and politically wrong.

As Lamar Alexander awoke that Wednesday morning, he was aware (although not nearly as tuned-in to the capitol hill rumor mill as Ned McWherter, John Wilder, and Bill Leech) of the dilemma his administration would have to face in a few days. He had no idea that he would be governor before the day was over. He had kept abreast of the press reports on Blanton's actions. He understood, as the public did, that there was wrongdoing afoot. For the moment that morning, the governor-elect could take satisfaction from the knowledge that by week's end he would have the power to lead a new administration that would bring an end to this disgraceful administration.

Alexander could not erase or reverse Blanton's constitutional pardoning power. The criminals Blanton let go would remain at large, unless and until convicted of some future crime. For now, the governor-elect could only focus on polishing his Saturday inaugural speech, and focus on the celebrative aspects of the occasion.

So the state faced a crisis, unprecedented in its history. No Tennessee governor, surrounded by scandal, had left office before the end of his term since Sam Houston voluntarily resigned in 1829 in the midst of a domestic relations controversy in which his wife, Eliza Allen, had abruptly deserted him in the midst of his reelection campaign. Poor Houston quit and promptly left the state. But this was a different time, a different century, a different situation. Blanton was not about to voluntarily walk away or surrender his power to pardon.

And so the coup occurred. It is hard to imagine, in this time of harshly divisive political partisanship, that Democrat and Republican leaders could come together—and act together—to find creative and responsible answers to the legal and constitutional crisis that confronted their state. But here they did, and in the course of a single, action-filled day they stopped the stampede of criminals from the state penitentiary—without offending the constitution.

This account of how and why they did it is the story Keel Hunt was never able to write during his decade as a professional journalist because it had not yet happened. Trained as a reporter and editor, he had left the *Tennessean* (where I was the editor) in 1977 to work for Lamar Alexander's campaign for governor. He was posited on the periphery of the events that "dark day" in January 1979—but was not close to the action. As he has written, that day he was teaching a class at Vanderbilt University, unaware like most Tennesseans of the tumultuous behind-the-scenes events that were shaking the foundations of state government.

It was late that day before he learned what had happened. This, then, is a story he has lived with, untold, for more than three decades. As readers of *Coup* will find, Keel is a gifted storyteller and a skillful interviewer. Because of it, the buried past is resurrected; the skeletal sketch I have briefly outlined here is disinterred, brought to life, given factual flesh in depth and fascinating detail. What has been a footnote to the history of the Blanton and Alexander administrations becomes a real-life drama with each of the players reading from a different script. It is a tragedy in which each of the performers changes his mind at least once during the crucial hours. Small wonder that Honey Alexander asked at one point, "Why can't somebody make up his mind?"

It begins with Hal Hardin deciding not to act as a federal official, declining to telephone his superior, Attorney General Griffin Bell in Washington, and acting instead as a citizen. He telephoned the governor-elect, and then the state officials, pleading with all of them to "do something" to stop the incumbent governor. Initially, not one of the state leaders thought he had the power to do what Hardin asked. And, Keel explains, for partisan reasons, they all were resolved *not* to act. Only legal research and reasoning finally moved them, across party lines, to change their points of view. They discovered, as the day of decision wore on, that they had the power to act—and that duty required the vision and courage to do so.

Keel Hunt has said to readers that he is not an academician or a historian. No matter. His book enriches history and reminds us again that in a time of crisis, on a dark day in Tennessee, there were politicians who were willing to act with courage and vision, across party lines, in the public interest.

John L. Seigenthaler
June 2012

COUP

CHAPTER 1

The Stranger

A LIGHT RAIN WAS falling on the small town square, at the end of the day on a Friday, when the man in the flowery green shirt appeared. He was holding a cigar in his hand.

He entered the door off the sidewalk on East Main Street, next to the Davis Dress Shop, and climbed the stairs to the law office on the second floor. He opened the office door, and the stale smell of the cigar moved with him into the small suite.

Inside he found attorney Jack Lowery alone, standing at the desk of his secretary Gail Crook, talking on the telephone. She had departed for the weekend just minutes before. Seeing the unscheduled visitor, Lowery put the phone down and greeted him.

The stranger introduced himself as "Bob Roundtree," but this was a lie. And the brief conversation that followed is how the world began to unravel for Governor Ray Blanton and his circle.

JACK LOWERY WAS A well-known figure in Lebanon, Tennessee, twenty miles east of downtown Nashville. He was also known at the state capitol.

To pay his way through Cumberland School of Law, he had once worked as a police officer in the town. He was elected to a term in the state legislature in 1966. Ten years later, on the day "Bob Roundtree" came briefly into his life, Lowery was a solo practitioner, with mainly a criminal defense practice. He was also Lebanon's part-time mayor.

The windows on the west side of Lowery's corner office overlooked the Lebanon town square. From his office he could see, in the middle of the square, the monumental statue of the Confederate general Robert H. Hatton, called the "Reluctant Rebel," killed in the Battle of Fair Oaks, Virginia, in 1862. Like Lowery, Hatton had been a graduate of the Cumberland School of Law, a successful lawyer in Lebanon, and a legislator in Nashville. His statue on the square faces south.

At this time—May 1976—Lowery had a client named Will Midgett, from nearby Watertown. Midgett had been convicted of second-degree murder in the death of a motorist. He was now serving his sentence in the state prison at Nashville.

"His family had prevailed on me to see if I could get executive clemency for him," Lowery told me. "I of course spoke to Eddie Sisk [Blanton's legal counsel] about it, because the governor would have to approve an executive clemency. I went and got the medical proof, the judge didn't object, and I filed all this information. Mr. Midgett said that if he got out, he would move to Florida. I delivered the information to Marie Ragghianti (then the staff extradition officer) because she was Eddie Sisk's right-hand girl.

"A few days later, a gentleman showed up in my office, late in the afternoon after my secretary left. He was wearing a green Hawaiian shirt, and smoking a cigar. Said his name was Roundtree."

Lowery recalled the following conversation.

ROUNDTREE: I need to speak to you. I believe I can help you.
LOWERY: What do you mean?
ROUNDTREE: I can tell you the terms of his release, when he'll be released, and he won't have to go to Florida.
[At this point, "Mr. Roundtree" also stated that his fee would be $20,000.]
LOWERY: I'll call you.
ROUNDTREE: No. I'll call you.

The stranger departed. Lowery moved to his west window overlooking the parking area, and he observed the man leave the building and get into the rear seat of a black sedan.

LOWERY SAID THE STRANGER'S mention of Florida "surprised" him "because nobody had that information, so I knew this man who had nothing to do with the state somehow had access to the file."

"I watched him get into a black Chrysler Cordova," Lowery told me. "I couldn't see the whole license plate, but I saw the number started with a '4' so I knew that meant the car was from Chattanooga. I was mayor at the time. I called the police chief, Royal Jones, and said we have to stop this car."

The vehicle from Chattanooga was stopped in Murfreesboro, south of Lebanon.

"In the car with this guy were two individuals who had robbed and kidnapped a banker in Georgia, and Georgia had been trying to extradite these two guys for over a year. Tennessee had not extradited these guys. I didn't know that information at the time, but learned it later."

Lowery said he reported the encounter to the district attorney, Tommy

Thompson, telling him, "I think it's a criminal act, so log the call." He said he phoned Ragghianti the next day and recalled that she expressed shock when he recounted the conversation, especially Roundtree's mention of the Florida detail. He says Ragghianti made the comment: "Oh, my God, I don't know how high up this goes." He never heard from "Roundtree" again. But Sisk phoned him two days later, asking about the encounter and the mysterious visitor. This conversation was brief.

"The guy [Roundtree] didn't call me back," Lowery remembered. "I did get a call from Eddie Sisk, at my house, on a Sunday night. Eddie says, 'Will you work with the TBI?' (Tennessee Bureau of Investigation)."

"I said, 'I just want my man Midgett out of jail.' Eddie asked me to write up a summary. I did, and I delivered it to Ragghianti."

Agents of the FBI later questioned Lowery about the incident and also asked him about his written report to Ragghianti. Apparently she had shown the report to an assistant US attorney, who had turned it over to the FBI.

Fifteen months later, in August 1977, Governor Blanton fired Marie Ragghianti as chairman of the Board of Pardon and Paroles.

Four years later, in 1981, Jack Lowery would testify in federal court about his late afternoon encounter with the cigar-smoking stranger. This sensational federal court trial put the governor's counsel, Eddie Sisk, and an accomplice behind bars for selling pardons for cash.

CHAPTER 2

The Sharecropper's Son
and Nixon's Choirboy

Most men are a little better than their circumstances
give them a chance to be.
—William Faulkner, *Go Down, Moses*

RAY BLANTON LIKED TO TELL his constituents that he was born "dirt-poor" in the cotton fields of West Tennessee, and this familiar story was true.

His birth, in 1930, came at the toughest of times for the American economy and for most American families, but Ray's father, Leonard, was resourceful. The Blanton family got by on hard work, love, and modest means. Leonard was a sharecropper and also worked on construction jobs in the area, when he could find them. Ray was one of three children, and the house the family lived in at this time, near the site of the Battle of Shiloh, was less than modest.

"I can remember visiting their home in Adamsville," his lifelong friend Shorty Freeland recalled years later. "There were cracks in the floor, and you could see the chickens underneath there. They would move one of the boards sometimes, and you reach under there and get eggs from a hen that just laid."

The combination of farming and construction jobs sustained the hard-working Blantons. In time Leonard established a family construction business that he named B&B Construction Company (for Blanton and Blanton), and over the next decade the enterprise began to grow on the strength of government building projects, chiefly road work for the counties and the state highway department. This was competitive work, highly prized among builders across the rural South, and it required good relations with public officials. That, in turn, stirred the father's suggestion that Ray consider becoming a politician himself. It could be good for business.

By now Blanton had worked his way through college, at the University of Tennessee at Martin. He was a handsome man, with wavy, dark hair above a high forehead, and he wore his sideburns moderately long in the style of the day. His handshake was sure, his winning smile easy, his dark eyes engaging. In his first campaign, in 1964, he ran for a seat in the Tennessee House of Representatives.

He proved to be a tireless campaigner. He enjoyed rising early, working late, and the long hours of small talk, listening, and handshaking on the town squares, and he won this first election.

As a freshman member, Blanton's desk was on the back row of the large house chamber. His biographical entry in *The Tennessee Encyclopedia of History and Culture* states that in his early service Blanton "distinguished himself by his habit of sitting in the back of the chamber, wearing his sunglasses, and observing the proceedings." But in the evenings he would ask administration officials—usually Harlan Mathews, then head of the Department of Finance and Administration, and Mathews' deputy, Tom Benson—to help him understand the proposed legislation.

"I first met Blanton when he came to the legislature," Benson remembered. "He would come downstairs almost every night to Harlan's office and ask us to explain to him how the bills worked. He was bright. He would ask good, intelligent questions about what the bills would accomplish. About half the time, he would offer to buy us dinner."

Blanton served only one two-year term in the state legislature. He gave up his seat in 1966, when he spotted an opportunity to run for Congress, challenging Congressman Tom Murray, a twelve-term incumbent in the Seventh District. Blanton defeated Murray in an upset and would go on to serve three more terms.

His time in Congress came to an end following the 1970 census, when the legislature combined his district with that of the popular congressman Ed Jones. Blanton bowed out. In 1972, he ran instead for the US Senate, challenging another incumbent, Senator Howard H. Baker Jr. Blanton won the Democratic nomination but lost badly to Baker in the November general election.

In all these campaigns, Blanton cultivated the same homespun and populist profile he had in 1964. He did the same when he ran for governor in 1974.

IN 1940, LAMAR ALEXANDER was born in Maryville to an elementary-school principal and a kindergarten teacher.

A *New York Times* reporter once wrote that Alexander "had grown up in a lower middle class family in the mountains of Tennessee." This description did not sit well with Flo Alexander, his mother, who considered the *Times* comment a slur on her family. When her son called home the next week, she was reading *Thessalonians* for strength.

"We never thought of ourselves that way," she told him. "You had a library card from the day you were three and music lessons from the day you were four. You had everything you needed that was important."

While both Blanton and Alexander grew up modestly, there was one major cultural difference. Blanton sprouted from the heartland of the Confederacy in West Tennessee, which had voted Democratic since Reconstruction. Alexander had descended from Lincolnites, East Tennessee mountaineers loyal to the Union. His great grandfather, when asked about his politics, said, "I'm a Republican. I fought for the union and I vote like I shot." The Second Congressional District, in which Alexander grew up, has not elected a Democrat to Congress since Abraham Lincoln was president.

But like Blanton, Alexander learned to work at an early age. He recalled that when he was ten the alarm clock was set to ring at four each morning. He pulled on jeans, tennis shoes, and a flannel shirt, stepped carefully down the squeaky stairs so as not to wake his sisters, raced on his bicycle to Broadway Food Market, and picked up seventy-five copies of the *Knoxville Journal*. He threw them onto porches one by one. By 5:00 a.m. he had crawled back into bed for another hour's sleep.

He was up again at six to practice the piano because this left his afternoons free for sports. He played the piano well enough to win superior ratings each year at music festivals, and as a high school student he won two state piano competitions. Piano playing, he said, taught him to practice, to be prepared, and to "play the piece just a little slower than you CAN play it."

Alexander was fair-haired, lean, and popular. He was elected class president three times and sang in the choir at New Providence Presbyterian Church. In 1957, he attended the American Legion's Volunteer Boys State, an intensive summer week of civic leadership training then held at Castle Heights Military Academy in Lebanon, Tennessee. The other delegates elected him their governor—by a landslide of three votes—and Tennessee governor Frank Clement spoke at the inauguration, exhorting the teenagers that "someday one of you boys will grow up to be the real governor of Tennessee." In his inaugural address Alexander, sixteen, defended the state's right-to-work law, called for lowering the voting age to eighteen, and urged civil rights for all races. This was the year President Eisenhower sent paratroopers into Arkansas to desegregate Little Rock's Central High School.

Alexander earned scholarships to Vanderbilt University, where he became president of Sigma Chi, helped set a school record in the four-hundred-yard relay, and edited the student newspaper, the *Hustler*. In 1962, as sit-in demonstrations mounted in downtown Nashville, his *Hustler* editorials chastised Vanderbilt administrators for refusing to admit blacks to the undergraduate college. This helped to provoke a campus referendum—in which students voted *not* to desegregate—but the controversy succeeded in forcing the Vanderbilt Board of Trust to open the university to African Americans later that year. (Not all Alexander's editorials were so serious; in another opinion piece, he recommended that Vanderbilt cheerleaders be attired in "good and short skirts.")

He earned honors in Latin American studies and joined Phi Beta Kappa. At age twenty-one he traveled to Paraguay, Peru, Chile, Bolivia, Argentina, and Brazil in a group of a dozen students from other college campuses, a six-week excursion organized by the National Student Association. (He later wondered if the trip had been sponsored by the CIA.) He was impressed with the student demonstrations he observed. Another member of the group, Duke student Karen Hanke Weeks of St. Louis, remembers the pro-democracy demonstrations as "transformative. Che Guevara was running all over South America urging revolution."

Vanderbilt nominated Alexander for a Rhodes Scholarship, and he was selected as one of Tennessee's two candidates but was rejected by the regional selection board. Instead, he accepted a Root-Tilden Scholarship to New York University law school. When he arrived in Greenwich Village in September 1962 (his first visit ever to New York City), he met another Root-Tilden Scholar in the registration line: a former Georgetown University basketball captain named Paul Tagliabue, later the commissioner of the National Football League. Alexander learned that Tagliabue had also been rejected by the Rhodes committee. The two young men became roommates and lifelong friends.

After law school, Alexander became law clerk to federal judge John Minor Wisdom of the Fifth Circuit Court of Appeals in New Orleans. Actually, he was Judge Wisdom's messenger, but the distinguished jurist agreed to treat the young man as if he were a law clerk. The messenger's salary was only $300 per month. To make ends meet Alexander played trombone, washboard, and tuba at night in a banjo band on Bourbon Street at a club called Your Father's Mustache. (Ten years later, his memory of that banjo band would give Alexander an idea that would become an important part of his campaign for governor of Tennessee.)

He returned to Tennessee following the New Orleans clerkship and worked in Baker's 1966 Senate campaign, first as a volunteer and later as a paid staff member. For the next few months, he lived with his parents at 121 Ruth Street in Maryville, "although my mother made it clear if I stayed longer than 2–3 months I would be paying rent." Baker won by more than a hundred thousand votes and became the first Republican popularly elected from Tennessee. After the election, Alexander worked for a Knoxville law firm for a couple of months, then drove his 1966 Ford Mustang to Washington, DC, to joined Baker's staff. He became the senator's legislative assistant in January 1967.

BLANTON AND ALEXANDER THUS ARRIVED in Washington in the same month of the same year—January 1967—but they did not meet at this point.

Their respective jobs generally kept them separated on opposite ends of the US Capitol building, Blanton beginning his first term as congressman from Tennessee's Seventh District, Alexander working for Baker, the Republican junior senator.

They would meet, in earnest, seven years later.

TOM INGRAM GREW UP in a strict Church of Christ family, and at David Lipscomb College in Nashville he studied to be a social worker. While an undergraduate, and to help pay his Lipscomb tuition, he became a campus correspondent for the Democratic *Nashville Tennessean*.

In the fall of 1966, Ingram was assigned to cover the US Senate campaign of the Republican nominee, Howard Baker. This was unprecedented inasmuch as the *Tennessean* was then known for attacking, not just covering, Republican candidates. The appearance of fair coverage in the Democratic daily probably caused some voters in Middle Tennessee to open their minds to Baker, the young Knoxville attorney, who was seeking to be the first Republican senator ever elected from Tennessee.

Ingram, then twenty-one, was riding on the Baker campaign bus when he met a Baker aide, Lamar Alexander, then twenty-five. Both remember that the long bus rides afforded time for conversations, and the two young men became well acquainted.

When Alexander ran for governor in 1974, he recruited Ingram as his campaign press secretary.

IN THE STEAMY SUMMER OF 1974, the race for governor in Tennessee drew sixteen contestants, including Blanton and Alexander. A total of twelve Democrats and four Republicans sought their respective party nominations this year, and in the languid months leading to primary day, in the heat of early August, each party confronted its own demons.

The challenge to any of the dozen Democratic candidates would lay precisely in the complications of that large number—twelve primary hopefuls on the August ballot. Tennessee had no constitutional or legal provision in its election laws for a run-off vote if anyone garnered less than 50 percent. This meant the winner needed only a plurality, not a majority, and in such a large cohort the prospect of any one candidate polling over half would be a virtual impossibility considering there was no single breakout personality in the crowded field.

The bane of Republicans, meanwhile, was not numbers but Nixon. The fresh memory of the 1972 Watergate break-in and the ensuing two years of continuing investigations, scandals, revelations, and trials—all very public on the nightly television news—still darkened the civic landscape all across America, everywhere roiling and embarrassing the GOP's politics.

This 1974 race for governor was also shaped by two statewide elections that preceded it, in 1966 and 1970. In short, Democrats in Tennessee, in 1974, were now scrambling to retake control of the state capitol.

By 1970, the Democrats—the party of Andrew Jackson—were no longer in power in Tennessee. They had lost the governor's office that year when Dr. Winfield Dunn, an affable Memphis dentist and a local GOP leader in Shelby County, had defeated colorful Nashville lawyer John Jay Hooker. This had been Hooker's second defeat in a statewide race. Four years earlier, in 1966, he had lost a bitter Democratic primary battle to the former governor Buford Ellington. (At this time, Tennessee governors were constitutionally limited to serving only one term in succession. From 1952 to 1970, in what pundits called "leap-frog" administrations, Ellington had alternated terms with Governor Frank G. Clement. After Clement died in 1969, and with Ellington term-limited, this regime came to an end with Dunn's election in 1970.)

Dunn was reared in Meridian, Mississippi, and his victory in the 1970 GOP primary was a surprise for a number of reasons to many, starting with virtually all the senior Republicans in the state. In some important respects, Dunn was a natural on the campaign stump. He was the son of a Mississippi congressman, Aubert Culberson Dunn, and had therefore lived in Washington, DC, with his parents in his youth. He was a faithful conservative and also an attractive, articulate speaker, but he was otherwise a political neophyte when it came suddenly to mounting a statewide campaign for governor.

He and his wife, Betty, had been friends with several other prominent Memphis couples, including Lewis and Jan Donelson, and this network of social relationships soon became the core of an ambitious political organization. Donelson's earlier efforts to establish a true two-party system in the county had been effectively stymied by E. H. (Boss) Crump, the longtime Democratic machine kingpin in Memphis. But the Donelsons and the Dunns—together with Congressman Dan Kuykendall and attorney Harry Wellford and their wives—persevered in their pioneering work. Dunn soon agreed to be chairman of the Republican organization in Shelby County.

The development of this nascent GOP structure in the largest city of West

Tennessee meant that Republicans now had bases in two regions of the state, not one. This contributed to the election, in 1966, of the East Tennessean Howard Baker to the US Senate, and his victory would in turn aid Republicans in the statewide elections of 1970.

In the early spring of 1970, with the encouragement of Wellford and others, Dunn decided to run for governor. No Republican had been elected governor in Tennessee in fifty years, but now the political landscape looked promising. Nixon was less than a year into his first term as president, Baker about midway through his first term in the Senate, and with Governor Clement's death, the leap-frog Democratic regime controlling state government had come to its natural end. The Republican field might even be competitive in 1970, but also no one was emerging with an established statewide political base nor even name recognition outside his own intrastate region.

Of the five Republicans who ran that year, the best known was the Nashville businessman W. Maxey Jarman. He had never been a candidate himself, but he was now retiring as chairman and chief executive of Genesco (formerly General Shoe Company), maker of the Jarman shoe and other popular brands. Under his direction, Genesco had expanded rapidly—acquiring a number of high-profile retailers including Bonwit Teller, Henri Bendel, and S. H. Kress—and was now the largest apparel company in the world. Its position as a leading employer in Middle Tennessee also positioned Jarman to be a civic leader in Nashville. He was also a devout Baptist and a prominent lay figure in the Southern Baptist Convention, headquartered in Nashville.

For his political steerage, Jarman relied on two other businessmen, Genesco executive Ben R. Murphy and John Hazelton, a stock broker with J. C. Bradford Company.

"In the beginning, Maxey viewed Winfield as just a dentist, and he thought a dentist was not going to be able to amass very many votes" Murphy told me. "As time went on, he began to see that Winfield was getting a lot of positive attention, so he changed his mind. He then called Winfield to come to Nashville to meet with him, and Winfield did come, but Maxey was a little late on that. If he'd done it a few months earlier, it might have made a difference." On at least two occasions, Jarman tried to persuade Dunn to drop out, describing his own preparations for a successful campaign and arguing that Dunn's candidacy would likely split the party vote among Middle and West Tennesseans, thus ensuring a victory for one of the East Tennessee candidates. Dunn was not persuaded. At the Nashville meeting, in a room at the Airport Hilton, Hazelton accompanied Jarman, and Dunn arrived with Kuykendall and Wellford. After lengthy discussion with no agreement, Hazelton slammed his fist on a table and shouted, "Dammit, Winfield, get out!"

"About that time," Dunn recalled in his autobiography, "we all figured the meeting was over. I responded that I was in the race to stay. We said good-bye. I don't recall further conversation among my group as we journeyed back to Memphis, but I am certain we felt we had done what we had to do under the circumstances."

In the campaign that followed, Dunn reminded audiences that Jarman had been a contributor to Robert F. Kennedy for president in 1968. The year before that, Jarman had publicly endorsed legalizing liquor-by-the-drink sales in Nashville in a local referendum campaign. Either of those positions probably cost him votes among conservatives in Middle Tennessee.

On August 6, 1970, a total of 244,999 votes were cast statewide in the Republican primary. Dunn received a full third of these in the five-man race—collecting 81,475 votes—and won the nomination. Jarman finished in second place, trailing the Memphis dentist by 11,055 votes. This outcome surprised most of the nominal Republican establishment outside Memphis, and it made visible the party's ascendance statewide.

It also set up a general election contest between Dunn and Hooker that would mark a turning point in the evolution of politics in Tennessee.

BOTH HOOKER AND DUNN, each an unlikely nominee for those different reasons, now needed serious organizational help for their fall campaigns. Two bright young lawyers stepped into the picture.

Dunn, through Wellford, reached out to Lamar Alexander, a young attorney now working in Washington, DC, to be his campaign manager for the general election campaign. A native of Maryville, Tennessee, Alexander had been a young member of Baker's Senate staff in Washington, soon after finishing law school at New York University. He had first become legislative director on the senator's Washington staff and was now working at the White House, reporting to President Richard Nixon's chief congressional liaison, Bryce Harlow. At about the time Wellford phoned him from Memphis, in August 1970, Alexander said Harlow was actually advising him against becoming a career Washingtonian.

"I was ready to come back to Tennessee and was encouraged to do so by Bryce Harlow," Alexander remembered. "He said, 'If you're gonna go back, you better go now, because Washington has a way of capturing you and you'll never go home.' That's what had happened to him, he told me. He'd come from Oklahoma to work for General Marshall, and he never went home. The second reason he encouraged me, I think, was he had a whiff of the kind of behavior in the White House that lead to Watergate, and he didn't want me involved in it."

When Winfield Dunn surprised the world by winning the Republican nomination for governor, in early August of 1970, he was a spectacular candidate but totally unprepared for a general election. That's not surprising because Republicans had never won a statewide campaign for governor—not even when Roy Acuff ran in 1948—since 1920 in the Harding sweep.

"Harry Wellford called me at the White House in early August and asked me if I'd like to come home and become the campaign manager. I said, 'I would like to come home, and yes.' I wasn't about to go by myself, so I recruited half of Howard Baker's staff to help me—which included Lee Smith, his legislative assistant, and Ralph Griffith, his press secretary. Sandy Beall and Sam Furrow came from Knoxville, and we all arrived in Nashville in late August.

"Senator Baker was surprised by that, and a little upset, because he had a pretty good relationship with John Jay Hooker. When I talked to him about it, he said, 'I have one word for you: *Win*'—because it put his reputation on the line. He was surprised by it. That's what he didn't like. He and Winfield were very close. He was strong for Winfield. But it was his staff that I was recruiting. He probably thought I should have come talk to him before I recruited them. He was fine with it. He just said, 'You better win' because, after all, he was up for reelection in two years. It was a state that was heavily Democratic, and if I didn't win he would have had a very unhappy Democratic governor working against him.

"The campaign only lasted two months, about eight weeks. Here we were—a bunch of kids—with no money, no organization, no advertising agency, and a candidate with a great personality but who'd never been elected to anything. We opened the Dunn headquarters at about Labor Day of 1970. We ran a campaign to save the state from John Jay Hooker."

HOOKER CHOSE BILL WILLIS, another young lawyer, to be his campaign manager. They had been friends, law partners, and fellow advisers to the publisher and editor of the *Nashville Tennessean*.

Willis and Alexander, both whip-smart and politically savvy, charted competitive campaigns that were technically smart. The first shot was Hooker's challenge to Dunn to meet him in a series of debates. Dunn's campaign team thought they were doing well enough without debates and did not want to do anything that might help Hooker interrupt their candidate's momentum. Alexander said his side knew they would have to agree to debates in some form but hoped to make them as insignificant as possible. He and Willis, meanwhile, agreed to meet for breakfast once a week in Nashville and, in the process, became good friends.

"We eventually agreed on a plan to have all the debates on one day, in October, in the middle of the week" Alexander remembered. "The day began at Rolling Mill Hill with an early morning debate at the garbage dump in

Nashville. The *Tennessean* reported there were women there for Dunn from Belle Meade wearing mink coats. Then we went to the Robertson County courthouse in Springfield, for a midday debate, and in the late afternoon we were in Jackson—and it was all over. Willis and I had agreed that Chris Clark, the anchorman for Channel 5, would be a fair and unbiased moderator, so he moderated the three debates.

"They made some news, but not nearly as much as they would have if they'd been on prime time on consecutive nights."

But in the end, it was Hooker's abandonment by the Democratic regulars and his own eccentricities that combined to defeat him. The establishment Democrats who had supported Ellington over Hooker, in 1966, still disdained the Nashville lawyer's center-left views and his Kennedy connections.

Hooker's own personal style had not helped him, either. After winning the primary vote in early August, he visited Governor Ellington in his office at the capitol, a common political courtesy and a show of respect to the titular head of the party. But the visit soured as soon as Hooker sat down. When he took his seat, Hooker leaned back and inelegantly put both his feet on the governor's desk, looked around the room, and said, "I think I'm gonna like this place." Ellington, feeling an insult and already having no reserve of kindness for the brash younger man, said little more. The meeting soon ended.

This scene is still credited, by the Democratic activists who remember it, as having sealed Hooker's fate. Ellington, already dismissive of Hooker for challenging him in the 1966 primary, now proceeded quietly to throw his support to Dunn.

ACROSS THE REGION, this turning away from moderate Democrats would also manifest most spectacularly in President Nixon's "southern strategy" to control Congress, a campaign that did oust Tennessee's Senator Albert Gore Sr. in 1970. (Gore, father of the future vice president Al Gore Jr., had been one of only three senators from the former Confederate states who had not signed the 1956 "Southern Manifesto" opposing integration. Gore's fellow Tennessee senator, Estes Kefauver, who died in 1963, had also refused to sign.) The elder Gore lost this election to Bill Brock, the Republican congressman of Chattanooga. Vice President Spiro Agnew campaigned for Brock, characterizing Gore as "the southern regional chairman of the eastern liberal establishment."

During this period, there was little ideological daylight separating the conservative establishment Democrats in Tennessee and the ascendant Republicans in the east and west counties. Reaction to the rising social issues across the country—especially school desegregation, but also other elements of the Great Society—had provided common ground to many conservative southern Democrats, Republicans, and independents.

IN HIS 2007 AUTOBIOGRAPHY, Dunn recalled a visit soon after the 1970 primary with Ellington's commissioner of safety, Claude Armour.

There was no more stalwart a Democrat and Clement-Ellington ally than Armour, and the message he conveyed to the Republican nominee was significant. He told Dunn he wanted to give him his personal endorsement and would do so publicly. He also shared with Dunn that he had offered to resign his current cabinet post in the Ellington administration, but that Governor Ellington himself had told him that would not be necessary.

"That position on the part of the governor," Dunn wrote of Ellington, "told us that he had no intention of endorsing my opponent, his fellow Democrat, John Hooker. I accepted Armour's support, and we immediately made plans to announce the good news." Dunn and Armour appeared together before reporters on September 28.

The signal from Ellington via Armour was only the first of several endorsements and other supportive actions from Democratic regulars that benefited Dunn that fall. Lee Smith, Dunn's political director in the 1970 campaign, told me one of his routine challenges following the August primary was to choose county campaign chairmen from a newly expanded field of hopefuls—between long-term Republican leaders well-known to Dunn, and new friends from the Ellington faction of the Democratic establishment.

Ellington's choice to abandon Hooker, while only semiprivate, proved to be lethal to the Hooker campaign. In November, Dunn was victorious on the double strength of an emerging Republican base and the votes of anti-Hooker Democrats. Dunn thus became the first Tennessee governor elected from his party in half a century.

The Dunn election accomplished, Alexander's duties now shifted to organizing the transition from the old administration to the new, including recruitment of the new governor's cabinet. Alexander remembers that many of the Ellington appointees at this time "expected to stay" in their state government posts, after observing how closely their boss and his lieutenants had identified with Dunn's campaign. In order to clear the slate for Dunn's own appointees, many of these would-be holdovers had to be flatly dismissed.

"One of the most conspicuous of these was Howard Warf, who was the commissioner of education, from Hohenwald, who had built his control over a powerful political machine through the educator corridors of the state. He fully expected to continue in his job. When the governor-elect asked to see him, Commissioner Warf thought it was to tell him how they'd be working together.

"He came in, and Dr. Dunn told him he was going to appoint someone else as the education commissioner. Warf was completely surprised. The conversation was over in about three minutes." There was now an awkward silence. The governor-elect looked at the crestfallen commissioner.

"Mr. Warf," said Dunn, the former dentist, ever polite, "I hope you don't mind my saying to you, what a fine set of teeth you have."

"Well, thank you very much, Dr. Dunn," Warf replied. He then departed.

Four years later, the dozen Democrats who entered the 1974 primary race were buoyed by the Watergate scandal, vexing to even the most ardent conservative Republican leaders. Watergate was a windfall for the Democrats, knowing that their nominee would have ready ammunition for the fall general election campaign, whoever the primary victor might be.

While there was no clear frontrunner at this point, it was nonetheless a star-studded field of formidable people. Those aspiring to the nomination included flamboyant Knoxville banker Jake Butcher; wealthy Chattanooga developer Franklin Haney; state treasurer Tom Wiseman; and a former back-bench congressman from southwest Tennessee named Ray Blanton, who had run unsuccessfully for US Senate two years before. (Hooker, twice defeated by this time, did not run again. Publicly, he cited his new responsibilities as chairman of STP Corporation, but he was also disappointed that he could not persuade the publisher and editor of the *Tennessean* to agree to support him a third time.)

On the Republican side, the best-known of the GOP candidates were Dr. Nat Winston, a psychiatrist who had been the commissioner of Tennessee's Department of Mental Health and Mental Retardation under two administrations; and Dortch Oldham, a founder of Southwestern Company, a publisher of Bibles and dictionaries that was known for its corps of eager young sales people who peddled those products door-to-door throughout the South. The youngest Republican in this primary was Alexander, who would turn thirty-four on July 3. After managing Dunn's victory in 1970, Alexander had now joined a new law firm in Nashville.

By the middle of June, there were so many candidates that the *Tennessean* chose to break with its own traditions. Instead of assigning a staff reporter to follow each of the principal candidates and filing news stories from the road each day, the newspaper adopted a zone coverage, establishing temporary bureaus in the larger cities across the long state and posting a news reporter in each of those. Each of the correspondents was expected to file short news updates on whatever candidates passed through their assigned territories each day. These multiple short reports were arrayed in equal fashion across the bottom of page 1 each morning, under one-column headlines.

On the surface, this was a way to cope with the large number of candidates, but this more visually balanced layout was also a response to criticism the newspaper had received for its lopsided coverage of Hooker in 1970, the one Democrat that the newspaper's publisher had so heavily favored. The capital city's morning daily had been stung by Hooker's defeat and was blamed by many Democrats for contributing to Dunn's victory.

THE MONTH OF JULY 1974 was a scorcher, with temperatures in the nineties and a heated campaign scramble to match, though by twenty-first-century standards both of the 1974 party primaries were rather tame and gentlemanly. This would be one of the last statewide elections in Tennessee to be waged in the old style: candidates appearing at dozens of courthouse squares and community bean suppers, with little television coverage and other news media often absent. The occasional "debates" were more so tests of crowd building and rhetoric than stages for the ad hominem attacks that would soon become commonplace across America.

On the first night of August, when the primary polls closed and the votes were counted, Alexander emerged as the GOP nominee with 120,773 votes, 50 percent of the total. Winston was second with 90,980. On the Democratic side, former congressman Blanton finished first with 148,062 votes—just under 23 percent of the total number cast in the field of twelve—Butcher second with 131,412, and Wiseman third with 89,061. With no runoff requirement for a primary in Tennessee, Blanton had the first statewide victory of his career.

Years later, after both Blanton and Butcher were in prison for unrelated crimes, Judge Wiseman said of his 1974 primary race against them: "I finished first among the nonfelons."

THE FALL CAMPAIGNS THAT FOLLOWED were a study in contrasts.

Blanton, with his rural drawl and roots as a West Tennessee farmer and small businessman, seemed to some the more authentic Tennessean. He often cited his "dirt-poor" childhood and his identification with blue-collar working-class families.

At his events on the campaign trail, the loudspeakers blared the anthem "We Need a Ray of Blanton Sunshine," adapted to the familiar tune of country music star Dottie West's 1973 hit "Country Sunshine" (first recorded as a TV jingle for the Coca-Cola Company). At many of these stops, Blanton was accompanied by the legendary sheriff Buford Pusser, native of Adamsville, the candidate's hometown. Pusser was a celebrity, popular for his storied career as a crime-busting sheriff, his life the subject of the 1973 movie *Walking Tall* with Joe Don Baker in the Pusser role.

Alexander, ten years younger than Blanton, seemed urbane and more polished in his campaign appearances. His Tennessee roots were as authentic as Blanton's, just different.

Alexander was born on the opposite end of the long state, in Maryville, between Knoxville and the Great Smoky Mountains. His schooling and work career—he was a graduate of Vanderbilt University and the New York University law school, and former staffer in the Nixon White House—distinctly separated and defined him.

Even so, with ninety days to go before the November general election, Alexander might have thought he would have a fighting chance to keep the GOP in power. His party still had control of the governor's office, with Dunn the incumbent. His political mentor, Senator Howard Baker, was ascendant, having won reelection two years earlier by trouncing Blanton. And Blanton himself, though victorious now as the Democrats' new nominee, had in truth performed most unimpressively in capturing his nomination with fewer than a quarter of the votes cast.

BUT NOW THE SHADOWS of Watergate lay darkly across American politics. As they lengthened they touched this election, too.

Just seven days after Tennessee's August 1 primary, President Nixon announced he would resign his office. On August 9, he boarded a military helicopter and departed the White House. That evening, the new president, Gerald Ford, declared to White House reporters that "our long, national nightmare is over."

One month later, on a Sunday morning, the phone rang at Alexander's home in Nashville. It was Baker, calling from Washington.

BAKER: What do you think about what Ford has done?
ALEXANDER: What has he done?
BAKER: He has pardoned Nixon.

President Gerald Ford, in what would become the defining decision of his short-lived administration, had announced that morning he had signed his name to a two-page document granting an "absolute pardon unto Richard Nixon for all offenses against the United States."

ALEXANDER: What does that mean?
BAKER: I think he just bought us a lot of trouble.

Alexander remembers thinking, "Since I was the one on the ballot, 'us' meant me."

NOTHING WAS THE SAME after this. Not only for Alexander, but for most Republican office seekers across the nation, the Nixon pardon began to roil the political landscape.

"I could feel the campaign, which had been rising, starting to sink," Alexander remembered. "I literally could feel it."

Larry Daughtrey, the senior political reporter, wrote in the *Tennessean* that week that there would not be another Republican governor elected in Tennessee for another fifty years. Throughout the fall, Blanton hammered Alexander for his earlier service in the Nixon White House. He even described Alexander as "Nixon's choirboy."

This comment prompted a rejoinder from a woman in Maryville, Mrs. Harry H. Proffitt, state vice chair of the Tennessee Farm Bureau, who had been Alexander's choir leader in his youth. She informed a reporter that Alexander had sung in her own choir at the Presbyterian church, and added, "Maybe politics could use a few *more* choirboys."

But the race was lost. On November 5, more than a million Tennesseans voted. Blanton won with 55 percent of the statewide total, to Alexander's 43 percent.

"On election day, people were so angry at the Republican Party—because of Nixon, that Ford had pardoned Nixon, on top of Watergate—that literally people were coming down out of the mountains who hadn't voted in years, and they were asking who the Republican candidate was just so they could vote against him. I lost, and Republicans lost at every level in Tennessee and across the country. There were only twelve Republican governors left serving in the fifty states after the Watergate election."

Counting his primary win in August, this was the second statewide victory of Blanton's political career.

It would be his last.

As Blanton and his team prepared for their new state administration, their hopes were high for both progress and patronage. State senator Douglas Henry recalled an early conversation with the governor-elect, in January 1975, during a visit with Blanton at the temporary transition offices in East Nashville.

"Senator, you don't know me," Henry remembers Blanton saying to him, "but I know who you are. And I want you to know that I want to be the best governor Tennessee ever had."

Henry would serve many years as chairman of the Senate Finance Committee, encompassing Blanton's one term in office. He remembers that Blanton's administration made genuine progress on a number of policy fronts, notably internal controls that strengthened the financial integrity of Tennessee's state government. But for this Henry chiefly credits William Jones, Blanton's respected commissioner of finance and administration.

"Governor Blanton had the good sense to appoint Bill Jones and let him alone," Henry said. "The debt went down, the credit rating went up, the number of state employees went down, the number of parks expanded. Of course, he [Blanton] made it impossible for those things to be remembered now."

BLANTON'S TERM AS GOVERNOR is remembered chiefly for corruption, but his administration also was noteworthy for some positive achievements in economic development. Under Tom Benson, his commissioner of economic development, the Blanton team boosted international markets for Tennessee agricultural products and also opened new doors for Japanese business investments in the state. This would lay a foundation for important location decisions by manufacturers, including Nissan Motor Manufacturing Corporation, that would come to pass after Blanton left office.

Benson credits his own predecessor, Dunn's commissioner, Pat Choate, for designing the modern international business recruitment program. But Benson said Blanton also deserves credit for establishing early relationships with leaders in Japan. This, in turn, eventually led to Nissan's decision to establish its small-truck plant in Smyrna, twenty miles southeast of Nashville. Benson told me he looks back with pride on the early years of Blanton's term, particularly the international program.

"We didn't have one before that," he said, "and we recruited thirty-eight international companies to Tennessee during that period."

In a related initiative, Blanton was host in June 1976 to an extraordinary meeting in Nashville of 101 delegates to the United Nations. It was the first time the UN members had ever met outside of New York City.

CHAPTER 3

The Red-and-Black Plaid Shirt

What is he thinking about? He'll be hit by a truck.
—Flo Alexander

ICE WAS FORMING ON THE DARKENED STREETS of Nashville by the time Lamar and Honey Alexander sat down in the warmth of their home for a candlelight dinner. It was the fourth day of January, 1977, their eighth wedding anniversary.

The two were now alone. Honey had tucked into bed the three children—Drew, seven; Leslee, four; and the two-year-old Kathryn—and had prepared veal piccata, the same meal that she and Lamar had shared in Washington, DC, in November 1968. That was the night he had proposed to her, at a restaurant on M Street, just days after Richard Nixon's election as president of the United States.

But this private evening in Nashville was soon interrupted—a telephone call from Senator Baker in Washington. Earlier that day, Baker had been elected Republican leader of the United States Senate. It was his third try for the position since the vacancy created by the death of his father-in-law, Senator Everett Dirksen of Illinois, in October 1969. Baker's margin of victory among Senate Republicans was only one vote, but he was elated.

"I want you to come to Washington to help me set up my leadership office," Baker told his former aide.

Alexander knew that Baker really was asking him to come back to Washington not just to "set up" the leader's office but to work in it with him permanently. Baker had a habit of turning again to aides he knew well, but on this call the senator was restrained in his invitation. He knew Alexander was trying to put down roots in Tennessee and remembered he had been turned down once before by this young protégé.

In 1973, Alexander had declined Baker's request to become minority counsel to the Senate Watergate Committee, recommending the senator hire Fred Thompson instead. Baker also knew that two years after that, Alexander had cited responsibilities at home when President Gerald Ford had asked him to help manage his 1976 reelection campaign. So Baker now said, "Come just for a few months and help me get started."

Alexander promised to call him back the next day. Returning to the dinner table, he told Honey about the invitation and said that, of course, he would not be able to accept. To his surprise, she said, "Why not? You're not really satisfied with what you're doing here."

Since his defeat in the 1974 governor's race, Alexander had been trying to find a satisfying path forward, remembering how *Tennessean* reporter Larry Daughtrey had predicted that Tennessee "would not elect a Republican governor again for fifty years." There was even a $25,000 debt left over from the 1974 campaign.

He had formed a new law firm with Lew Conner, Robert Echols, and Martin Simmons. To add gravitas, the young lawyers named the firm for their two senior partners, Bill Dearborn and Andrew Ewing. To earn extra money, Alexander had also formed a partnership with a real estate agent to buy dilapidated houses, fix them up, and sell them. This venture worked modestly well. Former senator Ross Bass bought one of the improved homes. Alexander also joined forces with Sandy Beall of Knoxville, ten years his junior, whom he had met on Baker's campaign train in 1972. Beall had dropped out of the University of Tennessee to found a restaurant named Ruby Tuesday's. Alexander became the company's lawyer and soon owned 10 percent of the stock.

He and Beall then borrowed $110,000 from Commerce Union Bank to buy Blackberry Farm, a run-down bed-and-breakfast outside Alexander's hometown of Maryville at the edge of the Great Smoky Mountains National Park. Each of the partners had wanted, one day, to build his own mountain cabin, and Beall and his wife, Kreis, dreamed of creating a fine resort.

Alexander and Beall also wanted to preserve the Blackberry Farm property from commercial development. They secured options to purchase two thousand acres in West Millers Cove between Chilhowee Mountain and the national park, although at this point they had no idea how they would pay for the land when it came time to exercise the options.

The Blackberry Farm project allowed Alexander to keep his official residence in the Republican-rich region of East Tennessee where he had grown up. With his young family he was already spending many weekends in West Millers Cove, staying at his father's modest mountain cabin on property that was adjacent to Blackberry Farm.

By now, Alexander had also found a way to elevate his public profile in Middle Tennessee. For nearly two years starting in 1975, he appeared regularly on television in Nashville.

He joined Democrat Floyd Kephart for twice-weekly appearances in a two-minute TV debate segment called Point/Counterpoint during the local news hour on Nashville's NBC affiliate WSM-TV. It was Kephart who had invited Alexander to appear on the recurring television segment. (Kep hart initially asked former governor Winfield Dunn, who declined). The two would take opposing sides of current state or national issues. At this time the WSM's local newscast was the most-watched television program in the Middle Tennessee region—stretching west to the Tennessee River and east to the Cumberland Plateau. The station's broadcast signal covered 40 percent of the state's voters. Dating back to the Civil War, this section had been heavily Democratic.

"Floyd takes the Democratic point of view," Alexander would tell audiences, "and I take the responsible point of view." He would later tell the story of walking into a gasoline service station in White County, on the eastern edge of the WSM's viewing area, where a station attendant recognized him. The fellow immediately asked, "Where's Floyd?"

"I knew right then that I had a big advantage in 1978 that I did not have in 1974," Alexander said. "People in a heavily Democratic area knew me as something other than a Republican."

SO IN JANUARY 1977, with his wife's unexpected encouragement and his law firm's permission, Alexander returned to Washington, DC. His desk now was in the new Republican leader's suite in the US Capitol building. His first assignment was to find Baker's new chief of staff. This process took four months and concluded with the hiring of James Cannon, a former *Newsweek* editor who had been an aide to both Nelson Rockefeller and President Ford.

When Alexander left Nashville for Washington in January 1977, prospects could not have looked worse for Tennessee Republicans. Jimmy Carter had defeated President Ford two months earlier, and the Watergate hangover had also helped Jim Sasser, Nashville lawyer and chairman of the Tennessee Democratic Party, to defeat the incumbent senator Bill Brock. In fact, every single office in the executive branch of Tennessee's state government was now held by a Democrat, and the state legislature was two-to-one Democratic. Except for Baker, the GOP gains in the 1970 and 1972 elections had been otherwise wiped out in Tennessee, and Baker himself was looking at a reelection campaign, for a third term, in 1978.

But not long after arriving in Washington, Alexander's political pessimism began turning to optimism.

"I remember standing at the steps of the Capitol," Alexander recalled, "watching Jimmy Carter make his inaugural address, and thinking, 'The man is already in trouble.' I was energized by the enthusiasm of the Republican US senators who were determined to challenge the Democratic stranglehold in Washington. My friend Wyatt Stewart introduced me to Doug Bailey, one of the political consultants responsible for advising twelve of the Republican governors still remaining in the country."

When Alexander returned to Nashville in April, he told Honey he was thinking about running for governor again.

"THERE IS NO NEED for Lamar to run like he did in 1974," Honey told a small group of advisers in early 1977. "He has to be more natural—be himself."

She was working furiously at her needlepoint as she said this, telling Doug Bailey and her husband just what she thought about the possibility that he might run in the 1978 governor's race. She well remembered the previous campaign.

"Last time, he spent all his time with the same Republican politicians," she said. "He has to get out and meet the people, walk down the street where they live. Campaigning the way people campaign today is really dumb."

Honey Alexander was accustomed to speaking her mind, in the way Texas women often will.

Her real name was Leslee Kathryn Buhler, but her baby brother had called her Honey, and ever since then so had everyone else. She had grown up in Victoria, Texas, amidst prickly pear, mesquite, and armadillos. Victoria was a town so rich in oil that when the O'Conner family decided to dig in their backyard for a swimming pool, they first invited a priest to pray that they wouldn't find oil. Honey's father, Frank Buhler, owned ranches and a savings and loan company but owned no oil or gas.

Honey's mother, Bette Jo Buhler, was a pioneer in the Texas Republican Party. In the late 1950s, in Wichita Falls, Bette Jo had met a five-foot-two-inch-tall teacher and former radio announcer named John G. Tower. He was also interested in politics, and they became fast friends.

In 1961, Tower maneuvered himself into a runoff to fill Vice President Lyndon Johnson's seat in the United States Senate, and he became the first Republican senator elected from Texas since Reconstruction. Bette Jo Buhler was a delegate to the 1964 Republican National Convention, in San Francisco, and she took her teenage daughter Honey along with her. (It was here that Barry Goldwater, the party's presidential nominee, famously proclaimed in his acceptance speech that "extremism in defense of liberty is no vice.")

Honey attended Smith College in Massachusetts, where she studied American history. Her classmates sometimes called her Honey the Hawk because of her support of the Vietnam War. When she graduated, in the spring of 1967, she moved to Washington to take a job as the receptionist in Senator Tower's office.

That summer, in an interoffice softball game, the Tower staff played the Baker staff. An outfielder on the Baker team, Lamar Alexander, remembers being so captivated by Honey's red shorts that he claims she slid into first base. (She denies this.) In any event, he pursued her for the next year while they both worked for the Nixon campaign, though they had different jobs in different locations. He was director of planning for Citizens for Nixon-Agnew and had moved from Baker's Senate office to space at the Willard Hotel on Pennsylvania Avenue. Honey campaigned with Senator Tower for Nixon, and this took her to two dozen states aboard a loaned Lear jet.

In November 1968, Nixon was elected, and Alexander was out of a job. He invited Honey to dinner at a Georgetown restaurant, on M Street, where he proposed marriage over a meal of veal piccata. To Bette Jo Buhler's shock, the wedding date was set for only six weeks later. On January 4, 1969, the ceremony was held at Trinity Episcopal Church in Victoria, Texas. Senator Tower attended the wedding.

Mrs. Buhler warned the young bride, "You may have politics in your future."

BY THE TIME OF THE WEDDING, Alexander had found his next job.

In the Nixon campaign, he had met famed Oklahoma football coach Bud Wilkinson, who became impressed with the young man. Wilkinson had telephoned his fellow Oklahoman, Bryce Harlow, and recommended Alexander. In due course, Harlow became Nixon's first appointee, as senior adviser in charge of congressional liaison, and Alexander became his executive assistant.

The newlyweds from Tennessee and Texas moved into a house at 3813 Forty-Eighth Street, near American University in northwest Washington. For the first six months of the Nixon administration, Alexander sat at a desk in Harlow's West Wing office, the same office that the vice president occupies today.

"I sat there twelve hours a day absorbing cigarette smoke and political wisdom," Alexander told friends. "I got a PhD in politics and government from one of the most admired men in Washington." A few months later, a small work space was created for Alexander just outside the Oval Office, a West Wing cubby hole that still exists today.

Honey became pregnant and, in the summer of 1969, quit her job in the Senate office. Their son, Drew, was born on September 21.

Alexander, now twenty-nine, at this point considered running for the Senate himself in the 1970 Republican primary. But he was dissuaded in a weeklong visit with a number of prominent Tennessee Republicans. The reaction of the mayor of Johnson City, Mae Ross McDowell, was typical.

"Mrs. McDowell, I'm thinking of running for the Senate," he said.

After a long pause she replied, "The *US* Senate?"

He did not run. The Chattanooga congressman, Republican Bill Brock, did, and he defeated the incumbent senator Albert Gore Sr. This was the same year that Winfield Dunn, the Memphis dentist, won the nomination for governor, upsetting several well-established candidates from Middle and East Tennessee.

Dunn was an engaging candidate but had never been elected to any office, and no Republican had been elected governor in Tennessee since 1920. Dunn, however, had one big advantage: The Democratic nominee was John Jay Hooker Jr., the charismatic but controversial figure who had split the Democratic party four years earlier.

It was at this point, in mid-August, that Wellford (later a federal judge) telephoned Alexander at the White House and invited him to become Dunn's campaign manager. Alexander quickly said yes and before the end of that month flew to Nashville to begin organizing the campaign. Honey packed up their house on Forty-Eighth Street and drove with baby Drew to Nashville. There the young family moved into a two-bedroom apartment at 4505 Harding Road.

When Dunn won in November, he asked Alexander to manage the transition between the old and new administrations. Alexander did this but soon moved into a private law practice with attorneys Bill Dearborn and Bob Warner. There were only three lawyers in the new firm, so the name on the door became "Dearborn, Warner, and Alexander."

While her husband helped start this law practice, Honey raised their two children—Drew and their infant daughter Leslee—and she also became active as a volunteer in the Nashville community. She was particularly interested in organizations providing prenatal care. She also raised money for the local public radio station, and she helped to found Leadership Nashville.

When her husband ran for governor himself in 1974 she pitched in, traveling to dozens of counties, in addition to caring for two children under the age of four. Some of the young women recruited to cheerlead at campaign stops were even called Lamar's Honeys. In June 1974, two months before the Republican primary, she gave birth to their third child, Kathryn. When Alexander lost his race to Ray Blanton in November, Honey was stoic and supportive, but not surprised.

IN 1978, ALEXANDER RAN a different sort of campaign, determined to shed the appearance of a big city lawyer. Ever after, he gave Honey the principal credit for making the difference.

He also had the friendship and loyalty of Tom Ingram. After the 1974 race, Ingram had worked as a business writer for the *Nashville Banner*. In 1977, when Alexander decided to try again, he and Ingram looked far and wide for a suitable campaign manager, but in the end Alexander decided that Ingram himself would be better than anyone else. He had a talent for team building and had the complete trust of the candidate.

Alexander also now had another formidable asset in Bailey, one of the nation's foremost political consultants to Republican campaigns. Bailey and his partner, John Deardourff, were credited with assisting the victories of seven of the dozen sitting GOP governors who had remained in office after the Watergate debacle. Early in his career, as a young doctoral graduate of Tufts University's Fletcher School of Diplomacy, Bailey had assisted Dr. Henry Kissinger at Harvard University in developing policy papers for New York governor Nelson Rockefeller. He met Deardourff, also a Fletcher graduate, during this period. Very soon after meeting Bailey in Washington, Alexander hired him for his second attempt at the governor's office.

Honey still doubted that her husband could win. Bob Clement, the son of a former governor, had overwhelming leads in the early polls, and Knoxville banker Jake Butcher seemed to have unlimited money. Moreover, there were practical family considerations. The new law practice was just getting off the ground. The family had little money, except for Honey's small inheritance from her father. And there was that lingering $25,000 debt still to pay from the 1974 campaign.

Bailey quickly helped Alexander assess the previous campaign and develop a new strategy and message. In the early summer of 1977, Alexander, Honey, Ingram, Bailey, and the author began to discuss a new concept that would help the candidate shake off any vestige of his unhelpful 1974 image—that of a lawyer in a dark suit and necktie, who was mainly seen at airport news conferences.

Alexander himself later credited Honey with prompting the imaginative idea of walking across the state. "She was the most realistic of the participants," he said later. These early planning discussions were usually held in the family room at 2322 Golf Club Lane, which had been the Alexander family's home since 1971.

"If you're going to run," she said, "you have to be yourself. Do the things you like to do."

She, Bailey, Ingram, and others quizzed the candidate. "What do you like to do?" He liked the outdoors. He liked music. He didn't like spending all his time with the same Republican leaders or speaking to civic clubs. He enjoyed meeting people.

"Then he could walk," Bailey suggested. So the idea was hatched: A walk across Tennessee. A thousand miles. Six Months. Shaking a thousand hands a day. Spending the nights in homes with Tennessee families along the way.

There was also discussion about what to wear on this walk.

"I can't walk across the state in a blue suit," Alexander said. He suggested that he would feel most comfortable in a red-and-black plaid shirt that he had in his closet.

At this point in this discussion, he left the den and went to the bedroom closet. He returned with the plaid shirt and also a pair of scuffed hiking boots, which he plopped down loudly on the coffee table. Someone mentioned adding denim jeans, but Alexander said he preferred khaki slacks. On rainy days, he would use a simple windbreaker jacket.

The group agreed to this ensemble, which in time became his trademark uniform for the campaign trail. Next day, Alexander drove to Friedman's Army Navy Store, on Twenty-First Avenue and purchased a dozen more plaid shirts.

All of this would supplant what Bailey called the "traditional Republican, Rotary Club kind of campaign" that, in 1974, was characterized by identical airport news conferences and other formal appearances in the principal media markets. The walk would enable a steady stream of encounters with normal folks, as well as with local reporters for smaller newspapers and radio stations in towns outside the urban media markets.

As THE WORD OF THIS PLANNED TREK of a thousand miles reached Alexander's friends, it was not met with uniform excitement.

While some allies saw it as a positive strategy, with potential to correct Alexander's prior image as citified and aloof, a few friends considered it corny. One of these was Judge Thomas Hull, who would later become Alexander's top legal counsel in the governor's office. When he was first informed of the plan, sitting in his small Greeneville, Tennessee, office, Hull candidly said the idea of walking across the state seemed strange, even oddball. He cautioned that such an announcement might be poorly received by Republican leaders. He nonetheless committed, in the same conversation, to support the walk strategy.

Even Alexander's mother declared, very privately, that she thought it was plain dangerous. Through no plan whatever, but a combination of coincidence and accidental timing, the job of informing his parents, Flo and Andy Alexander, fell to the author.

One of my early assignments as a member of the campaign staff was to preview the route of the candidate's walk, both to brief Alexander in detail on what he could expect and also to identify issue-related opportunities for the daily message. I had flown from Nashville to Knoxville to continue advancing the route of the candidate's forthcoming walk, and I stopped by Alexander's boyhood home in Maryville for a quick visit with his parents.

Mrs. Alexander greeted me and invited me to have a seat in the living room; the candidate's father soon joined us. She asked me what I was doing in town this time, and we chatted pleasantly for a moment. Then it was suddenly apparent to me they had not been told of the bold hiking strategy.

When I mentioned the general plan for the campaign and how the cross-state walk served to advance it, there was a moment of silence. Alexander's parents had both been teachers over their long careers—and both had that teacher's capacity for looking the unprepared student straight in the eye, waiting insistently for a response. Flo then spoke.

"What is he thinking about?" she asked. "He'll be hit by a truck, walking up and down those highways!"

I tried to return us to the rationale, but none of my points seemed agreeable. I chiefly remember thinking that I was in a difficult position. It was one thing to be at the office "on the carpet" talking to one's boss; I was now talking to the boss's parents, and their son hadn't even asked me to do this. Here, I was outnumbered. The room felt smaller. Nashville seemed far away.

On January 26, 1978, a winter morning in Maryville so cold the trombone player's slide froze, Alexander stood on the front steps of his parents' home at 121 Ruth Street. On this morning, he was wearing what became his campaign uniform: the red-and-black plaid lumberjack shirt, khaki trousers, the scuffed hiking boots, and warm socks.

To the assembled news reporters, he made a surprise announcement: He would walk one thousand miles across Tennessee. The route would take him from Maryville up to Mountain City, then west to Memphis and the Mississippi River. This would take the better part of six months, ending in early July.

He then stepped off the front porch and began walking east.

The idea sounded simple. In reality, it had required several months of detailed planning—mapping the specific route, crafting daily themes geared to local issues, identifying the families who would put the candidate up for the night along the way—and all this had been accomplished largely in secret. This was primarily to preserve the news value of the extraordinary announcement, but there was also some anxiety within the campaign team that the unusual concept might have been met with ridicule. The best course, they believed, was to announce it completely and well, all at once on the day it was to begin.

The announcement, like the rest of the campaign, featured music. Alexander's staff, working with Dr. W. J. Julian, the famed director of bands at the University of Tennessee in Knoxville, recruited four undergraduates—Bill Dickinson, Tom Gillespie, Kevin Kleinfelter, and Terry Tabors—to travel with the candidate as members of a new Alexander's Washboard Band. Alexander regularly joined in the music making, playing either the keyboard, trombone, or washboard as the spirit moved him.

Like many student ensembles, this band was actually quite good, and its performances also pulled together many elements of Alexander's larger campaign and personal story. Music had long been part of political history across the South. The band performed music familiar to Tennesseans, from the eastern high mountains to Nashville and on to Beale Street in Memphis. Not long before this, Senator Albert Gore Sr. had drummed up his own crowds with tunes he played on his own fiddle, and in 1948 the Grand Ole Opry star Roy Acuff had done the same in his own run for governor.

For Alexander himself, each campaign stop now was probably also a pleasant, though private, reminder of his time as a young man in the French Quarter, playing instruments like these, on those many evenings into the wee hours at Your Father's Moustache, the raucous club on Bourbon Street.

The name of this new band was an echo of Irving Berlin's 1911 classic "Alexander's Ragtime Band," a familiar piece of music that the campaign initially wanted to perform at every stop. The first plan, in fact, had been to use the famous Berlin tune as Alexander's official campaign song. It was peppy, perfect for drawing a crowd on courthouse squares, and certainly memorable. But performing the song publicly would have required getting permission from the Berlin estate, and the attempt failed. The answer came back from a representative of the heirs that Mr. Berlin had been a faithful Democrat throughout his life, that he would not have approved his song to be used in a Republican political campaign. So the classic song was dropped, but the phrase "Come on along" stuck. Those three words became a campaign slogan—and a fixture in Alexander's election-time vocabulary ever after on campaign signs, brochures, and other materials.

The journey proceeded, with Alexander walking along the left side of Tennessee highways, waving at curious passersby. At the end of each day's hike, he would mark an "x" with chalk on the asphalt where he stopped for the evening. He would then go to a local citizen's home for the night. During the daytime, this chalk-mark technique also made it possible to make detours for public appearances on the nearest courthouse square and still remain faithful to his pledge of the continuous statewide walk. He would always return and resume his walking at precisely that marked spot. No fudging, no cheating—for a thousand-plus miles.

For courthouse square events, in county after county, the young band members would drive the truck into town, hand out campaign materials to passersby, and start up the instrumental music. When Alexander arrived, he would join in on the trombone, keyboard, or washboard, and then he would speak to whatever crowd had assembled. Afterward, the band members would drive on to the next town, with their truckload of instruments and campaign paraphernalia, and set up for the next event.

For five months, this is how it went. From late January through June, Alexander would fly home to Nashville on Saturdays and return to the campaign trail the following Monday morning. Honey meanwhile raised the children, cooked meals, drove carpools, and with the help of a nanny, Jan Talley, somehow found time to maintain her own campaign schedule.

The red-and-black plaid shirt was getting recognized, along with the band and its music. Soon the campaign was auctioning the plaid shirts to raise money.

"I knew I was getting somewhere when people stopped laughing and someone paid $500 for my shirt at a rally in Columbia," Alexander said. The shirt became a symbol of a campaign to stay in touch with people.

FLO ALEXANDER, THE CANDIDATE'S mother, was right about many things. One of them was the possibility she feared, that her son might be hit by a truck. This did occur, though fortunately—for both the candidate and the campaign—it was a small truck and the accident did not happen on a highway.

His encounter with the white pickup did not occur until February. It was a Saturday morning, and he had dutifully marked his chalk "x" on the highway pavement near Morristown, in order to make a detour by car to campaign for a few hours in nearby Newport, Tennessee. At the town square, the candidate was making his rounds, stopping in shops, and greeting people on the street.

Suddenly, while turning to his right to wave at a woman on the sidewalk, he was struck by a pickup truck and knocked to the pavement. He suffered a sprain and was forced to leave the campaign trail for three days. His bright red windbreaker jacket ever after bore a smudge of white paint on the upper left sleeve. The next week, Alexander faithfully returned to the same "x" he had made on the road near Morristown, and he resumed his long walk.

Many places along the route were remote, and there were frequent stretches without telephone communication. This was the era before cell phones, pagers, and the Internet. Covering five to thirteen miles each day, walking on the shoulders of highways and rural roads, Alexander left the daily management of his campaign in the hands of Tom Ingram.

BY THE END OF THIS LONG TREK, when Alexander finally stuck a bare foot in the Mississippi River on July 6, he had covered 1,022 miles in just over five months.

By that day, while his unorthodox mode of campaigning had brought him a few sneers from traditional politicians, he had also generated volumes of news coverage in small-town newspapers statewide. His headquarters Rolodex now included thousands of new contacts and volunteers. The effort also harvested for him a wealth of real-life stories from Tennesseans he had met on courthouse squares and roadsides along the way.

When he concluded the walk at the big river, the August primary was just one month away.

By now there were three other Republicans in the GOP primary, and eight candidates on the Democratic side. But unlike the larger Democratic field in 1974, only three of these were considered to be serious contenders: Jake Butcher, the East Tennessee banking figure, Bob Clement, a former Public Service Commission member and son of the former governor, and Mayor Richard Fulton of Nashville—each with some semblance of an organized political base, owing to previous campaigns of one type or another.

THROUGH THE SUMMER, Butcher and Clement had a bruising battle. In multiple public appearances, Butcher would pointedly, and repeatedly, refer to Clement's height—calling him "Little Bob." Clement once responded: "It's true, I'm not tall. I'm only a quarter inch taller than Howard Baker!"

In further response to Butcher's ridicule, Clement's campaign spokesman, Tom Seigenthaler, also recommended that his candidate begin carrying an old-fashioned three-legged milking stool to his campaign stops. He suggested that Clement make a show of plopping the stool down, standing on it, and proclaiming, "There are a lot of little people in Tennessee." This apparently was pushing the metaphor too far for Clement's taste, and he rejected the idea.

As the August primary day drew closer, Butcher's rhetoric grew even more caustic and critical of Clement, with corresponding bitterness on the Clement side. These wounds never healed. In time, the Republican nominee would be the beneficiary.

ALEXANDER WON HIS REPUBLICAN PRIMARY over state representative Harold Stirling of Memphis by a wide margin. Butcher finished first among the Democrats with 41 percent of the vote. He had beaten Clement by more than thirty-one thousand votes. In defeat, Clement's loyalists were stung and angry at the callous treatment their candidate had received from the Butcher camp, especially at the end.

Seeing this split, rather than take a week off to rest as he had done following the 1974 primary, Alexander and his staff immediately worked through key volunteers to exploit the rift among the Butcher and Clement Democrats across the state. They did this by keeping it visible, and also offering the disgruntled Clement Democrats a place to land. One of Alexander's first visits following the primary was to the Crossville home of Clement's aunt, state senator Annabelle Clement O'Brien, sister of the former governor.

Several of Clement's top-level campaign leadership responded and joined the Alexander campaign within the month. One of these was Etherage Parker, a leading Clement fundraiser and businessman of Trousdale County. Another was Irby Simpkins, whose role as Clement's campaign treasurer meant his name had appeared on every Clement billboard, newspaper ad, and yard sign. It was quickly announced that Parker and Simpkins would be two of the five new statewide cochairs of the Alexander campaign. (Parker later served as Alexander's cabinet officer for tourist development. Simpkins, in 1979, became an owner and publisher of the *Nashville Banner* newspaper.) This maneuver deprived Butcher of unity across his own party. Together with Alexander's constant attacks on questionable practices at the Butcher banks, this kept the Democrat's campaign weakened and defensive through the fall.

BOTH NOMINEES WERE EAST TENNESSEANS, coming from small towns near Knoxville. Butcher's family was based in Maynardville in Union County, while Alexander's hometown was Maryville in Blount County. Butcher's circle considered Knoxville their stronghold, in particular, as it was the headquarters of his United American Bank organization.

This competition for votes within the heavily Republican east-state region was further complicated by Baker's reelection campaign. He was an East Tennessean, too. His hometown of Huntsville, in Scott County, was not far from Maynardville or Maryville. Baker, now running for his third term, had angered many in his own party by supporting ratification of the Panama Canal Treaty of 1977, proposed by President Jimmy Carter, to hand control of the canal over to the government of Panama. Also, Baker's Democratic opponent was Nashvillian Jane Eskind, a wealthy party stalwart and member of the Democratic State Executive Committee. With her nomination for Senate, she had become the first woman to win a statewide race in Tennessee. (She would lose this 1978 race to Baker but was elected two years later to a seat on the Tennessee Public Service Commission.)

"Butcher had anticipated, almost to the end, that Baker would run his own race, not be particularly hard on Butcher, and that that would undercut me," Alexander recalled. "What happened was that I ran my race and Baker ran his race, but in the end we both got on a train and went across the state. Instead of undercutting one another, our complementary races really helped each other, and we both won."

THE COMPETITION FOR VOTES was nonetheless fierce in Knoxville in particular, and this played out on two successive football weekends at the University of Tennessee.

Neyland Stadium, on the south side of campus above the Holston River, is one of the great temples of Southeastern Conference football. In this storied arena, with its orange-and-white checkerboard end zones, the Tennessee Volunteers won six national championships in the twentieth century (four of them under coach Robert Neyland). In the modern era, Peyton Manning played his popular college career here. The "Vols" regularly play before one of the largest audiences in college football. In 1978, the home stadium regularly held close to a hundred thousand fans on a Saturday afternoon. UT football boosters proudly claimed that game-day attendance made this venue "the fifth largest city" in the state.

The 1978 season opened with two home games in early September.

At the first, against UCLA, Alexander's supporters in the vast crowd looked up and saw a worrisome sight. A twin-engine plane was trailing a huge banner, for nearly a hundred thousand pairs of eyes to see, that read, "This is Butcher Country!" Attorney John King, a season-ticket holder and Alexander's Knox County campaign manager, remembers seeing the Butcher plane make continuous circles high above the stadium seats. He also remembers hearing boos from the crowd.

"The Butcher campaign was all over Knoxville," King remembers. "If there was a corner yard that didn't have Butcher yard sign, I wasn't aware of it. And, at the football game, they had a plane flying around before the game and during the game. It pulled a banner that said, 'This is Butcher Country.' It went around and around and around."

Tennessee lost 13–0 that afternoon. When the game ended, King found a telephone and called the Alexander headquarters in Nashville. He reported what he had witnessed, and a suitable response was discussed for the next weekend.

The following Saturday, as the Volunteers hosted Oregon State on the turf below, the same plane trailing the same Butcher banner was again visible in the sky above. "This is Butcher Country!" it read, as on the previous weekend. But now a second plane appeared in the sky, trailing a banner with red-and-black plaid trim and a different message.

"We got a plane," King recalled, "and I remember saying, 'I do not want that plane circling around forever—just make an impression and move on.' And it flew over only one time, just prior to kickoff. It went from the southeast corner of the stadium crossing to the northwest corner of the oval. It flew over real low, probably not really permissible, but flew over just the one time."

While the Butcher banner in the sky proclaimed, "This is Butcher Country!" the second banner behind the new plane read, "This is Your Country" on the top line, seeming to correct the other plane's message, then below that simply, "Vote Alexander."

"The crowd erupted, a spontaneous thing, just moments prior to kickoff,"

King remembers. Then the plane disappeared, "and it was almost like some sort of fighter plane strike. All of a sudden that plane appeared—and there was a rising kind of applause—and then it was gone."

It was a friendly applause, King said, either because Knoxvillians by now were already weary of Butcher's saturation campaigning in his hometown, or because the Alexander response was clever and lightning fast, or possibly just because there might have been more Republicans than Democrats in such a huge Knoxville crowd. Probably some combination of all three.

"It was the dueling airplane wars," said Molly Weaver, the young campaign volunteer who helped organize the Alexander side of this scene. "It was before people did that kind of thing at ball games. I remember finding the guy to do the sign. Our banner was a very funny combination of size, structure, and material. It needed to fly but be readable and be able to take off from Island Home Airport."

"I remember hearing boos when the Butcher plane went over," she said, "and when our plane went over there were cheers. There were people who thought the Butchers owned everything and had gotten too big for their britches. There were people who had Butcher signs in their yards, and I'm sure went into the voting booth and voted for Alexander. We thought it was a tremendous success."

TENNESSEE PLAYED OREGON STATE to a tie that day and went on to finish the season 5–5–1. As election day approached, polling by the Alexander campaign indicated a tight race at the ballot box, too, but this proved inaccurate. On election night, November 7, Alexander was the winner by an impressive margin, with 661,959 votes to Butcher's 523,495. This was a nearly exact reversal of the percentage difference by which Alexander had lost to Blanton four years earlier.

For Blanton and his circle, there would be more reversals to come—and soon.

CHAPTER 4

The Murders

I want to be remembered as the best governor Tennessee ever had.
—Governor-elect Ray Blanton to Senator Douglas Henry, 1975

IN THE MIDDLE OF THE ARC of his life, the sharecropper's son knew presidents and moguls and captains and kings, but at the end, only one name—Roger Humphreys—would be linked to his own above all others. In this low finale, both Shakespearean and mean, the governor was the master of his own misery.

They did not know each other, in the beginning. Blanton said so, later, in defense of his own actions. This was true. He had done what he did to help the young man on the recommendation of his topmost political adviser in East Tennessee, Jim Allen, who said the same after the going got rough.

Blanton and Humphreys were also a generation apart and certainly hailed from opposite places in different ends of the state—different both in terrain and politics—Blanton from the lowlands in the west, Humphreys from the mountains in the east. No geography is flatter or plainer than the plantation savanna of southwestern Tennessee. Blanton's hometown of Adamsville, ninety miles from Memphis, is on the edge of McNairy County and closer to Mississippi than it is to Nashville.

Humphreys was also reared in a placid neighborhood in a peaceful town. But his home was in the eastern highlands. Johnson City, one of the so-called Tri-Cities of northeastern Tennessee, together with Bristol and Elizabethton, is in fact one of the remotest places in the state in relation to the capital in Nashville. In Johnson City, when you stand on the Washington County courthouse steps, you are sixty miles closer to Canada than you are to Memphis.

Humphreys, in his youth, would have seemed an unlikely prospect for celebrity. His father, Frank, was a well-known retail merchant and a fixture in Johnson City's business community. Frank was also active in politics, a faithful supporter of the Clement-Ellington machine—a reliable Democrat in a region historically made up of staunch Republicans, one generation to the next.

Lee Smith, a fellow native of Johnson City, Tennessee, knew Roger from childhood and remembers his young neighbor as a quiet boy.

"Roger and I grew up together," Smith told me. "He was a few years younger than me, but he lived in the same neighborhood. Kids around the neighborhood would gather for ballgames and other activities. I knew him through my growing-up years, and he was a normal guy during those years. His father, Frank Humphreys, owned a retail sporting goods store. Frank Humphreys was always a supporter of Clement and Ellington; he was a Clement-Ellington Democrat. I knew he was on Blanton's patronage committee and tended to Blanton's affairs in upper east Tennessee."

But the lives of these two young neighbors would soon take dramatically different paths.

SMITH LEFT FOR NASHVILLE, to attend college and law school at Vanderbilt, and after that to Washington as a young staffer to Senator Howard Baker. He was recruited by Lamar Alexander to be the statewide political director in Winfield Dunn's 1970 campaign for governor, and there he worked alongside other young Baker protégés from Washington and Knoxville. In January, 1971, soon after Dunn took office, he appointed Smith to the senior post of counsel to the governor, and the young lawyer directed policy and planning throughout Dunn's term. When it ended four years later, the enterprising Smith launched a popular political newsletter called the *Tennessee Journal*.

Back in Johnson City, meanwhile, Roger Humphreys and Susan Garrett had married and also divorced, and in 1973 his life turned violent. Police found two people, a man and a woman, shot to death. They identified the female as Humphreys' ex-wife, Susan, and the male as her friend John Scholl, and they soon arrested Humphreys for the double murder. Investigators described a grisly scene, saying Roger had murdered the two with eighteen shots using a two-shot Derringer pistol—meaning he had had to pause eight times to reload. He was tried for the two homicides and convicted.

"I hadn't seen Roger in a long time, when my mother called me to say Roger had shot his former wife, Susan Garrett, and John Scholl," Smith told me. "Roger had found John and Susan together. He went to the residence where they were and just filled the both of them full of bullets. It wasn't long before the police tracked him down and arrested him. It came to trial, and it was major news in the area, as you would expect."

In October 1975, Roger was sentenced to serve twenty to forty years in the state penitentiary. He would not remain there long.

JUST TWO YEARS LATER, in early September 1977—in a pure coincidence—there was an unlikely reunion of two childhood friends.

Smith, now writing for his own *Tennessee Journal*, was not expecting a scoop. It was a quiet Thursday in Nashville. The afternoon had begun calmly enough when he dropped by the office of house speaker, Ned McWherter, at 1 Legislative Plaza.

"It was well before the legislative session, and I was talking to Ned McWherter about what he thought was going to be happening in the upcoming session," Smith recalled.

He was grateful for the appointment and interview, but Smith was also glancing at his wristwatch. He was anxious to get the information he needed as efficiently as possible. His deadline for news copy would fall later that evening. The newsletter was always printed and mailed on Fridays, and normally most subscribers received it on Monday. This following Monday, however, would be Labor Day, and most regular readers would probably not see the newsletter until Tuesday.

"I was talking to Ned, and Jim Kennedy [McWherter's top staff aide at this time] comes in and says, 'Mr. Speaker, there's a state photographer who wants to take a picture for your passport application. Do you mind if he does that now?' Ned says, 'OK.' Kennedy goes out, and in comes Roger Humphreys, and I almost fell out of my chair."

Smith recalled the following exchange:

HUMPHREYS: You're Lee Smith.
SMITH: Yes, Roger. How are you doing?
HUMPHREYS: I'm doing pretty well, under the circumstances.
[*Humphreys takes McWherter's photograph, and then departs.*]
SMITH [*to McWherter*]: I can't believe who just took your picture.
McWHERTER: What do you mean?
SMITH: That's Roger Humphreys. He's supposed to be out at the main prison—locked up behind bars—and he's up here taking pictures, supposedly for the state photographer's office.

This suddenly produced the second major news story about young Roger Humphreys: his strangely changed circumstances.

"I went back to my office and called the public information officer at the Correction Department," Smith said. "I asked her about Roger Humphreys' status, and she said, 'I'll have to call you back.' She called me back and said, 'Roger Humphreys is working as a trusty in the state photographer's office. He goes over there each morning and comes back to the state penitentiary in the afternoon.'

"I said, 'I can't imagine he is doing that. It was only a couple of years ago that he murdered his former wife and her friend, and his conviction got upheld. I can't imagine he's out running around state government. Is there anything you can say to explain that?'

"She said, 'The only thing I can tell you is that this was done on the direction of the governor's office.' I knew then," Smith told me, "that Frank Humphreys had called Ray Blanton and gotten this done for Roger."

Humphreys had been properly convicted of his heinous crime, but he had served only a fraction of his twenty-year prison sentence—only two months behind bars. Moreover he had been designated a prison "trusty" and given work-release status, which set him up for the outside job as an official state photographer.

Blanton's trouble didn't begin with Humphreys. There were already ongoing investigations by the FBI into liquor store licensing, government purchasing, and highway construction bid rigging. But it was this extraordinary case of a young double-murderer, with a day job carrying a camera for a state government agency, that became the flash point for the Tennessee's news media.

Smith's item in the *Tennessee Journal* of September 5 was brief—just a single paragraph on the back page.

"On Oct. 10, 1975, the Department of Correction received custody of Roger Humphreys of Johnson City on a 20- to 40-year sentence for two murders. Only two months later the department, acting on direct orders of the office of Gov. Ray Blanton, placed Humphreys at the Correctional Rehabilitation Center, a facility for minimum security prisoners outside the walls of the Main Prison. He was subsequently given a job as a state photographer in downtown Nashville. Humphreys is the son of Frank Humphreys Jr., the chairman of Blanton's Washington County patronage committee."

IN VIEW OF SMITH'S ELITE READERSHIP among Tennessee politicians and political writers, his short paragraph was long enough to get the attention of the region's newspapers and television news departments.

Soon other reporters began asking Blanton directly about the Humphreys case. The repeated questions seemed to irritate the governor, but rather than moderate his tone, he became more rigid in his defense of Humphreys' special treatment. The drumbeat of questions accelerated. Blanton became visibly annoyed, then defiant, then headstrong and unyielding. At one point, he vowed he would not "answer any more negative questions." Instead of tamping the story down, of course, this only added mystery to the subject for news reporters.

The governor was making the young prisoner famous, and the most devastating interview came on September 15.

THE GOVERNOR DID NOT CARE for Carol Marin, the chief state government reporter for Nashville's NBC affiliate, WSM-TV.

"Prisons, pardons, and paroles were my beat," she told me. "I had done a documentary on corruption in the Tennessee prison system. I ended up, on a regular basis, being inside prisons doing stories, and at the legislature all the time doing political stories, and the two distinctly intersected.

"Lee's newsletter broke the Humphreys story, and we took pictures of Roger Humphreys taking photos [in his trusty job]. We pursued that story aggressively—remarkable work-release relationships with politically connected people. Roger Humphreys' father was the chairman of the Blanton patronage committee in their county."

Marin said Blanton had declined repeated requests from her station for a face-to-face interview. At his official news conferences in his office at the capitol, which typically covered many topics with questions from multiple TV and print reporters, the governor would ignore Marin—obviously sidestepping her questions.

Suddenly, in early September, Marin got word from a station producer that a Blanton press officer had called. The governor would agree to an interview now but on one condition: The interview must be done "only live"—not recorded on tape for broadcast later. Blanton wanted his words to be heard in full, not selectively parsed by an opinionated editor.

Marin and her news director, Mike Kettenring, agreed to this condition.

"It was September 15, 1977, which happened to be my father's birthday," Marin remembered. "Blanton brought a lot of people with him. One of them told me later he had boasted he was going to 'get' me in the live interview. We then had to set up the interview in the Teddy Bart studio—next door to the regular news studio—because Blanton brought so many people."

THE INTERVIEW, ONLY SIXTEEN MINUTES long, was tense throughout.

Blanton, by turns, was fractious and petulant, accusatory and sarcastic. He lectured Marin, defended Humphreys, and commended the young man's behavior and personal progress behind bars. Humphreys, he said, was a "nice young man."

Then he threw gasoline on the fire.

"And I am going to announce to you now that before I go out of office he is going to be pardoned."

MARIN: Can you explain that decision, Governor.
BLANTON: Very simple. I felt like he merited it. You see, in a crime of
passion, the crime of murder . . . Mrs. Blanton and I request, whenever we have these inmates working for us out at the residence that

are around our children and our wives, we request murderers. For one very simple reason: They are rarely repetitious.

MARIN: Why not pardon *all* the murderers then, Governor, the crime-of-passion murderers?

Blanton insisted that not all murderers had earned release, as he claimed Humphreys had, through similarly good conduct and rehabilitation. Marin asked him about the influence on such decisions of his political friend Jim Allen. Blanton suddenly made a statement that seemed to open a new door.

"I have not sold a single pardon or parole," he said. "Neither has any of my people." He did not elaborate.

At this point in the live interview, Blanton claimed WSM in its news coverage had shown unfairness against him. Mentioning Kettenring, the news director, specifically by name, he accused the station of bias and unprofessionalism for presenting its "opinions" of him as news, rather than in broadcast editorials. He even suggested the station's FCC license possibly should not be renewed.

MARIN: Are you threatening our license, Governor?

BLANTON: And that is a good question, whether you should have your license renewed because of biased reporting under the guise of news, and not having the guts to come out and editorialize. Now, if you want to editorialize why not do it?

MARIN: Governor, we are interviewing you, asking you the facts instead. Rather than opinion, we are asking our chief executive.

BLANTON: I'm talking about what you have done in the past, not tonight.

MARIN: Are you saying, then, you don't have to explain Roger Humphreys? You will pardon him.

BLANTON: I have explained Roger Humphreys. I have explained Roger Humphreys. What else to you want to know? Ask me a question, not as a statement. Ask.

MARIN: On what information was Roger Humphreys released into minimum security two months after he was behind the walls?

BLANTON: Let me explain it to you as simple as I can, so you can understand it. Vocational aptitude, ability, trustworthiness, and the fact that he has performed. Now, can you understand that?

MARIN: Any politics?

BLANTON: No, no, I have just given you four reasons why. You want ten more?

MARIN: Thank you very much, Governor.

The interview was a bombshell.

Blanton's mention of a pardon was shocking. He had now added that word to the curious case of Roger Humphreys. Also, the governor's combative demeanor—argumentative, condescending, rude—had added a further dimension to the public's view of Ray Blanton. If there had been any chance before this that the Blanton-Humphreys story might fade from page 1, that possibility now vanished. The broadcast of Marin's interview gave the story a new life.

WSM's station manager, Tom Griscom, sent videotape copies of the recorded interview to other NBC affiliate stations across Tennessee. (At this time, before the advent of cable television with its hundreds of choices, the typical American set had only the local NBC channel and two or three others, meaning the Blanton interview received heavy viewing in each of the state's TV markets.)

"He was difficult," Marin told me. "He asked me if I knew the meaning of the word 'recidivism,' and I did. I even knew how to spell it. I remember the next day the switchboard almost melted down with phone calls, and in the next couple of days we got about two thousand letters from viewers furious at Blanton."

Humphreys' special status—together with the governor's growing petulance with news reporters—suddenly became the topic of intense media interest throughout Tennessee and across America. Correspondents for the *New York Times, Washington Post, Newsweek, Time,* and network television were now following the pardon story.

THE NEWS REPORTS QUICKLY ESCALATED into editorial condemnations. Over the following two weeks, Blanton was criticized in editorials statewide, with the notable exceptions of the opinion pages of the *Knoxville News-Sentinel* and the *Nashville Tennessean.*

- The *Nashville Banner* declared: "We suppose Humphreys' victims had families; most do. That's of no concern to the governor. Neither is justice."
- In Memphis, the *Commercial Appeal* insisted that "Blanton just doesn't care what people think about the way he governs Tennessee by the spoils system. He has been arrogant about everything. He is a hillbilly version of Richard Nixon, trying to establish his own kind of imperial government in this state, doing whatever he pleases regardless of what is right."
- The *Chattanooga Times* said Blanton "has successfully solidified his Republican opposition, increased the likelihood that Democratic candidates will discourage his support in future races, needlessly damaged the state's valuable work-release corrections program and,

interestingly, established an almost Nixonian disdain for the press and, perhaps, 'the people.'"

Smith's *Tennessee Journal*, in a related piece on prison overcrowding and the broader planning issues facing the state correction system, included the following comment that would seem prescient two years later:

"For the remainder of Gov. Blanton's term there is, unfortunately, no reason to expect that political interference in correction system justice will not continue. Barring any sharp change of policy, the only apparent solution to this problem is the inauguration of a new governor in 1979."

CHAPTER 5

The Madness

And there wasn't any Democratic party. There was just Willie . . .
—Robert Penn Warren, *All the King's Men*

As sometimes happens with public scandals involving senior elected leaders, the larger portion of the Tennessee Democratic Party establishment remained utterly silent on the Humphreys case throughout 1978. There is no record of minor politicians anywhere in the state urging Blanton to reverse his position on the pardon issue.

Why was this so?

First, it was more convenient and painless for most of these party regulars to remain invisible, to be unheard from. Though the pardon issue was clearly building as a public embarrassment, threatening the party's leaders and candidates, Blanton himself was known to react badly when criticized. He was considered mildly unstable owing to his alcohol consumption. It was much less risky, therefore, for any individual in the Blanton circle or in the broader party organization to simply keep one's silence and nod agreeably when the governor pointed to the meddlesome FBI as the cause of anybody's trouble.

For any individual operative, to do otherwise could result in the termination of a career, or of one's treasured access, at least for a good long while if not forever. It also would be too easy, with an ill-advised misstep, to run athwart the array of "Good Government Committees" (the five-member patronage review panels in every county), operating proudly if privately in their own small political fiefdoms. Any given local operative would expect that the committee in his own county could easily freeze him out of things, and probably would do so before the next weekend. Moreover, among minor elected officials, it was generally known and feared that if any legislator, mayor, county executive, or party chairman spoke up, he was likely to hear directly from either Shorty Freeland or Gene Blanton or some other enforcer in the governor's inner circle, if not from Blanton himself. Who needed that kind of trouble? Better to lay low. Even among major Democratic leaders in the state, there was a general silence.

One exception was Ned McWherter, a formidable politician who pushed back—because he could.

MCWHERTER WAS A FELLOW West Tennessean and a Democratic Party ally of Blanton's in their early careers, and he was the speaker of the Tennessee House of Representatives throughout the period of Blanton's term as governor. They did not clash in public; in most respects, McWherter was a constant supporter of the Blanton administration's initiatives and priorities. Instead, the speaker was emerging as the dominant leader in a legislature that was now becoming more independent of the executive branch.

Reflecting years later on their long association, McWherter said in an interview that the trouble with Blanton usually began when the governor started drinking. At first, it was the drinking in the afternoon. Later, it would start in the morning.

"Ray Blanton was a good person," McWherter said. "He got engaged personally, I think, in some things that caused him to 'bend the elbow' too much. When he got too much stimulation in his system, he would do crazy things."

McWherter's biographer, Billy Stair, described Blanton's administration as deeply marred by its governor's drinking problem.

"Plagued by alcoholism, Blanton was often detached from his duties and his staff, several of whom sought to use their offices for financial gain through the sale of pardons, liquor licenses and surplus state property," Stair recalled in *McWherter*, his volume on McWherter's career. "Many who worked with Blanton state that he acted responsibly in the mornings until he started drinking around lunch. The alcohol produced a crude personal style and an undisguised contempt for the press that made his term as Governor a period of constant controversy."

Bill Rawlins was a senior reporter and editor for the Associated Press for forty-five years and covered six Tennessee governors, including Blanton. In his 2001 memoir of the McWherter years, Rawlins described how the capitol hill press corps had downplayed its coverage of Blanton's drinking while he was in office.

"Blanton's alcoholism was rarely, if ever, mentioned in print or on radio or television, possibly because there were so many other juicy things to write about. In hindsight, this was wrong. The governor's problems with alcohol affected his ability to govern, if only because it impaired his ability to keep track of what was going on. . . . According to his intimates, Blanton began drinking a little about 10 a.m. and nipped a little more as the day went on.

This manifested itself in his news conferences. If he scheduled a morning news conference, he presented information he wanted to get across and answered reporters' questions without rancor. Afternoon news conferences, on the other hand, sometimes bordered on the sensational. The later in the day, the more argumentative he became, and his answers to questions were belligerent."

WHATEVER THE CAUSE, BLANTON'S personal style could be gruff, blunt, and at times crude, whether he was dealing with a subordinate or even with a private citizen, particularly one he felt might be aligned with his political enemies.

Mike Fitts, an architect and career state employee who eventually served as the state architect for nearly forty years, remembers such treatment on the day he met Blanton, in 1975, shortly after the inauguration in January. Fitts described the morning when his boss, Commissioner Bill Jones, who was Blanton's appointee over the Department of Finance and Administration, introduced him to the governor. Blanton immediately confronted Fitts about repairs to the base of the prominent statue of Ed Carmack that stands on the south side of the capitol grounds.

"We finished building the Legislative Plaza complex in 1974–75, and after the election I had already heard from Blanton's people, who said he wanted me to drain the pools on the plaza so all the people coming to see him would have room to stand at his inauguration. We didn't do that," Fitts recalled. "So one morning after the inauguration, Commissioner Jones and I were stepping off the escalator that connects the capitol building to the plaza, and we see the governor and some of his staff coming the other direction. Bill Jones asked me, 'Have you met Governor Blanton?' I had not."

Jones made the introduction. Blanton turned to Fitts and asked him about the railings that surround the Carmack statue. Fitts said he explained the status of the work, including the time required to match and select the proper materials for such a prominent focal point. Blanton then replied:

"Fitts, if you take as long fixing the toilets in the Legislative Plaza as it's taking you to finish the railing, we'll be up to our ears in shit."

Blanton then turned and walked away.

"That's how I met him," Fitts told me. "He was not very smooth."

EACH DECEMBER, BLANTON AND his staff would throw a Christmas party at the governor's residence for reporters in the capitol press corps and their spouses. Most reporters who attended remember these as relaxed, festive events.

Hank Allison, a reporter for the Nashville CBS affiliate WTVF-TV, and his wife, Sue, attended the last of these, in December 1978. In a keepsake letter to his son Robert, Allison later described a scene at the party involving the Blanton family dog:

"When Mom and I went to the residence for the party, he was in his last year of office and had a little dog. He asked me if I want to see him do a trick. I said yes. He said [to the dog], 'He's Republican!' and the little dog grabbed the cuff of my pants and started shaking it back in forth and growling."

Sue Allison, also an editor and reporter, said the incident was "an entertaining trick that seemed to amuse the governor mightily."

BLANTON'S EARLY CAREER in the family's construction business had prepared him and others in his inner circle to have a keen interest in state government building projects. The single largest capital project during his term was the new James K. Polk State Office Building in Nashville, a structure that was also designed (under the previous administration) to house the Tennessee Performing Arts Center, incorporating three theaters. Private-sector donors, led by Nashville philanthropist Martha R. Ingram, proceeded to raise a matching fund to build the TPAC portion of the new structure.

Mrs. Ingram had been a member of the advisory board of the Kennedy Center for the Performing Arts, which opened in Washington, DC, in 1970, and at that time she began to consider how Nashville might have a comparable facility. She and her associates worked closely with Governor Dunn, securing his support as well as speaker Ned McWherter's, for a public-private sharing of the capital costs. She recalled two encounters she had with Blanton in early 1975. The first meeting was at a reception to recognize the leading fundraising volunteers.

"The state had already approved $36 million for the project, but the new governor had the power to stop that, so I wanted to introduce myself," she said. "We were seated, and people were getting their recognition for having raised some money. It was just small talk before the ceremony, and I said what I thought was a polite compliment."

INGRAM: Governor, you're much more handsome in person than in your pictures.
BLANTON: Well, that's certainly a nice thing for you to say. I'd like to take you home with me tonight.

Ingram said she ignored the remark but felt "very uncomfortable" about the conversation. Her second encounter with Blanton was in the governor's office, on the following Monday, a meeting she had requested in order to ask formally for his support of the public portion of the funding for the TPAC project. This meeting did not go well, either, for any of several reasons.

Because of Blanton's suggestive remark at the reception, Mrs. Ingram asked her husband, E. Bronson Ingram, to accompany her. He was a prominent industrialist, a leading figure in Republican campaign finance, and he was also related by marriage to John Jay Hooker. (His sister Alice was the wife of John Jay's brother Henry Hooker.) Any one of these factors might have made the governor too uneasy about Bronson's presence and incline him to oppose whatever Martha was requesting. In any case, Blanton had been briefed on the subject and he wasted no time on pleasantries.

"He [Blanton] looked straight at me," Mrs. Ingram remembered, "and he said, 'Well, we're not going to build that project. We don't need any more damned THE-aters.' I said, 'But we've raised all this money.' He said words to the effect that 'Well, that's your problem.'

"I was stunned. I wasn't in tears; I was just too stunned to react at all. When we were back in the corridor, Bronson said he thought Blanton's comment was uncalled for, and he suggested that we go see Ned McWherter, if he might happen to be in town."

McWherter had endorsed the TPAC project in 1972, and his support as the new speaker of the house was important. He was in his office when the Ingrams arrived. Bronson explained the unfortunate meeting that had occurred just minutes earlier.

"Bronson said, 'Martha has obviously been traveling the state for two years, raising money' and I remember, very clearly, Ned putting his big arm around my shoulder and saying, 'Now, Martha, don't you worry about this anymore. I can handle him. Your theater is going to be built, like we said it would. We've given you our word. You've done what you said you would do, and we're going to do what we said we'd do.'

"I never talked to the governor again," Mrs. Ingram told me. "I never had to deal with him after that. The project worked out. The center opened in 1980, and the state did what they said they would do. I never asked Ned, 'What did you do?' I just thanked him."

For a time, in the early years of Blanton's term, the governor and his staff had cordial relations with reporters covering the governor's office, including those from the newsroom at the *Tennessean*. This flowed, in part, from the newspaper's endorsement of his campaign in the 1974 race, and the *Tennessean* and its staff were still considered friendly within the governor's circle.

When *Tennessean* reporter Jerry Thompson married in the summer of 1975, his colleague Frank Sutherland (later the editor of newspaper) used his connections as a capitol hill reporter to arrange an elaborate practical joke.

Sutherland asked Eddie Sisk, Blanton's legal counsel, if there were any way he might obtain mock extradition papers. He thought he could arrange for such a document to be "served" on Thompson immediately following his wedding ceremony in Coopertown, Tennessee, by a friendly deputy from the Robertson County sheriff's department.

Sisk obliged. But when Sutherland picked up the envelope, he saw inside that he had actually been provided with a genuine extradition document—complete with Governor Blanton's own signature, and even with the official state seal affixed—sending Thompson to the custody of authorities in Florida. If not for an understanding sheriff's office, cooperative in the joke, Thompson might have spent his honeymoon behind bars in the Sunshine State.

It was all in good fun. Of course, no one, at the time, gave much thought to who else might be signing the governor's name—and onto what other types of official documents.

DEEPER INTO HIS TERM, Blanton's behavior turned erratic, and his moods grew dark. In time, his circle grew smaller.

His rising notoriety had also complicated the lives of senior Democrats in the state, and this extended to leaders in the national party also. This tension combined with the continuing investigations by federal authorities, as well as news media, prompted some politicians to avoid public appearances with the governor.

It was not difficult for the elected officials in Tennessee's congressional delegation to avoid contact and joint appearances. Both Senator Jim Sasser and Congressman Al Gore Jr. were still in their first terms, following their elections in 1976. Sasser had defeated Senator Bill Brock, and Gore won the House seat that had been held for thirty years by Representative Joe L. Evins, who retired. Roy Neel, a young Gore staff member who would later serve as chief of staff to Vice President Gore, remembered the general attitude toward the governor.

"Most of us viewed the Blanton governor's office as a toxic waste dump of misbehavior and trouble, and nobody wanted to get near it," he told me.

BLANTON MIGHT HAVE RUN for a second term. A constitutional convention in 1977 had amended the state's charter to permit an incumbent governor to serve two consecutive four-year terms. Blanton could have been the first to take advantage of this new rule. Most of his longtime supporters figured he would do so. But by the spring of 1978, with the primary election only months away, Blanton and his inner circle were beset by scandal and investigations on several fronts. Controversy had swiftly overwhelmed his administration, isolating him from other leaders in his party.

Now, to the bitter disappointment of his most loyal partisans, Blanton surprised cabinet officers and friends by announcing that he would not run again. For this announcement, he chose an otherwise festive gathering, a watermelon picnic on the governor's residence lawn for several hundred men and women from across the state who sat on the ninety-five-county "advisory committees," more commonly known in the news media by now as the "patronage" committees. Shorty Freeland, Blanton's old friend and top staff aide and coordinator of the patronage committee apparatus, had arranged the event.

Even Shorty was surprised by the governor's announcement that afternoon. For the Democratic Party establishment, it meant there would be a chance to recover. It meant that, come summer, there would be an open primary.

BUT THE ROGER HUMPHREYS case did not disappear. Blanton was still the governor, with an unlimited power to pardon under the state's constitution. In the months leading up to the November 1978 election, that possibility figured significantly—though in different ways—in both Alexander's campaign and also for the Democrat Jake Butcher.

Following the initial uproar over Blanton's public pledge to pardon Humphreys, Alexander and his staff had enlisted two high-profile political leaders—Dunn, a Republican, and also John Jay Hooker, Dunn's Democratic opponent in the 1970 race—to oppose the pardon and publicly urge Blanton to recant. These former political opponents were enthusiastic with their new assignment, eloquent in its execution. They launched a round of news conferences across the state and announced their goal of collecting "one million signatures" on a petition urging Blanton to reverse his decision.

"It was a high use for Hooker. It was a high use for Winfield," Lew Conner remembered. "You've got to understand it took a whole lot of help from Democrats who had significant support, in order for us to win this election. One of them was Hooker, who still had his own very significant following. Hooker would've been elected in 1974 had he chosen to run. . . . We could not have won. If Blanton was gonna beat us, I think Hooker was gonna beat us worse. And the Clement family was very important to us."

As a political strategy, the petition drive had multiple benefits for the Alexander campaign as the November election drew near: unless and until Blanton recanted, it would keep the pardon issue clearly alive (especially as a wedge issue for Democratic voters); it would daily remind both voters and political writers in the news media of the broader clemency scandal surrounding Blanton's administration, and this potentially could isolate Alexander's opponent, East Tennessee banker Jake Butcher, from the base of Blanton loyalists in West Tennessee.

Butcher campaign leaders knew this. In their own extensive polling, they could see that the Humphreys case—together with Blanton's behavior, especially with news media reporters who questioned him about it—was eroding any advantage of having a fellow Democrat in the office. Clearly the long-running Humphreys controversy was taking a mounting toll on Democrats statewide. The party's nominees at every level, especially incumbent legislators, were at risk of attack and defeat, if it continued deeper into the fall, meaning their Republican opponents would likely use the gathering scandal as ammunition against them.

BUTCHER'S CAMPAIGN MANAGER, Karl Schledwitz, told me that Blanton by this time had become "a lightning rod"—drawing negative feelings toward himself and whomever he touched—and that the Butcher campaign plan therefore stressed the avoidance of any public association with the sitting governor.

The Humphreys issue was potentially very damaging to Democratic campaigns, because of Blanton's role as titular party leader, and especially for the Butcher campaign. The East Tennessee banker needed Blanton's base of supporters in West Tennessee, but because of the governor's dismal approval rating by this time, Butcher was loath to make the kind of joint public appearances that commonly benefit a nominee's general campaign when his own party controls the governor's office.

"We had a well-funded campaign, and the benefit of being able to do a lot of polling," Schledwitz told me, "and Blanton's numbers were horrific. Jake wasn't making joint appearances with Blanton. There was definitely an effort to avoid any appearance that we were connected to Blanton.

"It was a two-edged sword," he said. "We wanted access to his donor base and political apparatus, but at the same time you don't want the connection with him publicly. It was always a tightrope, a balancing act. We were trying to get Blanton to go away publicly as much as possible, and trying to have Jake not appear connected."

Accordingly, Butcher's team searched for ways to reach out and privately appeal for moderation on the pardon issue. They adopted a high-level brother-to-brother strategy. Leader of this effort on Butcher's side was the nominee's brother, C. H. Butcher, head of the C and C Banks in Knox County, and on the governor's side his younger brother, Gene Blanton.

"We were trying to do everything we could to get Blanton to tone it down," Schledwitz remembers. "C. H. was working through Gene Blanton—that was the main channel of activity."

Whatever the cause—either the very private entreaties from the Butcher camp, or Alexander's very public Dunn-Hooker petition gambit, or the combination of both—something worked. Blanton publicly backed off.

On Halloween, October 31, Blanton announced that "after prayerful consideration" he had reconsidered and would not be pardoning Humphreys after all.

This news took most of the steam out of the Dunn-Hooker juggernaut, but by then the damage to Butcher's campaign was done. It was not the only controversial issue that dragged Butcher down; from the Alexander campaign, a steady barrage of questions regarding Jake Butcher's banking practices had also gained substantial news coverage statewide in the latter days of the race.

BLANTON'S PUBLIC COMMITMENT TO back off the Humphreys pardon did not last long. Just long enough, some said later, for the cloud of controversy to clear and for the November election to come and go.

Election day arrived on November 7, and late that evening Alexander's margin of victory was eight percentage points, technically a landslide. Just ten days later, Blanton now told a young reporter for the *Nashville Banner* that he would pardon Humphreys after all. The question seemed to come out of the blue, but the governor answered quickly.

Peggy Reisser was barely six months out of journalism school. She had graduated from the University of Mississippi in Oxford on a Saturday the previous May and went to work at the *Banner* two days later. On November 17, she was assigned to cover a routine news conference in the governor's office, and before departing for the capitol, she chatted with senior reporters Mike Pigott and David Fox, the *Banner* chief political writer.

"You should ask him about Roger Humphreys," Fox said. By this time, because of Blanton's previous statement that a pardon for Humphreys would not be happening, the Correction Department was enjoying a somewhat lower profile in the news. Today's news conference was about other matters, mostly perfunctory announcements, and chiefly to make Blanton available to the capitol press corps.

The usual group of print, TV, and radio news reporters gathered in Blanton's office, a large rectangular space on the southeast corner of the capitol's first floor. The governor then stepped into the room and delivered his prepared comments. Then he invited questions.

"At the time, I was still learning about politics," Reisser told me. "I was knowledgeable about how to cover things, but I had been there only a short time. I said, 'Governor, do you still plan to pardon Roger Humphreys?'"

"Yes, I do," Blanton replied.

The room quickly erupted with a barrage of questions on the Humphreys pardon issue: When? How? Why? Whatever small thing Blanton had come into the room to announce was quickly forgotten. Humphreys was suddenly back on page 1.

And the cloud over the capitol, which in ten days had not drifted so far to begin with, now turned darker still.

Lee Lucas was twenty-three years old and hardly more than a temp in December 1978. The Alexander landslide had darkened her outlook also, as the newest and most vulnerable staff member of a governor who would soon leave office.

She had been hired as a receptionist in late September and reported to the governor's executive secretary, Dianne Turner. It was now clear that, in a few more weeks, a new governor would be sitting at the big desk in the next room—and most likely he would be bringing along a new receptionist, too.

Lucas' short time on the job had nonetheless brought its share of excitement. There was the morning in early November when she answered the phone and the caller was Lamar Alexander, the governor-elect, asking if he could speak with Governor Blanton about the transition plans.

She quickly figured this to be an extraordinary opportunity for herself and blurted to Alexander that she would love to keep her job as receptionist, if possible, after the inauguration in January. The governor-elect kindly took her name and said someone would follow up with her at an appropriate time.

Then there had been the staff Christmas party at the governor's residence in early December, a festive evening she attended with her mother and her twin sons. A keepsake photo was taken of the family, standing with a smiling Governor Blanton.

And there had been the afternoon of December 15, the day the FBI men came to visit.

SHE CANNOT RECALL THEIR NAMES, but she remembers the badge.

FBI agent Hank Hillin told me it was not him and claims she must be mistaken. But Lucas is firm in her recollection that three men in dark suits entered the governor's reception room at about 1:00 p.m.

This was the same December day that FBI agents, in a coordinated sweep in Memphis and Nashville, arrested three of Blanton's closest aides: his legal counsel, Eddie Sisk; the staff extradition officer, Charles Benson; and a Tennessee Highway Patrol officer, Lieutenant Fred Taylor, who had been assigned to the governor's security detail. Agents arrested Sisk at his ground-floor office at the capitol, one floor below the governor's reception room and office; Benson at the Nashville airport; and Taylor inside a motel room in Memphis.

Lucas described the scene in the governor's reception room:

"I remember thinking 'These are not tourists.' One of them—he had blond hair—came up to my desk and waited for me to get off the phone, and the other two went to other spots in the office. One of them went over to what we called 'the trooper's desk,' which was Fred Taylor's desk. I was on the phone, and this lead person just stood at the corner of my desk, waiting until I finished the call. He was very polite."

"Are you Lee Lucas?" the man asked, showing Lucas his badge.

"Yes, sir."

"Is Governor Blanton in the office now?"

"No, sir, he's not."

"Do you know if he is at the residence?"

"I don't know for sure."

"I want you to call the residence and determine if the governor is there. But don't tell anyone we're here."

Lucas quickly dialed the number at the highway patrol security desk on Curtiswood Lane. The sergeant who answered was positioned at a communications post on the ground floor, located just off the kitchen. From this position, the officer on duty could observe four black-and-white video screens displaying real-time images from the front gate down the hill and at other locations on the grounds. He was accustomed to receiving transfer calls throughout the day from Lee Lucas.

"Hey, Miss Lee," the trooper said brightly.

"Hello" she said. "Is the governor there?"

"Yes, ma'am, he is. Do you need to transfer a call?"

"Hold on a minute," she replied, still not grasping the purpose of all this, and not wanting to say the wrong thing. She quickly covered the mouthpiece of her phone and told the agent at her desk what the sergeant had asked.

"Give me the phone," the agent replied softly.

"Sergeant," the agent said, according to Lucas, "I want you to look at your security camera screen right now. At the front gate you will see one of our agents holding up his badge. I want you to ask the governor to come downstairs, so that we can talk to him."

Lucas recalls that all this happened very quickly, and remembers asking the agent at her desk: "Am I in trouble?" And he said "No, you're not. You've been very helpful to us. Thank you.' And they left."

What the agents asked Blanton that night, and how he responded, are not known. He was not arrested; more likely a subpoena and possibly a search warrant were served. An FBI agent later recalled that Blanton left his residence later that night, managing to elude agents who were posted there to follow him; he instructed at least two troopers to drive their unmarked cars through the gate and followed them in a third vehicle; the three vehicles were then observed heading in different directions, with the federal agents following two of them, but not the third in which Blanton, alone, was behind the wheel. A Blanton confidant told me the governor boasted to him days later that on this night—just hours after three of his own senior staff members had been placed under arrest by federal agents—he had driven himself unimpeded to the home of a female friend.

This was December 15.

EARLIER ON THIS SAME DAY, two hundred miles to the west in downtown Memphis, undercover agents had wrapped up a series of meetings with an unsuspecting source. Their guest was Fred Taylor, the veteran officer of the Tennessee Highway Patrol.

On these days, Lieutenant Taylor had been absent from his post in the governor's reception room in Nashville. Instead, according to federal prosecutors, he was in a motel room in Memphis talking calmly—and unwittingly—into a wire worn by the government's informant, Arthur Baldwin, the operator of a topless nightclub in Memphis. Several federal officials were in the next room listening in, watching video on television monitor screens, and recording it all for evidence.

By 1978, Taylor's precise "official" assignment had become something of a mystery within state government. When he was at the capitol, sitting at his post on the south end of the reception room, he was usually talking quietly into the telephone. He was frequently away. Whether official or not, his actual assignment was in service to the governor's younger brother, Gene Blanton. The younger Blanton was never a state employee, but he had a private office at the capitol, just off the reception room, a mere thirty feet from the governor's desk.

Federal investigators would later testify that Taylor was the main connection in the governor's office for families and friends of prison inmates seeking freedom for a price. FBI agents had skillfully recorded Taylor's numerous meetings with Baldwin. It was these encounters and taped conversations that had led to the coordinated arrests, on December 15, of Taylor in Memphis and of Benson and Sisk in Nashville.

The agents retrieved marked $100 bills from Sisk's pocket when they placed him under arrest in his office on the ground floor of the capitol building. At the Nashville airport, Benson was stopped just moments before boarding a plane for Memphis. Investigators said he was carrying clemency papers for one of the prisoners mentioned in the tape recordings.

The government later charged that all of this was connected: That the cash in Sisk's pocket was part of the payoffs for arranging the release of selected prisoners. On the clemency paperwork in Benson's briefcase, agents found the name of triple-murderer Eddie Dallas Denton.

In 1981, Sisk and Taylor were convicted on racketeering charges in federal court. Benson was acquitted.

FROM THE MIDDLE OF DECEMBER to the middle of January, with the controversy raging and the national media now paying attention also, speaker McWherter was apparently the only Democratic Party elder to make a direct appeal to Blanton. He reached out, privately, and sent a message to his old friend, imploring the governor to back down on the promised pardon.

The form of this message is now unclear. If it was a letter or note, the document is apparently lost to history. Neither McWherter's personal secretary Betty Haynes nor his longtime business associate Madelyn Pritchett remembered such a letter or could say where a copy might be found.

Stair, McWherter's biographer, told me his boss often wrote notes by hand, and therefore it was possible that no copy would have been retained. Seigenthaler had heard of such a letter but speculated that Blanton might have been so angry "he tore it up." If Blanton kept such a note, which is doubtful, it did not end up in his catalogued official papers at the Tennessee State Library and Archives, as governors' correspondence properly should.

In any event, McWherter's message to Blanton was simple: "Issue a bunch of commutations here at the last, and the legislature will inaugurate Alexander early."

AT ABOUT THIS TIME, McWherter also phoned Hal Hardin, the US attorney for Middle Tennessee.

"This is when I first heard that he [Blanton] was planning to release a group of inmates," McWherter recalled, in an interview years later. "I called the United States attorney the week before this happened, and I told him I did not know my constitutional responsibilities, that I was also going to call Attorney General Leech, and asked them if they thought I had any constitutional responsibilities I wanted them to let me know."

Hardin's memory of this brief conversation is profound. McWherter spoke slowly, somberly, and he even addressed the US attorney as "General," which is an honorific usually reserved for county prosecutors. Recalling this brief exchange, Hardin said he remembered there was "something about his voice, so sincere, that I just sat motionless for some time."

> MCWHERTER: General, this is Ned McWherter. I just want to let you
> know that if you ever need my help, I'm here to help you.
> HARDIN: Thank you. Thank you very much.

In our interview, Hardin said he regarded McWherter's call as extraordinary, coming from a senior state government official, and highly significant.

"I felt later that he might have been inviting me to reach back out to him. I've thought a lot about it. Was he thinking I was the only one who would do anything? Had something happened I didn't know about? In the end, I believe he was just frustrated and wanted me to know that, no matter what, he was there if I needed him."

ON MONDAY, JANUARY 15, early in the evening, John M. Parish and his wife, Cile, were spending their first night in their new apartment in downtown Nashville.

In five days, on Saturday, Parish would be starting to work as Alexander's press secretary, following the inauguration ceremony. He was already assisting the transition office with occasional announcements of other new cabinet appointments. The political editor and a columnist for the *Jackson Sun*, and one of the most senior members of the capitol hill press corps, he had been recruited by Alexander in December.

In the beginning, Tom Ingram had wanted this job. He was unquestionably Alexander's closest adviser, had been the campaign press secretary in 1974, and was elevated to campaign manager for the 1978 race. After Alexander's victory, Ingram had privately hoped to be the new press secretary by the time of this triumphant week in January. But *Tennessean* editor John Seigenthaler had different advice. He had known and admired Ingram, both as a former member of his own news staff and later as an astute political operative, but nonetheless the editor now gave Alexander a contrary view about filling this key position.

"John Seigenthaler gave me a book by George Reedy, called *Twilight of the Presidency*," Alexander recalled. Reedy had been President Lyndon Johnson's press secretary.

"I read it for one thing—to learn about executive leadership. Reedy said a president needed to do three things: See a need, develop a strategy to meet the need, and persuade at least half the people you're right. But Seigenthaler gave it to me for another lesson: to not surround yourself with people who were too close to you to begin with. John said to me that in the midst of the Blanton scandal and the lack of confidence in state government, Ingram was too close to me to be the press secretary.

"He said you should pick the meanest, toughest, most independent reporter you can find in the state, make him the press secretary, tell him he can come into any meeting unannounced, and to always tell the truth. That definition fit one person—John Parish, the crusty *Jackson Sun* political reporter—so I asked him to do it, and he did. Tom became the deputy to the governor, which he excelled in, but he gave up his opportunity to be the press secretary."

THE PARISH'S NEW APARTMENT was on the twelfth floor of the Capitol Towers, on James Robertson Parkway, at the foot of capitol hill. In an unpublished memoir of his career, Parish described the view out his apartment window, which faced south, and the scene up the hill:

"I could look out my window and see the lights burning late in the Capitol," Parish wrote. He probably did not learn until the following day what business they had been up to. "Governor Blanton and Secretary of State Gentry Crowell were signing last-minute pardons and commutations that would turn a lot of criminals out of prison—some of them with political connections and some who allegedly had bought their freedom.

"My instincts as a newsman made me want to get right over there and cover this big story. It was difficult to be a spectator when something like this was taking place."

LATE ON THIS MONDAY EVENING, Blanton was sipping scotch as he signed clemency papers for fifty-two state prisoners. Only three of these were outright pardons. The convicted double-murderer Roger Humphreys was one of them.

It was an extraordinary, shocking event under the circumstances. Behind the privacy of his closed office door, shielded from news reporters waiting outside in the first-floor hallway of the state capitol, as the calendar rolled down to barely five days left on his time in office, Blanton did the unthinkable. In the group of fifty-two, he had commuted the sentences of twenty-three convicted murderers, many of them released for time served—meaning they could immediately walk free through the prison gates. Moreover, thirty-six of the fifty-two were prisoners who had *not* been recommended for release by the state's Board of Pardons and Paroles.

With him were three people. Retired Nashville judge Robert Lillard, who had replaced Eddie Sisk as the governor's legal counsel the month before, had worked through the entire day preparing the fifty-two clemency documents. The commissioner of the Department of Correction, C. Murray Henderson, stood nearby, apparently silent. Secretary of State Gentry Crowell, whose attesting signature was required, sat with Blanton as he executed the documents.

Crowell described this scene later for *Tennessean* reporter Doug Hall. Crowell said that when Blanton came to the paperwork for Humphreys, he paused and looked up at the secretary of state.

"This takes guts," the governor said.

"Some people have more guts than brains," Crowell replied.

Blanton then looked back down, put his pen to the pardon certificate, and signed it. Crowell, as he had done with the other documents, dutifully affixed his own signature as a witness. The governor then handed the Humphreys pardon to Henderson.

Blanton put on his trench-coat, and the four men walked through the office door leading to the first-floor corridor, where about a dozen news reporters and photographers were waiting for any update. As Blanton paused there briefly to answer questions, Crowell walked down the hall to his office with his record of what documents had been executed. Henderson, unnoticed in this commotion, quietly left the building and walked to a waiting car.

COMMISSIONER HENDERSON NOW MOTORED down capitol hill to Charlotte Avenue, where he turned right and traveled the six miles to the Tennessee State Penitentiary, a gloomy castle-like structure in an industrial area of western Davidson County.

The state's main prison, opened in 1898, looms as a foreboding shape against the night sky. Its fortress architecture is arresting—massive stone walls, medieval corner towers topped by high conical roofs—all surely designed to instill helplessness and fear. It was closed in 1992 after a judge declared the place cruel and unusual, but the vision of it has lived on. It has since been a favored location of movie directors wanting a venue to convey the essence of Maximum Security Prison, a vision of hopelessness and doom for all who entered: it was featured in *The Green Mile* (1999), starring Tom Hanks and James Cromwell, and in *The Last Castle* (2001), with Robert Redford and James Gandolfini. In its day, however, this place was not fiction, but all too real.

On this cold Monday night, the commissioner's car rolled to a stop at the front door of the reception building, on the south side of the prison complex. Humphreys' attorney, David Pack, promptly stepped out of the darkness to greet him. Pack had been the state's attorney general until 1974. He had resigned to run for governor, only to become one of the eleven Democrats who lost to Blanton. He was now in private practice in Nashville, and no lawyer in town had a client with a higher profile.

Henderson handed him the pardon certificate, the ink of the governor's signature barely dry on the paper. Pack now walked through the heavy door of the penitentiary gatehouse and presented this document to the officer on duty. A moment later, the same door opened once again and Humphreys appeared, holding his packed suitcase in his hand.

He turned to his lawyer and asked one question.

"Am I dreaming?"

Silently now, the most famous double-murderer in America climbed into another sedan, closed its door, and disappeared into the January night.

CHAPTER 6

A Man of Great Promise

The most fatal thing a man can do is try to stand alone.
—Carson McCullers, *The Heart Is a Lonely Hunter*

THE FIRST US ATTORNEY to be posted in Nashville was Andrew Jackson. During his early career, in 1788, the future president was appointed solicitor of the Western District.

Like Hal Hardin 190 years later, Jackson served at different times as the federal government's attorney and also as a trial judge. Both men were tall and physically imposing, and both bore a visible facial scar on the right cheek, from their youth—Jackson's from the sword of an angry British soldier, Hardin's from an automobile accident when he was thrown through the windshield, requiring 188 stitches. Hardin's great-great-grandfather, Obediah Hardin, served in Jackson's army in the Battle of New Orleans.

President Jackson is regarded as the founder of the Democratic Party. But for all his achievements and fame, his name has been forever controversial—as much so among Tennesseans as he has been across the nation—even to the present day. His war against the national bank stirred opposition, but the most persistent criticism of Jacksonian domestic policy, over generations and continuing today, has centered on his championing of Indian removal. Hardin, in fairness, counts himself among those critics. (Jackson's fellow Tennessean, Congressman David Crockett, opposed the president on many issues and lost his own House seat in 1834 before meeting his fate with other Tennessee volunteers at the Alamo. "You may all go to hell, and I will go to Texas," Crockett famously said, before heading west.)

Hardin, too, was a life-long Democrat, and by 1977, when President Carter named him the US attorney for the Middle District of Tennessee, he might have felt a debt of gratitude to Governor Ray Blanton. He had not been a Blanton supporter in the 1974 election but had nonetheless become the new governor's first judicial appointee as a state circuit judge. Blanton had also appointed him to serve on the Tennessee Law Enforcement Commission.

Yet, in the kind of irony that will happen in state and local politics, it was Hardin who in time would initiate the maneuver to oust Blanton from office.

HARDIN WAS THE SON of a tenant farmer near Old Hickory, Tennessee, a dozen miles northeast of Nashville. His mother wanted him to be a preacher, but Hardin insisted he wanted to work for the FBI. After finishing high school, in 1959, Hardin set out to travel across the country, both to begin working his way through college and also for the experience and the adventure. One of his jobs was on a commercial pea farm in Walla Walla, Washington, where he met another young man from Nashville named Frank Woods.

Along the way on his western journey, Hardin attended five different colleges, and in fact he did take a job as a fingerprint technician in the FBI headquarters in Washington, DC. He then joined the Peace Corps—all before finally earning his college degree at Middle Tennessee State University. (There are still tales told among some Nashville lawyers that Hardin, during his Peace Corps service, was in reality working for the Central Intelligence Agency. He denies this.)

In the Peace Corps, in 1963, Hardin was assigned to duty in the jungles of Colombia near the Rio Magdalena and the town of Plato. In a 1965 interview for a profile in the *Tennessean Magazine*, Hardin told writer Max York that he had initially been cautious about the available food in the remote villages, thinking it was unhealthy. There was no refrigeration, so the local diets often included spoiled meat as well as contaminated water, so Hardin said he avoided them. A large man—six feet three inches tall—he lost forty-three pounds, down from 210, before putting his apprehension aside.

"After a while I decided that wouldn't do," he recalled. "I couldn't bond with the people if I was separating myself from them in that way. I thought 'If these folks can eat it, so can I.' After that, I stopped losing and gained back a few pounds."

Years later, he remembers being "forever changed by the experience" in the South American jungle. Hardin formed cooperatives, including tobacco and savings co-ops to eliminate middlemen, and community action groups that improved sanitation and nutrition for poverty-stricken local citizens. The teams he organized installed eight hundred latrines and built better roofs for shelters. Before he departed the jungle, Hardin had gained the respect of local families and village leaders, for his own leadership skills.

When he returned to Tennessee, he finished his last year of college at Middle Tennessee State and entered law school at the University of Tennessee at Knoxville. (One of his law school roommates in Knoxville was T. Edward Sisk, who in 1975 would become legal counsel to Governor Blanton.) During this period, in the summer of 1966, Hardin left law school to join the campaign of John Jay Hooker, who was running for the Democratic nomination for governor of Tennessee.

A HANDSOME MAN with movie-star good looks and a jovial manner, Hardin soon found political campaigns to his liking. In Hooker's 1966 primary campaign, Hardin reported directly to the candidate, first as a driver for two weeks and then as a traveling aide. He operated from the state campaign headquarters in the old Andrew Jackson Hotel, with its view of the state capitol across Memorial Square.

Through the summer he worked the long hours typical of a young gubernatorial campaign staff member, and here he encountered Frank Woods again and Frank's brother Larry Woods, among several other young attorneys then also in their early twenties.

These included Bill Willis, Bob Brandt, Charles Bone, Aaron Wyckoff, Charles Burson, and Charles Susano, as well as the candidate's brother, Henry Hooker. By this time, Frank Woods had married Jayne Ann Owens of Paris, Tennessee, also a lawyer. (She was arguably the biggest celebrity in the group at the time, having been crowned Miss Nashville and the first runner-up Miss Tennessee in 1964.) As all these friendships developed over the following years, most of the young lawyers connected to the Hooker campaign would become important politically themselves. Most would go on to roles in other Democratic campaigns and, for some, into new law firms they formed together. Three of these (Susano, Brandt, and Hardin) would become judges, and another (Burson) would be Tennessee's attorney general. Jayne Ann Woods would later serve with distinction as commissioner of the Tennessee Department of Revenue on Governor Blanton's cabinet.

After Hooker lost the primary in early August, he asked his young aide to come to work in his Nashville law office, and Hardin accepted. Hooker then persuaded Alexander Heard, the chancellor of Vanderbilt University, to arrange for Hardin's admission to the Vanderbilt School of Law. Hardin received his law degree there in August 1968. The next state bar examination was not scheduled until the following February; Hardin meanwhile took a job as acting director of the St. Louis Job Corps Center for Women, an agency that was part of a company run by Frank Woods at the time.

SIX MONTHS LATER, HARDIN RETURNED to Nashville and passed the bar exam, and the local district attorney, Tom Shriver, offered him a job in the county prosecutor's office. He remembers telling Shriver he would take the job on one condition: That he be assigned as "the third man" at the prosecution table for an upcoming trial that some were already calling the "master trial of the century"—the 1969 murder trial of Nashville car dealer William Powell, accused of killing his business partner, Haynie Gourley. The opposing lawyers in this case were the two most celebrated attorneys in the city at the time: Jack Norman Sr., for the defense, and John Jay Hooker Sr., father of the recent gubernatorial candidate, serving as a special prosecutor on Shriver's team. These two celebrated lawyers were personal friends and longtime competitors, and they had not faced each other in a courtroom since the famous Jimmy Hoffa trial.

Shriver agreed, and the spectacular murder trial was everything Hardin had hoped it would be. Both Powell and Gourley had been socially prominent, and there was high news media interest in the state capital. The *Tennessean*, believing Powell to be guilty, had aggressively pushed for facts during the police investigation. Once the trial began, both the *Tennessean* and the *Banner* published full transcripts of each day's court proceedings. Seigenthaler's son John Michael Seigenthaler (later known as John Seigenthaler Jr., when he was the weekend anchor on *NBC Nightly News*) was a thirteen-year-old copy clerk for his father's newspaper at the time. His assignment, each evening, was to fetch the court transcripts by taxi from the court reporter downtown and deliver them to the *Tennessean* typesetters for publication the next morning.

Powell was acquitted, with Norman's defense prevailing over the senior Hooker, and this would be the last time these two legal titans faced off in a Nashville courtroom. A year later, Hardin entered private practice, joining Norman's law firm. There he met his future wife, Pia, Norman's granddaughter, who was employed as an office assistant.

OVER THE NEXT EIGHT YEARS, Hardin established his own resume as a trial attorney as well as state and county prosecutor. He had occasional involvement in other political races, including serving as treasurer for Karl Dean (later the mayor of Nashville) in his first run for county public defender, managing Shriver's race for Congress, and also Randall Wyatt's run for a local judgeship. In 1975, Blanton, in his first judicial appointment as governor, selected Hardin for a vacancy on the state circuit court of Davidson County. He had probably come to Blanton's attention through recommendations from several friends, including Woods and Willis.

On the day of his swearing-in, standing behind Blanton's desk with the governor looking on, Hardin raised his hand and took the oath administered by Justice William J. Harbison, an associate on the five-member Tennessee Supreme Court. Harbison had been one of Hardin's law professors at Vanderbilt, in his civil procedures course, but their families also shared a connection dating back three generations to the Civil War.

Their great-grandfathers—William Matthew Harbison and Isaac Henry Hardin, son of Obediah—served together in the Confederate army and fought at the Battle of Fort Donelson above the Cumberland River, northwest of Nashville. After four days of Confederate bombardment, not a single federal gunboat had been able to pass Fort Donelson. But the advancing Union army, under the command of General Ulysses S. Grant, ultimately prevailed, capturing the fort and taking many prisoners. This was Grant's first important victory and opened the way to Nashville, which became the first Confederate capital to fall.

The captives at Fort Donelson, including Harbison and Hardin, were taken to a federal prison in Illinois. This probably saved their lives. Had they escaped south, they might have had the misfortune to meet Grant's army again, at the bloody Battle of Shiloh. From Fort Donelson, Grant advanced to Shiloh, near Adamsville and Savannah, Tennessee, where the casualties on both sides would surpass twenty-three thousand.

IN 1977, LESS THAN two years after his swearing-in by Justice Harbison, Hardin's fellow judges elected him the presiding judge of all Nashville's courts, and later that same year, President Carter nominated him to be the US attorney for the Middle District of Tennessee. Hardin was only seven years out of law school at this point, and in this position he followed some of the attorneys he admired most.

One was James F. Neal, who had prosecuted Jimmy Hoffa for jury tampering, and in 1973-74 served as the special Watergate prosecutor. Neal would go on to defend Exxon in the *Exxon Valdez* environmental disaster in Alaska; Ford Motor Company in the Ford Pinto litigation; and Elvis Presley's physician, George C. (Dr. Nick) Nichopoulos. Another of Hardin's predecessors as US attorney was Gil Merritt, who would later be named by Carter to a judgeship on the US Sixth Circuit Court of Appeals. (Hardin's father had been a tenant farmer and manager on the Lebanon Road farm owned by Merritt's father.)

As a presiding judge in Nashville, Hardin had instituted some procedural reforms, distributing assignments of some criminal and civil cases to all the sitting judges, and he started holding court on Saturdays. Now, as the US attorney, he likewise continued long hours. He worked hard and earned a reputation, both in his own staff and also among agents of the FBI, as tenacious and thorough in prosecuting criminal defendants and representing the government in many civil proceedings.

These included public officials, as well as white-collar criminals and drug traffickers. Over his nearly four years in the position, the young US attorney established a conviction rate of 98 percent.

HARDIN'S CAREER WAS ON a decidedly fast track. He was also considered by some at this time to be an attractive candidate for public office. There was no Democrat in the state with a more promising future.

This was quite the achievement, in fact, at a time of such overwhelming Democratic Party dominance in Tennessee. It is difficult now, three decades later, to convey how thoroughly Democratic the Middle Tennessee political environment was during this period. Although Baker, Brock, and Dunn had won important Republican victories in statewide offices, the state's middle section was still firmly Democratic. Not only had Blanton retaken the governor's office for the party, but in 1976 Nashville attorney Jim Sasser, longtime chairman of the state Democratic Party, had won the US Senate seat that Senator Albert Gore Sr. had lost to Brock in 1970.

In this partisan environment, Hardin was known as a loyal Democrat and an experienced campaigner with an appealing manner, and he had a sterling reputation as an attorney, judge, and prosecutor. When politicians talked about particular upcoming races, Hardin's name was typically mentioned. One Nashville radio reporter even ordered up "Hardin for Governor" campaign bumper stickers. He would not be moved by this flattery and dismissed any such suggestions.

It was precisely this work record and reputation for party allegiance, in a context of such strong Democratic Party dominance, that made what happened over the next six hours on January 17 all the more extraordinary.

CHAPTER 7

The Dominion of the Editor-in-Chief

The way to right wrongs is to turn the light of truth upon them.
  —Ida B. Wells-Barnett

THE MULTILINE ROTARY PHONE on the editor's desk, nearly hidden behind the clutter of newspapers and circulation reports, rang insistently. The initials on the blinking button read "ACE."

"Can you come up here?" asked Amon Carter Evans, owner and publisher of the *Nashville Tennessean*, the morning newspaper, and John Seigenthaler's only boss in the world.

The editor-in-chief stood quickly, walked out the door of his third-floor office, and strode through the busy newsroom. Bypassing the slow elevator, he bounded up the dim stairwell to Evans' suite on the floor above. He strode down the corridor to the opposite end of the building, smiled at the publisher's secretary as he passed, and stepped into Evans' private office.

Governor Ray Blanton was sitting there, holding a glass in his hand. Seigenthaler remembers that Blanton appeared to be "slightly drunk" and unfocused on this mid-November afternoon.

It was not unusual for Blanton to be in Evans' office, though this was the first such visit in several months. He was, by traditional measures, a friend of the newspaper. But Seigenthaler, based on his own staff's reporting, had grown to dislike the man as crude, venal, and possibly corrupt.

"Hello, Governor," Seigenthaler said.

Blanton nodded, but he was visibly annoyed. Normally, people sitting in this particular room with the publisher and editor of the morning newspaper for an audience—and especially the occasional elected official—were supremely focused on any business or political topic that was at hand, usually solicitous of both the publisher and editor, eager to engage them in conversation.

But not today. When the editor greeted him, Blanton did not rise from his chair. Evans spoke next.

"Ray," the publisher said, "tell John what you just told me."

"Well . . . I've decided I'm going to pardon Roger Humphreys after all," the governor replied. "Amon and I were just talking about it." Blanton added that he was scheduled to speak in Jackson the next day, that he would be flying there on state aircraft, and that he thought he would call a news conference for the time the plane would return him to the National Guard hangar in Nashville.

Turning to Seigenthaler, Evans said: "Now, John. Tell Ray what you think about that." The editor shook his head and then answered bluntly.

"If you pardon him, they'll impeach your ass before sundown."

This produced what Seigenthaler remembers as "this long silence"—Blanton remaining seated, his drink in his hand, looking back at Evans, waiting for him to say something. But Evans said nothing more.

"Well, by God, I'm going to do it," said the governor. Seigenthaler left the room.

UNDER NORMAL CIRCUMSTANCES, in the middle of November of an election year, a governor might have been seated in that particular chair reflecting on his reelection victory. He might have been visiting with the publisher and editor thanking them for their newspaper endorsement and the non-threatening campaign coverage. The glass in his hand might have been for the purpose of a toast.

But Blanton's life and his time as governor had not worked out in that normal way, and most certainly this had not been a normal year. He had not sought reelection, and he was now on a path to a very different future. By this time, he had all but stopped keeping office hours at the capitol, preferring to operate from the privacy of the governor's official residence on Curtiswood Lane in South Nashville.

By the second week of November, on the afternoon of this meeting with Evans and Seigenthaler, Blanton had already been through a full year of controversy, bordering on scandal, and with much of his grief coming from the FBI and the rest of it from the news media.

IT HAD NOT STARTED OUT this way.

In his early years in politics, Ray Blanton had been a friend of the newspaper. The *Tennessean* had supported his campaigns for Congress and governor. His positions on a few standard issues—opposing the death penalty, favoring a state income tax—were in alignment with the paper's traditional editorial views and center-left politics.

He had known Evans first but soon came to know others in the publisher's inner circle, including William R. Willis and his Nashville law firm. Willis was Hooker's law partner, and the most prominent client of the Hooker, Hooker, and Willis firm was the capital city's morning newspaper, then called the *Nashville Tennessean*, with its activist young publisher and tenacious editor-in-chief.

This tight network of publisher, editor, attorneys, and friends began in the early 1960s and over the following decade proved to be a dangerous territory—a political snake pit of trouble—for any public official it opposed. And any opponents of politicians the newspaper supported would, sooner or later, come to respect this closeness of politics and journalism—activist publisher and editor, and connected attorneys—out of a fear born of painful experience.

Nashville's morning daily came of age in the great middle period of American newspaper journalism, between the early proliferation of a thousand independent pamphlets and broadsheets in the eighteenth and nineteenth centuries and the era of rapid consolidation and large-chain ownership in the late twentieth. Concentrated ownership within publishing families was nothing new in some larger cities, of course, as exemplified by the Ochs family's properties in New York City and Chattanooga, the Hearst's in New York and California, and the Medill's and McCormack's in Chicago, New York, and Washington, DC.

In the early and middle years of the twentieth century, aggressive journalism was also being practiced in other US cities—under the ownership of families who were less nationally recognized at the time—in Atlanta, Louisville, Nashville, Memphis, Raleigh, Austin, Miami, Philadelphia, and also in smaller cities across the South including Anniston, Alabama, and Jackson, Mississippi, among others. Most of these were then independent of chain ownership. In Nashville, the *Tennessean* was controlled over four decades by the Evans family. Their ownership had its origin in the New Deal, and this particular political heritage infused the newspaper with a liberal spirit that flowered in the 1960s.

The newspaper's founder had been Colonel Luke Lea, a Nashville financier and lawyer, who also organized the American National Bank in Nashville and the Central Bank and Trust Company in Asheville, North Carolina. Silliman Evans Sr., meanwhile, was working in Texas as a reporter for the Fort Worth *Star Telegram* and its publisher, Amon G. Carter, a leading citizen of Fort Worth and an early investor in American Airlines. Evans became an influential Washington correspondent for the *Star Telegram*—and also an effective political operative for Carter and his interests in the nation's capital. Evans later became an executive in businesses that Carter controlled.

The story goes that the Nashville newspaper was the ultimate reward to Evans for his political work, in the summer of 1932, at the Democratic National Convention in Chicago. There he helped his boss, Carter, to promote the candidacy of New York governor Franklin D. Roosevelt for president. When the convention began, Roosevelt had not yet announced the name of his vice-presidential running mate. He was also struggling to collect the required two-thirds majority of delegate votes that the nominee would need to win the party's presidential nomination. What Roosevelt needed was the support of Texas delegates who were committed to their favorite-son congressman, House Speaker John Nance Garner.

With Evans acting as messenger, Carter and Congressman Sam Rayburn worked for days to persuade their fellow Texans to support Roosevelt. They argued that this move would close ranks and prevent a disastrous division in the national party. To fail in this, they said, would benefit only the Republicans in the fall election. By the evening of July 1, a dealt was struck: in return for Garner's ninety Texas delegates, Roosevelt would announce Speaker Garner as his running mate. This clinched the nomination for Roosevelt at Chicago, and the Democratic ticket was victorious later that year.

For their hard work on the convention floor, Roosevelt's operatives were eventually repaid, each in a manner important to him. With Garner as vice president, Rayburn's stature in Congress rose, and he became Speaker of the House himself in 1940. Evans would be compensated much sooner—but the story is also more complex.

Four months after the 1932 election, in early March 1933, the *Nashville Tennessean* was placed under federal receivership. The publisher, Lea, and his son, Luke Lea Jr., had been indicted in 1931 in connection with the failure of their Asheville bank. Littleton J. (Lit) Pardue, a local lawyer who once had been an editorial writer at the newspaper, was put in charge of the struggling paper, essentially serving as publisher for a time. But the financial losses continued, and the federal Reconstruction Finance Corporation acquired a controlling stake in the newspaper company. In 1935, the agency sold the bonds it held to a Nashville banker, Paul Davis, the president of First American National Bank in Nashville. The newspaper was sold at auction in 1937. The successful bidder, for $850,000, was Roosevelt's trusted ally, that former reporter from Fort Worth, Silliman Evans Sr.

Evans was now the new publisher of both the morning newspaper and its afternoon sister publication, called the *Evening Tennessean*, and he soon struck new operating agreements with his competitor, James G. Stahlman, publisher of the *Nashville Banner*. Evans' plan was a new business model in the newspaper industry called the "joint operating agreement." It provided an exemption to federal antitrust laws for certain newspapers. In its infancy, only three JOAs were established during the decade of the 1930s, including Evans' plan in Nashville. The practice had been tested first, in 1931, in Albuquerque, New Mexico, where the pooling of resources helped to save the afternoon newspaper. (The practice was reconfirmed by Congress in 1970, with passage of the Newspaper Preservation Act, though it became one of the early controversies over concentrated media ownership in America.

Nonetheless JOAs eventually saved the poorer-circulation afternoon newspapers in some two dozen US cities.)

At the time Evans got to town, Stahlman was publishing the afternoon rival *Nashville Banner* five days a week and also an edition on Sunday. With the JOA model, Evans and Stahlman formed a third entity, called the Newspaper Printing Corporation, that enabled a cost-sharing deal through which the two publishers could share advertising, printing, and circulation support services. They would also share space in the same building, at 1100 Broadway, near the city's railroad depot and central post office. As part of this business alliance, Evans agreed to cease publication of his afternoon edition, and Stahlman agreed he would no longer publish a newspaper on Sunday.

Evans also lost no time putting his partisan Democratic stamp on the morning newspaper. *Time* magazine once described him as a "hell-for-leather Democrat" and quoted the acerbic Nashville publisher as having said that "no Republican is fit to hold public office." He was also an ardent progressive toward Tennessee politics, editorially battling the entrenched Crump-McKellar machine, excoriating its favored candidates, and promoting virtually anyone who opposed it. In his own will, Evans exhorted his heirs in their stewardship of the morning newspaper to defend and support the Tennessee Valley Authority—the region's crown jewel of Roosevelt's New Deal—and to "continue to oppose the political machine until it and all its evil works are exterminated."

Editorially, the *Tennessean* and *Banner* maintained their respective independence. They did this so exuberantly, in fact, that their opposing viewpoints and competing news staffs became locally famous—the *Banner* staunchly Republican, the *Tennessean* Democratic. The publishers even took opposing stands on the issue of daylight saving time, and this actually spilled from their editorial pages onto the sidewalk outside the office. The clock on the building above the Broadway entrance then had two faces—one facing east and the other west—and for years they marked different time, with one hour difference.

Evans died in Texas in 1955 at age sixty-one. He was in Fort Worth attending the funeral of his mentor, Amon Carter, when the heart attack came. The board of the Nashville newspaper, controlled by Evans' widow, Lucille, together with the trust department at First American Bank, selected Evans' elder son and namesake, Silliman Evans Jr., then thirty, to take over as publisher. But the son did not share the father's zeal or passion for political combat, and the *Tennessean* now entered a less active phase, with a noticeably lower profile with respect to machine politics at city hall and the state capitol.

Journalistically, however, the *Tennessean*'s profile would never be higher than on Silliman Jr.'s watch. This period, from 1955 to 1962, was characterized by investigative reporting and the highest national prizes in the newspaper business. In 1957, editorial cartoonist Tom Little won the Pulitzer Prize. Coverage of the emerging civil rights movement in the South included reporting by the young David Halberstam, Tom Wicker, Wallace Westfeldt and Fred Graham. The newspaper's crusading reports on abuses in organized labor earned the 1962 Pulitzer for reporters Nat Caldwell and Gene Graham.

Another staffer during this period, who also departed for a brief time, was an aggressive young reporter named John Lawrence Seigenthaler, who had been a favorite of Silliman Sr.

Seigenthaler was a Nashville native and one of eight siblings in a large German Catholic family. He attended Father Ryan High School and worked afternoons as a soda jerk at the West End eatery called Candyland. After high school, he joined the air force, and when his hitch ended, in 1949, he was hired at the *Tennessean* (where his uncle Walter Seigenthaler was boss of the circulation department) by the editor-in-chief, Coleman Harwell. The young Seigenthaler took courses at George Peabody College during this period, but he more quickly took to the rhythms, late hours, and intrigue of the newsroom—where everyone worked under the influence of partisan publisher Evans and the day-to-day direction of Harwell.

He flourished in the newsroom, learning from Harwell and other young journalists on the staff. (There were bumps in the road early on, as there are for most fledgling reporters who are trained on the job. Years later, Seigenthaler recalled a tense moment when as a rookie he turned in his first short news item for publication. The stern city editor, Ed Freeman, quickly read the piece, made a few marks, then looked up at his cub over the rim of his eyeglasses.

"Let me tell you something," Freeman said. "I don't know how much longer you'll be working here, but we try to put a verb in every sentence."

But Seigenthaler's grammar came into harmony with his nose for news soon enough, and he excelled as a tireless reporter. In 1953, he won the National Headliner Award for his investigative reporting that revealed the location, in Texas, of a Nashville man who had disappeared in 1931. In 1954, he talked another man out of jumping to his death from a Cumberland River bridge.

In 1957 his investigative reporting on the Teamsters union in Tennessee resulted in the impeachment of a judge in Chattanooga. He also went to Washington, DC, to cover hearings of the US Senate committee investigating organized labor, and here he met two brothers who would influence his work and life ever after. Senator John F. Kennedy of Massachusetts was the second-ranking Democrat on the committee, and his brother Robert F. Kennedy was the committee's chief counsel. Teamsters' activities in Nashville were of interest to the investigating committee, and Seigenthaler was now regarded as an expert on the subject because of his recent reporting.

All of this helped Seigenthaler, in 1958, earn an invitation into Harvard University's Nieman Fellowship program for journalists. His one-year sabbatical at Cambridge coincided with Senator Kennedy's 1958 campaign for reelection, and during this time Seigenthaler arranged separate campus visits for the senator and also Bobby Kennedy to meet with the Neiman fellows. Bobby Kennedy invited Seigenthaler and his wife, Dolores, to come to Hickory Hill (his home in McLean, Virginia) for Christmas that December. During this holiday visit, the younger Kennedy brother asked Seigenthaler to help him write and edit a book about corruption in the US labor movement, centering on the findings of the 1956–59 McClellan committee investigation. Seigenthaler accepted this invitation, as well, and after completing his Harvard Fellowship in 1959, he returned to Washington to work on the manuscript. The result was Kennedy's 1960 bestseller *The Enemy Within: The McClellan Committee's Crusade against Jimmy Hoffa and Corrupt Labor Unions.*

By the time *The Enemy Within* was published, Seigenthaler had returned to the Nashville newsroom as the weekend city editor of the *Tennessean.* Back home, he quickly became one of a half dozen journalists leading the newspaper's coverage of the developing civil rights movement across the South, including the lunch-counter sit-ins in Nashville. Their work was groundbreaking, but the young reporters soon ran into the contrary preferences of a new editor, Edward D. Ball, who had been hired by Silliman Evans Jr. to replace Harwell. Born in Marion Junction, Alabama, and a graduate of Auburn University, Ball had been a war correspondent, Nashville bureau chief for the Associated Press and, most recently, executive director of the Southern Education Reporting Service. Soon after he was named editor, Ball summoned the news staff to a meeting.

Ball said his impression was that the reporters had been manipulated by the Nashville students who organized the lunch-counter sit-ins. "I think you have been manipulated by these black students," he told the team of reporters who had covered civil rights. He then informed them that the newspaper's aggressive attention to the issue would now cease. The young journalists— including Halberstam, Wicker, Westfeldt, and Seigenthaler—were stunned. Their crusading coverage of a major social movement was being called into question. In fact, to their amazement, it was being stopped. The staff meeting ended quickly, but outside the newsroom and after hours, the young men continued their discussion of what it meant. They met at Blackie's, a restaurant down the street.

"Suddenly, it all changed for us," Seigenthaler wrote later. "Ed Ball, a veteran executive from the Associated Press, became the new editor, and the paper's effective and thorough reportage on the civil rights conflict ended. No more was the civil rights struggle a priority at the paper. . . . The *Tennessean*, we were told, was out of step with its readers. That decision forced a 'stay or go' decision on some of our staff members."

Within months, Halberstam, Wicker, Westfeldt, and Seigenthaler had all left Nashville. Halberstam and Wicker departed for the *New York Times*, Westfeldt first to a six-month writing job with the US Civil Rights Commission and then to NBC News in New York, where he produced *The Huntley-Brinkley Report*. For Seigenthaler, who was the second of them to leave, Ball's new policy sealed his own decision for a second departure from the *Tennessean* newsroom in three years, and once again his leave would involve the Kennedys. He joined the JFK presidential campaign as administrative assistant to Robert Kennedy, the campaign director. Soon after the election, when the president-elect chose his younger brother to head the Justice Department, the new attorney general offered Seigenthaler a job as his administrative assistant in Washington.

Seigenthaler's service to Kennedy was brief but would become famous, particularly in the South, for his role as a Justice Department liaison during the most contentious period of the civil rights movement. Only four months on the job, Seigenthaler was assigned by Kennedy to serve as liaison between state officials in Alabama and the Freedom Riders, who had been trained in nonviolent protest tactics in Nashville and were now traveling by bus from Birmingham to Montgomery. When an angry mob chased two of the young Freedom Riders as they exited the bus at the Montgomery station, Seigenthaler attempted to shield one young woman. He was struck behind the left ear, by an assailant wielding a pipe, and lay unconscious and seriously injured on the pavement for several minutes.

Just two months after this, in July, Silliman Evans Jr. died of a heart attack on board his thirty-three-ton ocean-going yacht *The Tennessean Lady*. (A young Hal Hardin, while a law student in the 1960s, was employed for a time as the vessel's dashing, white-uniformed captain.) Evans was only thirty-six years old, and the suddenness with which he vanished from the publisher's office caused a serious transition issue. His younger brother, Amon Carter Evans, at twenty-nine was considered too young and unprepared for the job by Mrs. Evans and her trust partners. Instead, they named a veteran reporter on the staff, John Nye, to succeed Silliman Jr., but his appointment lasted only eight months. In March 1962, Mrs. Evans announced that her son, Amon, was now the publisher.

The younger Evans had worked in the newsroom with Seigenthaler, who had helped train him as a reporter. Now, at the urging of the newspaper's attorney and Evans confidant John Jay Hooker, Evans promptly phoned Seigenthaler, then thirty-four, in Washington and offered him the top editor's job. Seigenthaler accepted and departed the Kennedy administration, though he would remain close to Bobby Kennedy and his family. (He took a leave of absence in 1968 to join Kennedy's presidential campaign, assisting with the management of the western primaries. He was in San Francisco when heard the news that Kennedy, only moments after claiming victory in the California primary, had been assassinated in a Los Angeles hotel. Seigenthaler returned to the *Tennessean* newsroom in Nashville the following week, still visibly stunned and deeply saddened. He was a pallbearer at Kennedy's funeral in New York City.)

Through the 1950s and early 1960s, the *Tennessean* came to be regarded in the newspaper industry as a productive training ground for reporters and editors destined for larger newspapers. This gave rise to a generation of outstanding reporters, most with an investigative bent owing to their tutelage by Harwell and Seigenthaler and to the atmosphere of role models past and present within the vibrant newsroom. During this period, Wallace Westfeldt left for NBC News and became senior producer of *The Huntley-Brinkley Report*. Halberstam, Tom Wicker, Bill Kovach, John Hemphill, and later Reginald Stuart all "graduated" to the *New York Times* early in their careers. Fred Graham also went to the *New York Times* and later CBS; Rudy Abramson to the *Los Angeles Times*; Wendell Rawls to the *Philadelphia Inquirer* and later the *New York Times* and *Atlanta Journal-Constitution*; Jim Squires, Jack Hurst, and Joel Kaplan moved on to the *Chicago Tribune*; Rob Elder to the *Miami Herald* and later *San Jose Mercury News*; John Haile to the *Orlando Sentinel*; Elaine Shannon to *Newsday* and later *Newsweek* and *Time*; Kathy Sawyer and Eve Zibart to the *Washington Post*; Kenneth Jost to *Congressional Quarterly*; and Doug Hall to the *Detroit Free Press*.

This tradition, and the ongoing aspirations it engendered in the *Tennessean*, also produced award-winning journalism by other reporters who remained in the Nashville newsroom—all working under the influence of the young Seigenthaler with his sharp eye, competitive spirit, and rising prestige and reputation in the industry.

As in prior decades, journalism at the *Tennessean* continued to be intertwined with local and state politics. Squires, who himself rose from young library clerk in the *Tennessean* morgue to become editor-in-chief of the *Chicago Tribune*, wrote about this mixture in his own 1996 memoir *The Secrets of the Hopewell Box*. He recalled that Seigenthaler returned home in 1962 "streetwise and tough . . . polished by a year as a Nieman Fellow at Harvard and steeled by the daily mental combat that came from constant association with the iron-willed Bobby Kennedy."

"He returned home," according to Squires, "bearing not only the Kennedys' clout but their passion for politics, committed to cause, and—as Tennesseans would soon learn—the same willingness to seize and exercise power in pursuit of both. Under his hand the *Tennessean* would become the dominant power in Tennessee politics."

BY THE TIME RAY BLANTON ran for governor in 1974, Seigenthaler had reigned as editor at the morning newspaper—and, by extension, over much of Nashville's municipal politics—for a full dozen years. Much of the influence that he and Evans wielded derived from Seigenthaler's own forceful personality (less so to Evans', as he often deferred to his editor's judgments) and also from the newspaper's role in a number of momentous local issues over the turbulent decade.

The *Tennessean* had editorially supported the 1962 referendum vote to consolidate the city and county governments in Nashville, which brought Mayor Beverly Briley to consolidated power also, and passage of the 1967 liquor-by-the-drink referendum, which ushered in the city's modern hospitality and tourism industry. The newspaper also published editorial appeals for moderation and racial understanding as social turmoil followed the assassination of Dr. Martin Luther King Jr. in 1968, in Memphis, and in 1970 following court rulings requiring cross-town busing for school desegregation. The latter touched off bitter unrest in neighborhoods across Nashville, as well as in Charlotte, North Carolina, and other US cities.

Because of this unabashed tradition of Democratic politics, assertive journalism, and reform zeal, the morning newspaper and its forceful editor had by the late 1960s become, for politicians seeking public office, the larger force to be reckoned with—an influence over local perceptions, patronage, and politics that any enemies ignored at their peril.

It did not last much longer, arguably only one decade more. But while it did last, Evans and Seigenthaler were at or near the center of virtually every important political match that was played in Tennessee's capital city—supporting their friends, opposing others.

In the fullness of time, Ray Blanton would experience both.

IT WAS THE 1966 RACE for governor in Tennessee that proved to be the climax of the rollicking *Tennessean* tradition of influence in statewide races. In that year, the newspaper's support of Hooker bled from the editorial page and suffused the news section also.

The *Tennessean* had developed a long record of enmity toward the so-called leap-frog administrations of Governors Frank Clement and Buford Ellington, and now Hooker was Evans' chosen candidate to oppose the long-running regime. Reporters covering the Hooker campaign favored him in their daily reports, while doing the opposite in their coverage of Ellington.

This phenomenon—mixing journalism and politics—was not exclusive to the *Tennessean*. It was practiced also at the afternoon *Nashville Banner*, still under the ownership and influence of Jimmy Stahlman. In fact, the afternoon *Banner* provided its own brand of reverse balance—favoring Ellington in news reports as well as editorials, while attacking Hooker. A top Ellington aide at the time, Bo Roberts, told me of one end-of-the-day conversation that he observed during the 1966 primary race. At a restaurant dinner table in Jackson, Tennessee, the *Banner* chief political writer, Kenneth Morrell, was holding court.

"Somebody at the table asked Ken if he was objective," Roberts said. "Ken looked at the fellow and said, 'Objective? Yeah, I'm objective. My objective is to elect Buford Ellington governor.' Of course, you had the same feeling on the other side, at the *Tennessean*. As a journalism school graduate myself, it was pretty amazing to watch."

Another sharp *Banner* knife was wielded by the brilliant editorial cartoonist Jack Knox, whose remorseless sketches of Hooker were often featured on page 1. Through the summer of 1966, Knox ceaselessly linked Hooker to Bobby Kennedy, his well-known political friend, as well as to business arrangements that the *Banner* said qualified Hooker as a "wheeler-dealer" who identified more closely with wealthy folks than the common man. In the frame of every Knox cartoon was an overfed cat (labeled "fat cat" lest anyone miss the metaphor) carrying a sign that read "Bobby says Hello!"

In the 1966 race, Ellington trounced Hooker, winning the Democratic primary in early August, and the nominal general election also in the following November. In so doing, Ellington and his supporters not only kept the governor's office in the hands of the heirs to the aging Crump-McKellar machine, but they also shepherded a quiet resentment of Hooker among party regulars. This enmity would prove to be politically disastrous for Hooker four years later.

The 1970 race would be the last statewide election in Tennessee to occur on Stahlman's watch. Through the fall campaign leading to the November general election, the *Banner* as expected resumed its negative attacks on Hooker, while this time favoring the Republican Dunn. The *Banner* fed the old resentments of the Ellington machine, stoked them, compounded them—once again using both words and pictures.

In place of the references to Kennedy, who had died two years earlier, Knox now visually linked Hooker to the 1968 failure of his "Minnie Pearl's Fried Chicken" business venture. Knox now included in his Hooker cartoons the image of a decrepit, featherless chicken, sometimes on crutches, always croaking the words "Pluck, Pluck, Pluck 'em."

Meanwhile, the coverage by the *Tennessean* was more restrained than in 1966, its partisan volume now lower, its political activism and influence reduced to the point of eclipse, as the new decade opened. By the time of the

1970 election, in fact, the crusading middle period of newspaper journalism in Nashville began to close more generally. And the political landscape was clearly altered.

Clement was dead, Ellington was ready for retirement, and there was no obvious heir to the long-running leap-frog regime. The most likely prospect might have been Jared Maddux of Cookeville, a five-term state senator and Clement stalwart who served four terms as lieutenant governor, but his health had declined following a heart attack in 1966. He died in 1971, at age fifty-nine.

Changes in the ownership of both the Nashville newspapers also contributed to a new landscape for a new day. By the end of the decade, Gannett had purchased the *Tennessean* from the Evans family, and the old joint operating agreement with the *Banner* was terminated, too. The afternoon paper eventually folded, in 1998.

HOOKER STILL REMEMBERED.

His memory of Ken Morrell's relentless attacks during the old campaign wars would come back to haunt Morrell, now the editor of the *Banner*. By this time, the ownership of Stahlman's newspaper had changed not once but twice, and oddly Hooker himself was one of the new proprietors. A former *Banner* staff reporter, Bruce Dobie, recalled the moment in a 1998 article in the *Nashville Scene* after the current *Banner* owners, Irby Simpkins and Brownlee Currey, announced they would finally cease operations.

"In 1972 Stahlman sold his paper to Gannett for $14 million," Dobie recalled. "Then, in 1979, Gannett decided to sell the *Banner* and buy the *Tennessean* instead. In an ironic twist of fate, Hooker engineered the deal and joined Simpkins and Currey as one of the paper's three owners. After landing at the *Banner*, Hooker walked into the newsroom, picked up the telephone, and fired Ken Morrell."

In that same piece on the demise of the *Banner*, Dobie also wrote: "Over time, the papers' political alignments would grow more blurry. The *Banner* became less Republican under Simpkins; *The Tennessean*, under Gannett, became less Democratic. As a result, there would be less contrast between the two papers, and their editorial voices, unfortunately, would become almost indistinguishable. With the rough edges gone, there was less for the newspaper-reading public to enjoy."

The *Tennessean* staff remained largely intact under its new ownership. Foremost among these new Gannett employees was Seigenthaler. As part of the sale agreement, he was named president, publisher and editor of Gannett's Nashville enterprise going forward, and his influence over politics and politicians would continue.

THE RIFT THAT THE Humphreys pardon opened between Blanton and the *Tennessean* front office would never heal.

When Blanton met with Evans and Seigenthaler in November 1978, what no one outside the Blanton circle yet knew was a transaction—not uncovered by the *Tennessean* until two years later—that would send him to prison. This involved liquor store licenses, favors for a friend and contributor, an oil field in Texas, and an otherwise unrelated loan at a Nashville bank. It would lead to Blanton's ultimate undoing and put him behind bars.

By 1980, the newspaper's top investigative reporter was Joel Kaplan, a Vanderbilt graduate barely a year on the job. At the office one afternoon, Kaplan told Seigenthaler that he had received a tip that Blanton was connected to a deal involving oil leases somewhere, possibly with a payoff involving someone within the governor's extended circle.

The words "oil" and "Texas" reminded Seigenthaler of a visit at his home, some six months earlier, with his next-door neighbor and longtime friend Henry Hooker (brother of John Jay Hooker Jr.) who had introduced the editor to an oilfield developer from Texas.

"The guy wore boots and blue jeans and a denim jacket," Seigenthaler told me, describing the meeting at his home on Vaughn Road. "They sat down in my front room and spread all these maps out, and Henry was selling these lots in this development at, I don't know, $25,000 or $50,000 a pop. I listened to them and made no bones about it that I didn't have any money."

The editor told Kaplan about this meeting, and they discussed how to develop a news story about it. Kaplan spent most of the day talking to sources. When he returned to the editor's office later in the day, Seigenthaler said, the reporter told him, "The deal was cut at Commerce Union Bank, and it was Jack Ham. He's paying off that loan." The following day, this information was published in a *Tennessean* news story.

Seigenthaler's first visitor that next morning was Hank Hillin, the FBI agent in charge of the bureau's Blanton investigations. Hillin questioned the editor about the article.

"Where in the hell did this come from," he says Hillin asked him.

"Look, Hank, I can't talk to you about it," Seigenthaler responded, "but it shouldn't be too damned tough. You know [from the published article] where we've been." Hillin and his fellow agents questioned Ham, who would eventually become the government's star witness in the federal court trial that ended with Blanton's conviction.

"So, by this time, I know Blanton was a crook," Seigenthaler said, "and I know that investigation is ongoing."

Ham had been the second largest contributor to Blanton's 1974 campaign, and now he was one of the central figures in the liquor store licensing scandal that was enveloping the governor. He acquired a lucrative retail store license in the Green Hills area of Nashville, then was granted a transfer to the Donelson community on the opposite side of town, with assurance that no competitor would be permitted in his new territory—all through the influence of the governor's people on the staff of the state Alcoholic Beverage Commission.

At Blanton's trial, in 1981, prosecutors presented videotaped testimony by Ham, stating that he had owed Blanton a $20,000 payment for his role in the store license decision. Also, he said, Blanton had wanted to dispose of his stock in the Texas oil leasing venture, which Blanton now considered worthless. The solution was that Ham would take back the oil leasing stock at a loss, and pay off Blanton's loan at Commerce Union Bank.

CHAPTER 8

The Attorney General and the Rule of Law

> . . . before I can live with other folks I've got to live with myself. The one thing that doesn't abide by majority rule is a person's conscience.
> —Harper Lee, *To Kill a Mockingbird*

WILLIAM McMILLAN LEECH JR. was the son of a judge, and though his career centered in the urban state capital of Nashville, throughout his life he was firmly rooted in the more rural counties beyond the city.

He was born in 1935 in the small town of Charlotte, just west of Nashville in Dickson County. The Leech family was politically connected to the Clement family—Governor Frank Clement was born in the same county, in the larger town also called Dickson—and Bill's father, William M. Leech Sr., had served on the governor's cabinet as head of the Tennessee Department of Highways before his judicial career began.

Bill Jr. was the second of two children. He and his brother, Earl Warren Leech, fourteen months older, were both athletes and played together on the same football teams at Charlotte High School and at Tennessee Tech University in Cookeville. Bill attended Tech on an athletic scholarship and was a standout player. He was recruited by the Chicago Bears but declined the offer.

He worked summer jobs in Tennessee and Mississippi driving trucks and bulldozers for an asphalt paving company. After graduation he joined the US Army and was posted in Germany. When his tour of duty ended, he worked as a teacher and high school football coach. After this, he entered law school at the University of Tennessee, in Knoxville. One of his classmates at the UT law school was T. Edward Sisk, the same Eddie Sisk who would later serve Governor Ray Blanton as his staff legal counsel.

(Earl, unlike his father and brother, chose the military for his career, not the legal profession. He was an officer in the Korean conflict, served two tours in Vietnam, and later was aide-de-camp to General William Westmoreland when he was commanding officer of the 101st Airborne Division at Fort Campbell, Kentucky. Earl retired from the army in 1978, with the rank of lieutenant colonel, and had a twenty-year career as a banker in Nashville.)

After finishing law school in 1966, Bill Leech made his home in the small unincorporated village of Santa Fe (pronounced "Santa FEE") near Columbia, the county seat of Maury County, south of Nashville, the "Mule Capital of the World."

His first job was as an assistant district attorney under District Attorney Arnold Peebles. Leech and Peebles' son then established their own law firm. Leech also served as a municipal judge in Columbia. He later formed a second law firm with Tom Hardin and Bob Knolton. Leech became respected both as a lawyer and civic leader; he was president of the Maury County Bar Association and the county Chamber of Commerce. In his private practice, he represented, among other clients, the Tennessee Farm Bureau.

In 1971, Leech was elected to represent Maury County as a delegate to the state constitutional convention in Nashville. Once there, he was elected its president. The primary issue was property tax reform, specifically the re-ordering of property tax assessments based on use. This had been a policy priority of Leech's longtime client, the Tennessee Farm Bureau Federation. Some at the time referred to the 1971 convention as "the Farm Bureau Convention," and indeed it produced an amendment to the state's constitution, called Proposition 1, that gave farm property the lowest percentage classification for assessment of taxes.

In 1974, Leech was one of several lawyers across Tennessee who assisted in the extraordinary statewide campaign of five Democratic nominees to the Tennessee Supreme Court. The candidates were Ray Brock, Robert Cooper, incumbent justice William H. D. Fones, William Harbison, and Joe Henry. They largely eschewed political fundraising, but they had the political guidance of Speaker Ned McWherter. Their team approach proved successful, and the Democratic slate was elected in August of that year.

Three years later, Leech was elected to the 1977 constitutional convention. It was a much briefer affair, but one significant amendment the delegates approved was to permit a governor to succeed himself and serve a total of two consecutive four-year terms. (This provision would become applicable to the current governor, meaning Governor Blanton would be the first to be eligible to do this.) When this convention adjourned, Leech and his fellow delegates received a commemorative gift for their service—a small oak tree sapling—and this Leech planted at his home on Highway 7 at Santa Fe.

Ever after, he called it the Constitutional Oak. In time, it grew stout and towered high, where the gravel drive turns and leads up to the white house on the hill.

TENNESSEE IS THE ONLY STATE where the attorney general is appointed by the state's supreme court. In 1978, when the incumbent attorney general Brooks McLemore retired, Bill Leech applied for the job.

The five justices knew him, though they were much more familiar with his father, who by this time was a judge of the chancery court in Dickson County. But the son was now a prominent attorney in Nashville, and the five justices knew him to be a Democrat. He had also aided them in their election four years earlier. The chancellor's son was promptly considered and was appointed within a few days.

One of the surviving justices, Robert Cooper Sr., told me there were actually two ballots, occurring on the same day. In the first, Cooper dissented, making the vote four to one. He argued that the court should keep with longstanding tradition of naming an attorney general from the section of the state that was represented by only one justice. (Cooper and Brock were from East Tennessee, and Harbison and Henry from Middle Tennessee, with Fones the only West Tennessean.) Cooper felt the new attorney general should therefore be selected from the west not the middle, where Leech lived. Nevertheless, with four justices wanting Leech—and Henry arguing that the court ought to be "unanimous" in its selection—Cooper demurred. The sectional tradition came to an end at this point.

For his installation, Leech asked his father, Chancellor William Leech, to do the honors. The oath was administered in the supreme court chamber in Nashville.

LEECH QUICKLY BEGAN TO MODERNIZE the attorney general's office and its procedures, and he grew the staff with an emphasis on professionalism and collegiality. Reporting to Leech was the chief deputy C. Hayes Cooney, who was senior to a group of six deputy attorneys general and a number of junior associates among whom different types of cases were assigned. But in practice, the group functioned more openly than its formal organizational chart would suggest.

Leech's top deputies at that time say the office operated much like a modest-sized law firm, with junior members commonly dealing directly with the attorney general himself depending on the nature of their assignments. Cooney, now in private practice in Nashville, was the chief deputy from 1976 to 1980. Under Leech, he says, the office had an "open-door policy" that invited junior associates to ask for help and do their work in a "collegial, collaborative" manner.

Leech faced his share of controversy during his tenure in the office. But as the *Nashville Banner* chief political writer, Mike Pigott, observed in a 1981 profile: "The controversy and criticism, however, seem to slide off Leech like water off a duck's back." In one famous opinion letter, Leech had declared it was unacceptable on constitutional grounds for public high school football coaches to lead their teams in pregame prayers. This produced an outcry from parents as well as coaches statewide.

"I have been especially disappointed with the coaches for their lack of understanding on the issue," Leech told Pigott. The coaches, he said, "don't realize the importance of secular freedom in this country—that the government will not involve itself in people's religious beliefs. Many of our ancestors came to this country after they were imprisoned in Europe for their religious beliefs. It wouldn't hurt those high school coaches to learn and teach a little government. They apparently lack understanding of how it works. They are not being true to their oath as teachers."

ATTORNEY J. W. LUNA, who later headed two state departments in Governor Ned McWherter's administration, was an assistant district attorney in Coffee County during Leech's tenure as attorney general.

"Leech was an interesting fellow, much more a legal scholar than many people realized," Luna told me. "He would bring a team together. He would rely heavily on the individual talents of his team. He was a great manager like that, of the talent around him."

As attorney general, Leech was one of four "constitutional officers" in state government, so called because of the recognition of their particular offices in the Tennessee constitution. While he was an official of the state's judicial branch, the other three were elected by the legislature: the secretary of state, Gentry Crowell; the comptroller of the treasury, William Snodgrass; and the state treasurer, Harlan Mathews.

Leech's widow, Donna, says they did not regularly socialize with the other constitutional officers and their wives, preferring to keep to themselves at home in Santa Fe. She remembers he was sparing in his use of the state-owned automobile that was available to the attorney general. When they would go out, she told me, they would take her blue Plymouth, or occasionally his aging, gray pickup truck. They would leave his official state car—a gleaming black sedan—parked at home.

In his personal life, Leech was a family man; an avid fisherman and quail hunter; a gentleman farmer, Civil War reenactor, and breeder of mules on his Santa Fe farm near Columbia, Tennessee. He prized his friends, his mules, his tractor, and his barn, where he liked to relax on evenings and weekends. Leech had two daughters from his first marriage, Anna and Becca, and they lived with their mother in Nashville.

He met his second wife, Donna, who was born in Oak Ridge, when she came to work as a legal secretary in his Columbia law office, on South Garden Street, in the old Daily Herald building. When they married, in January 1978, Bill adopted her daughter, Katie.

On the family farm, there were horses, cattle, bird dogs, a pet goat named Nanette, a donkey named Howard Baker, and his mate, Myrtle. Leech's two daughters recalled life on the farm.

"My father picked us up pretty much every Friday afternoon, and we spent pretty much every weekend on the farm," Becca Leech remembers. "My sister, Anna, was really into horses. My father had mules, and we would have to help him herd them from field to field. I hate mules to this day because of it. Donkeys are a different story. Howard Baker [the donkey] was the leader of the cows. I loved the goats. The mules stampeded once and killed a mother goat, and the baby had to be bottle-fed. We called her Nanette, and some days my father would load her up and take her with him to the law office in Columbia, and he would bottle-feed her in the kitchen at the law office."

Katie and Becca both described their father's gray pickup truck. He would use it to haul animals, and on weekdays he would take his girls to school in it also. "This awful truck," as Becca remembers it, was a source of pride for him, and a source of common embarrassment for her and Katie.

"It was terrible," Katie remembers. "There would be dead birds—quail—in the front seat that you would have to scoot over. There was also something wrong with the muffler—it was very loud. So everybody at school would know I was coming. They could hear it from a mile way."

But the girls also remember the Santa Fe farm, on its hill off Highway 7, as their father's favored refuge—his place of rest and peace. With its rolling fields, corral, barn, and smokehouse and its ever-changing menagerie of animals, the children called the place Green Acres.

"I think he was definitely happiest at the farm," Katie told me.

THE ATTORNEY GENERAL WAS RECOGNIZABLE by his tall, slender, lanky frame and horn-rimmed eyeglasses. He seldom appeared in any attire other than his dark, three-piece suit.

Had they ever met, the movie director Robert Mulligan might have cast Leech (and not Gregory Peck) for the role of Atticus Finch in the 1962 film *To Kill a Mockingbird*.

Years after Leech's death, Becca, now a teacher and mother of two, took her children to see that same film and told them afterward: "If you ever want to know what your grandfather looked like when he was headed off to work, or what his attitude toward his work was, you can look at Atticus Finch. He always talked about integrity, doing what you love, but doing it following your conscience."

"HE WAS CONSTANTLY BEING APPROACHED to run for this or that office," his law partner, James M. Weaver, remembered, "but he had zero interest in that. Could he have been a politician, yes. Could he have been elected to the Senate or to the governor's office, Lord yes. He could have been the congressman from the Fourth District, from Santa Fe, for as long as he wanted.

"He had no desire for power. All he wanted to do was watch his kid grow up, cut his hay, and raise cows—and hunt and fish. If he had wanted power, he could have had it. Bill Leech was a handsome, six-foot-two-inch man, 235 pounds, with gray hair and this great Southern gravelly voice, and a weathered face. He could have been in politics, but he wouldn't even consider it."

His health was generally good, Donna remembered, but he was also a chain-smoker. He also enjoyed a good drink.

"When he was at home," she said, "there were constant conferences. It's who he was. He enjoyed it. I remember his compass was so correct—truly he would zero in on a problem and really get it right, even if it was difficult. Once he got his facts and made his decision he knew what he needed to do.

"I remember he said he was concerned about civilization, and he said he wondered whether it would survive," Donna continued. "He appeared to manage everything, and I think he did. I think that's why bird hunting, fishing, coming to our farm at Santa Fe, putting on his boots and going out to the horse barn, going downtown [in Santa Fe] and having coffee at Betty's restaurant—he needed that time. These things let him decompress a bit. He loved living in the country and having his time out here, but he loved the law and loved doing what he did. And he loved lawyers—really good lawyers—and also young lawyers, giving them responsibilities and seeing them becoming excited over issues."

OUTSIDE HIS IMMEDIATE FAMILY, Leech treasured most his relationships with other lawyers and his all-male fishing excursions with a close circle of these best friends. With these, he would talk about life and the world and politics and the rule of law.

Charles A. Trost was Leech's law partner twice, at firms in Columbia and Nashville. He called Leech "a die-hard, yellow-dog Democrat" but also a respected lawyer who "promoted the careers of so many people in this town. You could write a book about all the people he promoted in the legal profession."

"Bill had such credibility, such an amazing capacity to connect with people, this air of rectitude about him, and he was not all puffed up with his own importance," Trost told me. "He had an amazing ability to meet people on even ground. Bill was just as 'at home' drinking coffee at Betty's Café in Santa Fe and talking with farmers and neighbors, as he was sitting in the

Oval Office with Ronald Reagan. Wherever Bill was, he was the same person. I've never known anybody else like that."

Weaver remembered Leech's "intuitive nature" about the law.

"While he was extraordinarily savvy and wise, spending one hour in the law library reading cases was *not* something he liked to do," Weaver told me, "but he had an innate sense of the law, and he surrounded himself with smart people, as smart as he could find. We called it 'Leech Law.' He would say, for example on a telephone call with a client, 'Here's what I think the law is.' Then he would say to me, 'I hope I was right. Please check that.' He would 'pontificate' as he liked to called it. He had an intuitive nature about him, with regard to anything—either relating to the law, or where the smallmouth were hiding in the river on a summer day. It was wisdom, guided by experience."

Trost recalled a story told by the dean of the UT law school, Richard S. Wirtz, who had appealed to Leech for help when the school ran into accreditation trouble over the inadequacy of the law school library. Leech told Dean Wirtz that he would "see what I can do." Leech returned days later and asked the dean, "Will $15 million help?" The attorney general had meanwhile discussed the issue with McWherter and Wilder, and they assured him of the new funding.

"Someone said Bill Leech can get through doors where nobody knew there were doors," Trost added.

His closest friends called him Bubba.

At the end of a long day, whether in government offices or courtrooms, friends remembered Leech would often wrap things up by saying, "Let's go to the river." Like Trost and Weaver, most of Leech's fellow fishermen were attorneys, and they often wet a line together in the Middle Tennessee streams of the Duck River, Jones Creek, and the Harpeth River.

Some of them also enjoyed hunting trips with Leech to Montana and South Dakota and exotic fishing excursions to Belize, in Central America. These included Tom Peebles, A. B. Neil, J. Stanley Rogers, Cleve Smith, Bobby Holloway, Seth Norman, Ted Davis, Justin Wilson, Waverly Crenshaw, Philip Davidson, Weaver, and Bill Farmer.

"He had a passion for hunting and fishing," Peebles wrote, in a 1996 memorial edition of the *Tennessee Law Review*, after Leech's death. "He scrambled up and down practically every hill in Maury County following his favorite bird dogs. He floated the Duck and Buffalo Rivers after smallmouth bass, and he waded the saltwater flats off the coast of Belize in search of bonefish and tarpon. All along the way, no matter where he was or what he happened to be doing at the moment, he made friends."

On the Missouri River outside Pierre, South Dakota, a ten-day outing was typical, Weaver recalled. "We would hunt pheasant in the morning until we got our limit, and we would hunt sharptail grouse in the afternoon."

Of the sporting trips to Belize, the central purposes were fellowship and fun as much as the hooking of silvery tarpon and taking the feisty bonefish from the blue water. These close friends would join in these excursions in the tropical sun and evenings of laughter, lie telling, and scotch drinking. In later years, young Will Leech, the son of Bill and Donna, would accompany his dad on such manly adventures.

But at the end of 1978, as the holidays approached and winter came, young Will had not yet arrived. Donna Leech was an expectant mother, her due date in the middle of January.

Hal Hardin, second from right, poses with Colombian villagers at his Peace Corps post in the rural town of Plato, 1963.

Aboard the campaign bus in 1966, Hardin and candidate John Jay Hooker consult a map of Tennessee to plan their daily campaign stops.

John Jay Hooker, candidate for governor in the 1966 Democratic primary, shakes hands with supporters at a campaign event. His personal aide, Hal Hardin, shadows him from behind.

US Attorney General Robert F. Kennedy confers with his young staffer John L. Seigenthaler, circa 1962.

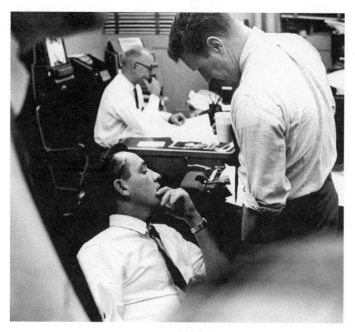

In the *Nashville Tennessean* newsroom in 1968, editor-in-chief John Seigenthaler chats with his boss, publisher Amon Carter Evans. Behind them is the managing editor, Ed Freeman.

Seigenthaler was a pallbearer in the funeral of Senator Robert F. Kennedy, 1968. In this photo, he is second from left, behind Kennedy's brother-in-law Steve Smith and the senator's young son, Bobby Jr.

Three generations of Wilders on the steps of the family business, the Longtown Gin and Supply Company, near Braden, Tennessee, in 1947. The future lieutenant governor, John Wilder, is holding his infant son, Shelton Wilder.

John Wilder, center, welcomes Alabama governor George Wallace to Nashville, circa 1975. Wallace had been paralyzed in an assassination attempt in Maryland in May 1972 while campaigning for president, but later that year won Tennessee's first Democratic presidential primary.

Major General Joe Henry, seated at right in this 1954 photo, was the state's adjutant general, leader of the Tennessee National Guard, during the first administration of Governor Frank G. Clement, left. Standing are Lieutenant Colonel Murray M. Johnson Jr., left, and Brigadier General William Johnson. Photo by Bill Preston.

Henry greets Winfield Dunn, the first Republican governor of Tennessee in fifty years, at the 1971 Gridiron Show in Nashville. Of Dunn's 1970 election, Henry remarked that "the fifty-year plague of political locusts struck again." Photo by Bill Preston.

The five Democratic candidates for the Tennessee Supreme Court in 1974.
Seated, from left, Robert Cooper, William H. D. Fones, and Joe Henry; standing,
William Harbison and Ray Brock. Photo by Dale Ernsberger.

Gov. Ray Blanton, right, with members of the Tennessee
congressional delegation in 1975. From left, Representative Richard
Fulton of Nashville; Senator Howard H. Baker Jr.; Representative
Joe L. Evins, the dean of the state's delegation in Washington; and
Representative Marilyn Lloyd of Chattanooga.

Alexander and Blanton appear together at a 1974 campaign event at a synagogue in Nashville.

Blanton, candidate for governor in 1974, appears with Eddie Sisk at a Nashville news conference.

Beneath a portrait of President Andrew Jackson, and with Governor Ray Blanton looking on, Hal Hardin is sworn in as circuit court judge, 1975. Supreme court justice William Harbison, Hardin's former law professor, administers the oath.

US Attorney Hal Hardin, left, shakes hands with Billy Carter, brother of President Jimmy Carter, at a reception hosted by United American Bank in Nashville circa 1978. Carter is flanked by attorneys Frank Woods and Jayne Ann Woods, husband and wife.

A young Lieutenant Ned McWherter in his Tennessee National Guard uniform at Camp Shelby, Mississippi. McWherter joined the Guard in 1948 at age seventeen, and forged many of his most lasting political friendships with fellow guardsmen. He resigned the guard, with the rank of captain, after he was elected to the state legislature in 1968.

McWherter, seen here at the 1976 Democratic National Convention in New York City, was leader of the Tennessee delegation and an important ally of Georgia governor Jimmy Carter, who was nominated at this convention.

Speaker Ned McWherter, far right, appears with a number of ranking Democratic and Republican politicians in this undated photo from the McWherter family collection. From left, Bill Hamby, senior aide to Senator Howard Baker; attorney Bill Willis; unidentified; Eleanor Willis; John Jay Hooker; Fred Thompson; Sarah Thompson; businessman Tom Beasley, later chairman of the Tennessee Republican Party; unidentified.

Opposite: Because of his size, McWherter was frequently said to resemble the character Hoss Cartwright on the popular TV western *Bonanza*. In this undated photo from the McWherter family collection, the Speaker, right, appears at a political fundraiser with the actor Dan Blocker, who played Hoss, and US senator Albert Gore Sr.

Bill Leech wore number 44 for the Tennessee Tech Golden Eagles and was a standout player. He was recruited by the Chicago Bears but declined the offer and joined the US Army instead. After his discharge he became a teacher and coach before entering law school.

Below: Leech is sworn in as Tennessee's attorney general in the Tennessee Supreme Court chamber in 1978. This moment of laughter occurred when Leech momentarily flubbed his repetition of the extremely long oath of office, and his father, Chancellor William M. Leech Sr., who was administering the oath, remarked, "Am I going to have to go halfway with you, son?" Photo by Gerald Holly.

President Jimmy Carter is greeted by Lieutenant Governor John Wilder (center) and Speaker Ned McWherter on a presidential visit to Nashville in 1978 to boost the Democratic slate of candidates. Jake Butcher, the party's nominee for governor, is at far right.

CHAPTER 9

The New List and the Ticking Clock

All we have to decide is what to do with the time that is given us.
—J. R. R. Tolkien, *The Fellowship of the Ring*

THE BABY CAME AT A QUARTER OF NINE on the morning of the fateful day.

The birth of Will Leech (seven pounds, ten ounces) on Wednesday was joyful and otherwise uneventful. It was also a relief. Donna Leech, thirty, had been ordered into Baptist Hospital on Monday by her obstetrician, Dr. Larry Arnold, concerned about her elevated blood pressure. The Leech family home in tiny Santa Fe, Tennessee, was more than fifty miles distant. At Baptist Hospital in Nashville, which boasted having the region's first neonatal intensive care unit, Donna's condition could be closely monitored with those advanced resources at arm's reach, not two counties away.

Donna's husband, Bill, the attorney general of the state of Tennessee, was bone tired himself. Just the afternoon before, he had flown home from Washington, DC, ending a quick trip full of stress of different sorts.

Leech and two associates—Deputy Attorney General William C. Koch and Assistant Attorney General Mike Terry—had been in the nation's capital all day Monday and Tuesday. Leech was scheduled to make his first appearance before the US Supreme Court on Tuesday morning, arguing the state's position in *Rose v. Mitchell*, in which a Tennessee prisoner had filed a criminal habeas corpus suit, challenging his confinement. The case might have been mundane, but a lawyer's first time before the nation's highest court never is. Because this was to be Leech's first appearance, he asked his senior US senator, majority leader Howard Baker, to introduce him. When the Tennesseans arrived at the supreme court building around 8:30 a.m., no one had gotten much sleep.

Late into Monday evening and well past midnight, Leech had been in his room at the Hay-Adams Hotel, across Lafayette Park from the White House, but there had been no time to enjoy the postcard view out the hotel window. His original plan for this evening was to prepare, with Terry's help, for the high court argument the next morning. But Leech's time had been constantly interrupted by phone calls to and from Nashville relating to Blanton and the climaxing clemency controversy.

These calls began around 11:00 p.m. Washington time, just minutes after reporters in Nashville learned that Blanton had pardoned Roger Humphreys. This news immediately touched off a round of calls from Nashville to Leech involving C. Hayes Cooney, his chief deputy, and other officials in the state capital.

At the Hay-Adams, Terry and Koch remember, they were both seated on the hotel room floor, with paperwork from the *Mitchell* file arrayed around them. Terry took the lead in prepping Leech as the staff attorney most familiar with the Mitchell case. Leech was on the bed, propped up with a pillow against the headboard, jacket off but still wearing the navy-blue vest and trousers of his trademark three-piece suit, necktie still on but the knot loosened. In one hand, he held the phone to his ear, and with the other, he sipped a bottle of Heineken beer. After dinner, he had ordered a six-pack for the evening prep.

Terry estimated later that Leech was on the phone to Nashville 80 percent of the time, and the prep session was given up not long after midnight. Koch and Terry then departed, with Leech still on the phone. The next day, after the court session ended Tuesday morning, Leech confided to his opposing counsel, Nashville lawyer Walter Kurtz, that he had been awake until 3:00 a.m.

Whether fatigue played a part in Leech's Supreme Court appearance cannot be known. Terry said his boss performed masterfully, especially considering the much-interrupted prep session the night before. At one point during arguments, Chief Justice William Rehnquist interrupted Leech, asking him where Covington, Tennessee, (the scene of the crime) was located. Leech paused and said he did not remember.

"I remember," said Kurtz, who became a state circuit judge in 1982, "an observer saying he thought Bill was distracted that morning. I don't remember that, but I do remember he wasn't as up on the facts as he might have been, because he was focused on something else. My parents had come down from Elmira, New York, to see me in my first appearance before the Supreme Court—which is the pinnacle of your career—and I remember wanting to introduce Bill to my parents. He said, 'Well, yes, but I really can't stay but just a moment, because I've got to get back. There's a real crisis going on."

The high court ruled 7–2 to send the *Mitchell* case back to US district court in Memphis for another hearing.

The attorney general would not learn until later this day, on Tuesday afternoon, that he had a further legal issue to deal with relating to Blanton—an issue that involved his own office.

All of this—the travel, the court preparation interrupted so often by calls from his home office, the strain of hearing troubled news, appearing before the Rehnquist court on Tuesday—must have contributed to the weariness Leech now felt, back in Nashville on Wednesday morning.

He had taken a room at the Sheraton Hotel on Broadway, across the street from the city's main post office, to be closer to Donna at the hospital. At the Sheraton, he would be only a few blocks away from her bedside and would also avoid the hour drive to and from their Maury County home.

At the Sheraton, in room 416, he had slept a few hours on Tuesday night, but through the early morning of Wednesday he had mainly been pacing the hallways and the waiting room at the hospital. There was much on his mind—Donna's condition, the baby soon to arrive, and also the rising volume of news about Governor Blanton.

Shortly before 9:00 a.m., Leech heard the most important news. His son, Will, had been born and was a healthy baby, and Donna was doing fine. Normal delivery. No complications. For the Leech family, this was the happiest of mornings, fatigue and all. Bill's first glimpse of young Will was through the glass of the hospital's nursery window. Then he visited with Donna in her private room, staying as long as he could.

Nothing else about this cold winter day would be either normal or uncomplicated. Donna remembers the anguish in her husband's voice when he told her he must leave quickly.

"Sweetheart, I love you," he said. "I'll be able to explain everything later."

Almost immediately, he departed his wife's bedside, stopping in the corridor to visit briefly with their Columbia friends Mr. and Mrs. Ted Davis, who had driven to Nashville for the birth. Then he left the hospital.

"When Bill left, he planned to return to be with us later in the day," Donna told me. "He did not come back for hours. He called me sometime later in the afternoon and said that he did not have time to explain but to 'watch the news' and I would then know why he had not made it back to be with us at Baptist.

"It was at this point that I realized his fatigue was much more than the trip to Washington, the rigors of the Office of the AG, my hospitalization. . . . He was deep in the trenches. The next time I saw his face was on television that night."

The attorney general would not hold his newborn son in his own arms for another four days.

AT ABOUT THAT SAME MOMENT, ten blocks east, on the eighth floor of the Kefauver Federal Building on Broadway, the US attorney was also pacing.

Through the early morning, Hal Hardin had been restless, worried. He was weighing the growing implications of information coming in from the gathering field investigation by the team of agents of the Federal Bureau of Investigation in Memphis and Nashville. Compounding that now was a mushrooming volume of news coverage—in newspapers, on television, locally, and also nationally—about Tennessee's defiant Governor Ray Blanton.

So extraordinary was Blanton's action late on Monday evening—five days before he was to leave office as governor—that it escalated the news coverage of the so-called clemency-for-cash scandal to the stratosphere, and the state's political establishment recoiled in outrage. By Tuesday morning, the operative questions had become: Who else might Blanton release before the inauguration ceremony on Saturday morning? And what possibly can be done to stop this madness?

Hardin now paced the eighth-floor corridor of the federal building, hands jammed into his rear pockets, those questions stirring in his mind—and other questions, too, including what is the standing of a federal US attorney to take any action at all in this obviously state-level predicament?

As Hardin strode the long corridor that connected his office on the east end of the floor with the chambers of US district judge L. Clure Morton, two deputy US marshals, Don Benson and Lex Lancaster, approached him in the hallway. They exchanged greetings. Benson asked Hardin what he thought would happen about Blanton.

"I told them I felt helpless about the situation," Hardin said. "I was also critical of the state political leaders, because they were not taking enough action."

SIX BLOCKS FURTHER DOWNTOWN, Lee Lucas arrived for work, as normal, at her desk on the first floor of Tennessee's state capitol building. She had now been the governor's receptionist less than four months but by this time was already quite accustomed to working alone.

Now, most days at the capitol were quiet, and especially in this reception room with its grand murals of the state's history. The real business of state government, as distinct from the ceremonial, was being seen to in other offices in other buildings. Beneath this vaulted ceiling, Lucas' routine work now consisted largely of greeting the occasional tourists, answering the phones, and transferring calls as necessary, usually either to the press office down the hall or, when appropriate, to the governor himself at home.

On this quiet Wednesday morning of January 17, the governor's reception room was silent once again except for the occasional ring of the office telephone. Routine calls to answer, the occasional tourists to greet, a reporter arriving now and then, whom Lucas referred to either the press secretary, Jim Gilchrist, or his deputy, Betty Nixon, in the press office down the hall. No doubt, the snow, the slush, and the winter chill were combining to keep the tourists away.

What Lucas did not know at this hour was that FBI agents were in the capitol once again. One floor beneath her.

At 10:30 on this January morning, FBI agents John Gisler and Hank Hillin returned from the early visit to the capitol to their field office at the Kefauver Federal Building. The phone at Gisler's desk was ringing.

"We had just gotten back in the office," Gisler told me, "and I received a call from a source of mine I had cultivated in the capitol building regarding what had been going on."

"My source told me a new list had been prepared. There were names I was familiar with that were on the list. I asked about certain names and was given some names that were on there, names we were extremely concerned with, individuals that we didn't want released. I went right up to the eighth floor, met Hal, and told him what was going on."

Gisler reported the new information to Hardin. He explained that the phone call he had received moments earlier from his source in the capitol had yielded a new list of names. These were described by the source as additional prison inmates for whom clemency paperwork was being drawn up, for the governor's signature before the weekend.

One of the names was Eddie Dallas Denton, who was serving time for three murders. He and certain other prisoners on this new list had also appeared on the previous "list of thirteen"—the same names that had been mentioned in undercover surveillance sessions in November and December in Memphis.

Hardin, recalling this hallway conversation, said Gisler appeared "dejected."

GISLER: This is really disgusting.
HARDIN: How sure are you about this information?
GISLER: I am damn sure this is going to happen.

This new list was seriously problematic for the FBI and threatened to jeopardize the prosecution of the burgeoning clemency-for-cash scandal. If these individuals now went free and vanished to parts unknown, the federal probe could be set back months, certainly, if not years. But even this was outweighed by the implications of the release of convicted felons and the risk it posed for public safety.

Hardin told me he had felt strongly at this point that Blanton must be stopped, but he had misgivings about the appropriateness of his role in such an action as a federal agent.

"I thought, holy hell, this is really not the business of the United States attorney," he told me. "I'm dabbling in state politics. This thing could blow up.

"One of my principal concerns," Hardin said, "was there were all sorts of allegations flying around that 'the FBI is on a vendetta' and 'the US attorney's office is on a vendetta against the Blanton administration,' and I wanted to separate my client and my office from this event in case it went bad. I dealt with one FBI agent [John Gisler] and no one else, and John did not know exactly what was going on [between Hardin and the state officials]."

And, apart from any alleged vendettas, Hardin knew that he himself might be seen as politically motivated, being occasionally mentioned by others as a possible candidate for state office.

> HARDIN [*to Gisler*]: Look, I do not want you to ask me any questions, because you do not want to know anything. Don't tell anybody else about it.
> GISLER: What are you going to do about it?
> HARDIN: John, you really don't want to know. I'll get back to you later in the day.

The day was now advancing toward noon and the lunch hour. Hardin returned to his private office, at the east end of the corridor.

He closed the door and walked to the window and looked out to the east. On the horizon, across the Cumberland River with its traffic of barges and boats, lay East Nashville; in the middle distance the traffic of lower Broadway, with its honky-tonks and other shrines to country music, in constant motion, day and night.

He remembers looking at the big clock, across Eighth Avenue, on the high stone tower of the weatherworn old Customs House. From his office window, the clock was at about eye level.

The time was 11:30 a.m.

CHAPTER 10

The Turmoil

... in real life, the distinction between good and evil
is never as clear cut as the "good guys" and the "bad guys"
or the characters in *Star Wars*.
—The Reverend William J. Carl III,
inaugural sermon, January 21, 1979

HARDIN RETURNED TO HIS DESK on the east end of the eighth floor of the Kefauver Federal Building and sat down for a long moment. He then took a step that in the short space of a dozen hours would change the trajectories of a dozen careers, including his own.

In this momentary pause, he made a few notes and looked out the window facing the old Customs House. This time, the hands on the clock of the high tower across the street seemed to be racing forward to bad events. In his solitude, Hardin considered his options—which were now extremely limited.

THE US ATTORNEY HAS ENORMOUS POWER in the federal system. The Justice Department includes ninety-four US attorneys scattered throughout the nation and its possessions, and they are the government's chief law enforcement authorities with respect to federal laws. They are appointed by the president, with the advice and consent of the Senate, and report to the attorney general in Washington.

Each US attorney, among other duties, represents the various federal agencies and in that capacity works closely with the field agents of the FBI to coordinate investigations and prosecutions of federal cases. All search warrants, arrest warrants, and grand jury subpoenas must have his approval and are then valid and enforceable on US citizens throughout the world. State governments meanwhile are sovereign with respect to state constitutions and statutes, however, and officers of the state and federal governments are sensitive to this "delicate balance," as courts have described it, with each obliged to respect the authority and prerogatives of their counterparts in the "other" government.

Both the formal requirements and the informal traditions of this complex federal system were among many issues on Hardin's mind this morning. But so were the gathering evidence from the field, the rising public and private furor over the release of prisoners, and the implications of that ticking clock across the street. He had served earlier in his career as a state prosecutor in Tennessee's trial courts, had subsequently been associated as a practicing attorney with two of the preeminent icons of the state bar—Jack Norman Sr. and John Jay Hooker Sr.—and he had been a state court judge as well. And, yet, now Hardin was the nation's chief law enforcement officer for the Middle District of Tennessee, and he was certain something drastic had to be done.

He was worried that the state officials whom he believed had the direct power to act were not acting or, at a minimum, were moving much too slowly. In contrast, Hardin believed Blanton was making the most of his own shrinking time frame—acting swiftly, starting on Monday evening, to release a large number of prisoners before his absolute power to do so as governor expired, on Saturday.

What would Blanton now do with this new list, Hardin wondered, and how quickly might he do it? Fifty-two signed on Monday, a new roster now in preparation for tonight or tomorrow? How many more names—how many more lists—might surface before Saturday morning?

BY THIS TIME, a new and more disturbing name had been mentioned: James Earl Ray, the convicted assassin of Dr. Martin Luther King Jr., was the most notorious prisoner in any of Tennessee's penitentiaries. He was kept in maximum security at Brushy Mountain State Prison, in the remote mountains north of Knoxville. Under a broken, corrupt system of clemency for cash, if cash payments were all that stood between Ray and freedom, might he be next?

In a 2011 interview, US district judge Tom Wiseman mentioned Ray as one whom authorities feared might be released in January 1979. Wiseman was a new federal judge in January 1979—his appointment by President Carter had been confirmed only five months before. I wanted to speak with him chiefly for his recollections of McWherter's rise to power. But early in our conversation, he asked me to help jog his memory by reviewing the chronology of the Humphreys case.

When I finished the story and said the investigators were subsequently worried that other, more hardened criminals might be paroled by Blanton, the judge interrupted and finished the sentence for me.

"—worried that they might let James Earl Ray out, too."

THERE WAS NEVER ANY FURTHER INDICATION that Dr. King's assassin was on the to-be-released list during Blanton's term. Possibly he never asked or, if he did, possibly neither he nor his agents could meet the quoted price.

But Hardin told me that undercover agents themselves mentioned Ray's name at one point—just to test the limits of how far the governor's men might go, of how audacious their process had become. This exchange occurred at a nondescript motel near the Memphis airport.

"At one of the meetings, I was with [FBI agent] Corbett Hart and others in a motel room next to where Arthur Baldwin was talking with Fred Taylor," Hardin said. "The FBI was monitoring their conversation, and we had pretty much all the statements that would be needed, so a break was taken. Baldwin goes out to the parking lot to smoke a cigarette, and Taylor remains in the room. I recall one of us saying something like, 'Let's see how far they'll go. Who's the meanest SOB in the pen?'"

One of the agents suggested that the "meanest" currently might be Larry David Hacker from Hamilton, Ohio, then serving a twenty-eight-year sentence at Brushy Mountain for armed robbery and safecracking. Hacker, thirty-three, was officially considered "hardcore, aggressive." He might have come to mind for several reasons—but the chief one was that he and Ray with five other inmates had briefly escaped from Brushy Mountain the year before, in June 1977.

It was Ray's disappearance, not Hacker's, that made international headlines, but prison officials speculated at the time that Hacker was the real mastermind and ringleader of the brazen escape. It had been meticulously planned. They had used a makeshift ladder, assembled with some twenty sections of pipe, which Hacker would have had access to in the prison plumbing shop where he worked. There was also early speculation that the daring escape might even have had the assistance from prison employees, a thought that Blanton's Correction Department commissioner, C. Murray Henderson, immediately denied as "absurd, irresponsible, and absolutely untrue." Nonetheless, with Tennessee and its prison security now in the national spotlight, Governor Blanton said he would activate members of the National Guard to aid in the search. He also told reporters he was keeping US Attorney General Griffin Bell regularly briefed on the status of the manhunt through the rugged Cumberland Mountains.

Hacker was captured two days later. Ray was found hiding in the underbrush the next night, just three miles from the prison. He was tracked down by two bloodhounds, sisters named Sandy and Little Red, whose photos were transmitted worldwide by the Associated Press.

IT WAS DECIDED THAT Baldwin would return to the room and ask Taylor another question.

"Go back in there," Hardin told the agents, "and ask him how much it would cost to spring Hacker and James Earl Ray."

When the agents returned to their monitoring post, Hardin told me, what they heard next was chilling, and at this point Hardin said all the agents concluded "there was no limit to what they would consider."

Taylor's reply, as Hardin recalls, was to the effect: "Whew! I don't know about that—that's pretty hot. But . . . maybe we can help him *escape*." Meaning, escape again.

Hardin recalled that as a result of this conversation, together with other evidence from the monitoring sessions, he became convinced there was nothing the collaborators would not do for money.

"Literally everything was for sale—in for the fix," he said.

Hardin's sense of hopelessness was deepened when he remembered his phone call weeks earlier to Bill Willis, his friend and former law office associate, who had been Blanton's lawyer. In that call, Hardin asked Willis to speak to Blanton about the rumored clemency actions, and encourage him to desist, but this had proved fruitless.

"Bill and I had been in a lot of cases together—with each other, and against each other—and we were both kind of proud of the fact that we were still friends," Hardin told me. "I called him and said, 'Bill, this guy Blanton is just crazy. He's out doing these idiotic things, and I know you're close to him. Can't you just tell him to stop?'

"Bill said, 'Hal, nobody can talk to him right now. He's not coming into the capitol, he's staying in the mansion, and by 10:00 in the morning he's hitting that vodka and he's drunk. He's out of control.' I knew then, from Willis, that we were dealing with somebody who was out of control and not a rational man. If he wouldn't listen to Bill Willis, he wouldn't listen to anybody."

Now, Hardin believed, there must somehow be an extraordinary intervention, possibly an unorthodox one. Suddenly it came to him there was but one way to proceed.

This same Wednesday was also moving day for the Alexander family, a gray winter's day of unsettledness and upheaval for the young family in the middle of an otherwise festive week that would end on Saturday with inauguration and parties and family in from out of town.

On this morning, Alexander was anticipating a quiet day of tying up loose ends and working on his inaugural address. This had been a physically demanding period. In addition to organizing the new administration, recruiting new cabinet members, and overseeing the inaugural planning, he and his wife were flying each night to a different city for thank-you receptions, greeting hundreds of friends and well-wishers. Tonight, in fact, he and

Honey were scheduled fly out of town once again—to Jackson, Tennessee—
for the final reception. Many attending these events would not be able to
come to Nashville for the weekend of celebration.

He was, in his own words, "bone tired" by this Wednesday. Fortunately,
the evening event in Jackson was the only public engagement on Alexander's
calendar for this day. He would therefore have, at last, a day for reflection,
for his own private thoughts, and for writing. The gloom of the gray weather
outdoors, in fact, made this a good day to work in solitude indoors.

Honey, now five months pregnant, had been caring for their three children throughout the campaign. On this day, she was overseeing the final
day of packing for the move. The last large moving van was being loaded,
and the three young Alexander children—Drew, nine, Leslee, six, and
Kathryn, four—were in varying stages of helpfulness. Leslee was suffering
from a cold and would not be going to school today. Her mother asked the
movers to leave one mattress behind so that Leslee could rest during the
day. Otherwise, the furniture and virtually all the family's clothing were in
boxes on the final moving truck by mid-morning for the delivery to Curtiswood Lane. At the end of this day, they would all lay down their heads in a
new home.

THE NEW HOME, the official residence of the governor, was vacant now.

Governor Blanton and his wife, Betty, had welcomed the Alexanders to
the residence during a social visit in late November and, in keeping with tradition, offered to move to their new private home on Jefferson Davis Drive in
the Oak Hill section of Nashville well in advance of the inaugural weekend.
This would permit the Alexanders to move in at their leisure, as part of the
orderly transition period.

It was during this earlier visit that the Alexanders made a resolution to
alter the residence staffing. Traditionally, the kitchen and housekeeping staff
were selected from state prison trusties, in many cases individuals who were
serving sentences for capital crimes. (Alexander remembered that Blanton
summoned his house staff to the sunroom and asked them to tell the governor-elect about the crimes they had committed.) The Alexanders decided
they would end this practice.

Honey's close friend, Carole Fant Martin, had been helping with the
move during the morning, watching the workmen load boxes of clothing
and other possessions onto two large moving vans at the Golf Club Lane residence. When the last truck was loaded and closed, she drove to Curtiswood.
She would be stationed there through the afternoon to supervise the unloading and coordinate the routing of the boxes of clothing to their designated
bedrooms upstairs.

AROUND 9:00 A.M., ALEXANDER departed the Golf Club Lane house, with Trooper Herchel Winstead, for the five-minute drive to his private transition office on Hobbs Road.

This office, two floors above a Shoney's restaurant, was a quiet collection of rooms at the south end of the Green Hills commercial district. Here, for two months, Alexander and his aides had conducted most of the private interviews with prospective cabinet members, selecting the men and women who would lead the government's principal departments under his new administration.

Winstead, forty, was a sixteen-year veteran of the highway patrol and one of three troopers assigned to Alexander's plainclothes security detail on election night the previous November. He is an affable but imposing man at six feet four inches tall. He played basketball during his two years at Lincoln Memorial University in Harrogate, Tennessee, then joined the marine corps, where he was assigned to the military police. (In retirement, he still wears a cap that reads "Once a Marine, Always a Marine.") After graduating from Aquinas College, Winstead joined the Tennessee Highway Patrol in 1963 with the aid of his sponsor, Hub Walters, whom Governor Frank Clement later appointed to the US Senate.

"I picked him up at his residence, and we drove to the office," Winstead told me, recalling the daily routine. "We'd walk down to the end of the hall, to the last office on the right, and I'd be right behind him. His office was on the right, where he would interview people, and we had a little desk there outside his office where we had a phone. I would receive all phone calls."

As Alexander sat looking through his notes for his inaugural speech, he thought about the rising level of news coverage, controversy, and clamor that his predecessor had ignited over the previous thirty-six hours. That spectacular round of commutations on Monday night had raised many questions, and there had been some immediate stirrings about whether the new governor ought to take office early, and put a stop at last to Blanton's unfettered power to pardon.

But on this Wednesday morning, the controversy seemed to have died down somewhat. Alexander took this as a good sign, and a source of personal relief.

"The idea of an early swearing-in seemed, to me, to amount to a coup—a taking of the office—which seemed inappropriate, probably unconstitutional, and, so far as I knew, there had never been anything like it in American history. I was relieved that it was now Wednesday and another day had passed, closer to the regularly scheduled inauguration on Saturday, without further talk of an early swearing-in."

THERE WAS ALSO IN THE AIR, on this Wednesday morning, a growing sense of anticipation of a happy sort.

Virtually all the work was done, and a festive weekend was coming up. Planning of the weekend events was settled. Across the state, dozens of high school marching bands were rehearsing, eager to be in Nashville for Saturday's inaugural parade and possibly a chance to appear on television as their units marched proudly past the new governor's reviewing stand.

Hotel rooms were booked for families, special guests, political supporters, and campaign staff, some of whom had worked for five years to achieve this inauguration. Thousands of campaign supporters were eager for the trip to Nashville and the joyful celebration, or if unable to attend in person, to watch it on television. Some might already have attended one of the regional receptions.

Tonight, in Jackson, would be the last of these.

TODAY, THEREFORE, SHOULD BE a calm day, Alexander thought, a quietly productive day. His inaugural address was not yet finished. He wanted to project an upbeat tone on Saturday morning—the triumphant end to a long campaign, the proud beginning of a new administration—so the young governor-elect set about his writing.

For the next two hours, the only interruptions were brief meetings with at least three of his closest advisers. He visited with Fred Thompson, the lawyer he had recruited to Howard Baker's campaign and now a senior adviser to the transition planning. This conversation was brief because Thompson was scheduled to fly back to Washington, DC, shortly for a meeting with his own clients at Westinghouse Corporation.

Alexander also met with two other men who had been announced as new cabinet members before the holidays, Lewis Donelson, of Memphis, and Gene Roberts, of Chattanooga.

Donelson was in fact the first to be announced, in early November. Alexander had persuaded him to leave his established law firm to become "the CFO of state government"—the new commissioner of the Department of Finance and Administration. In this forthcoming role, Donelson had been working steadily over the holidays helping Alexander formulate his first budget for presentation to the legislature. He had been meeting with Blanton's finance commissioner, Bill Jones, and his staff throughout this period. Donelson was in the Hobbs Road office this morning to update Alexander on his progress.

Roberts, a former FBI agent, was at this time the elected police and fire commissioner of the city of Chattanooga. His appointment as Alexander's new commissioner for the Safety Department, which included the Tennessee

Highway Patrol, was announced four days before Christmas. Roberts had flown into town this morning to discuss executive security arrangements with the governor-elect, including protective services for the Alexander family and other arrangements for the governor's residence. Roberts would also depart shortly and return to Chattanooga in the early afternoon.

In these meetings, Alexander was relaxed, wearing khaki slacks and a t-shirt.

"Wednesday morning," Alexander said, "it seemed to have settled down. The talk about an early swearing-in had settled down, and so I was sitting there in the office—having campaigned for five years, walked across the state, family moving, dead tired from recruiting a cabinet, and spending every evening traveling to Memphis and upper East Tennessee for these receptions—and I was sitting there looking forward to having a few hours to work alone on my address for Saturday."

Then, shortly before noon, the telephone rang.

CHAPTER 11

The Call

Never be afraid to raise your voice for honesty and truth and
compassion against injustice and lying and greed. If people all over the
world . . . would do this, it would change the earth.
    —William Faulkner, commencement speech
      at Oxford High School, 1951

HARDIN LOOKED AGAIN OUT his office window at the clock in the high
tower across the street. Time seemed to be moving faster. He then decided
he would call Alexander, directly and immediately, but that he would do so
"as a Tennessean," not as the US attorney.

After all, he had not yet conferred with any of his superiors in the Justice
Department. He had not given so much as a heads-up to his big boss, Griffin B. Bell, the seventy-second attorney general of the United States. Bell, the
courtly Georgia Democrat, was (like Hardin) appointed by President Carter.
Hardin said later he did not call Bell at this point, thinking he would not be
able to reach him quickly enough—and feeling that such a delay would effectively end any possibility of an accelerated swearing-in of Alexander before
the day was out. Across the street, the minute hand had moved forward.

"Governor Blanton was getting ready to release several individuals, some
of whom were targets in the federal grand jury investigation," Hardin recalled in our interview. "One of them was Eddie Denton, who was serving
time for a triple murder [in Newport, Tennessee, in a tavern shooting in
the early hours of Christmas morning, 1975]. I decided 'I can't stand by any
longer. This is it.'

"I decided to call Lamar and tell him that I was calling as a Tennessean,
but that I felt it was my obligation as a chief law enforcement officer for the
Middle District of Tennessee to convey to state authorities any information
I had about impending criminal activities or irregularities or improprieties
about to occur."

He also believed that he alone should phone Alexander, rather than delegate the task to his number 2, Joe Brown, the chief assistant US attorney,

"for basically two reasons: Joe was the lead prosecutor in the case, and it would look improper for him to have to call the incoming governor and advise him about information concerning a target of investigation, that is the present state government. Defense attorneys would have a field day with that in court. And also I did not feel that Joe could get the attention of the right people and, perhaps, not even be able to get through to them."

HE KNEW HE WAS stepping into a gray area, where the proper path was not clear.

"I knew, as a principle of law, US officials ought not to be messing around in state government that closely," he told me. "I think it's a dangerous precedent. But I had to let him know."

Hardin also felt he "had to keep the information away from as many federal employees as possible" so that if the maneuver failed he alone would take the heat. "I was concerned that eventually the defense attorneys would use my involvement—sharing sensitive information about the case with state officials, and blocking established state procedures—as a basis for appeal. Everybody involved was concerned this thing would go south.

"I was trying to shield my staff and the FBI from knowing as much as possible. The FBI was my client, and I felt an obligation to my client. I felt an obligation to my staff also. I can't be out there being accused of dabbling at politics, or 'Hardin wants to run for governor' or 'He's doing it for some political reason.' If it had to come, I wanted it to be from me. I'm not trying to be a martyr here—I'm just trying to tell you."

Except for his brief conversation with Gisler in the hallway moments earlier, Hardin had not consulted anyone in the FBI about this new information—to say nothing of taking the extraordinary step of sharing sensitive investigative information directly with a state government, let alone an official so visible as the governor-elect three days before inauguration day, urging him to take office ahead of schedule.

Gisler, in an interview, said he felt that Hardin was deeply concerned over how the story would play out if events proceeded on the current course. He told me that he and Hardin had a high level of "mutual trust" and that by this time he had developed a deep respect for Hardin's fidelity to the cases they worked together. He trusted the US attorney implicitly. In return, Hardin trusted Gisler and the integrity of his work as an investigator.

Gisler said he believed that Hardin "was trying to provide me with some insulation" when he gave him the terse "You don't want to know" reply in the hallway. Yet, for all that, Hardin was now about to phone Alexander to alert him to the findings of a current FBI investigation.

"I made it a point not to advise the FBI," Hardin told me, "because I did not want it to be said in the future that they participated in such a move. They were my clients—a client in an ongoing sensitive investigation."

And time was short. The time, by the clock on the tower across the street, was a few minutes after noon.

Hardin reached for the black phone set, picked up the receiver, and punched in the number he had for Alexander's home on Golf Club Lane. After several rings, he heard only the recorded voice on the Code-a-Phone answering machine ("We're not in right now . . ."). Next, he dialed the number for Alexander's transition office, formerly the Republican candidate's state campaign headquarters, on Crestmoor Road.

Betty Street answered. Hardin identified himself and his office, then asked to speak to Governor-elect Alexander. Street asked him to wait a moment and placed the call on hold, and then she buzzed Tom Ingram for guidance. Ingram, thirty-two, had by this time changed roles, from Alexander's campaign manager to director of his post-election transition planning team. As a young newspaper reporter in Nashville, Ingram had known Hardin as a young attorney, a Democratic political operative, and judge. Ingram sensed that this call was unusual and must be important enough to involve Alexander directly, whereas most incoming calls were more commonly routed to members of the campaign and transition staffs.

Ingram instructed Street to give the US attorney the unlisted phone number for Alexander at the private Hobbs Road office, located less than a mile away. Hardin now dialed this third number.

At this moment, Winstead was returning to the Hobbs Road office with lunch—a sack of hamburgers from the Wendy's restaurant across the street. This was the trooper's second trip out of the office since arriving there mid-morning. He had also driven across town to the Nashville airport, at about 11:00 a.m., to pick up Roberts for his scheduled meeting with the governor-elect, escorting him to the third-floor suite, before departing again for the quick lunch run.

When Winstead returned this second time, he noticed the door to Alexander's private office was closed, as expected. The meeting with Roberts and Donelson was apparently still in progress. As soon as Winstead walked the few steps to own desk, the office phone began to ring.

"I answered the phone," he remembers. "I opened the door and said, 'Governor, you have a call. It's Hal Hardin, the US attorney.'"

Suddenly, there was no time for hamburgers.

This first call was brief.

Hardin quickly explained the situation, but Alexander remembers that his first thought was to question the veracity of this caller.

"I remember the words," Alexander recalls. "He said, 'The governor is about to release some state inmates who we believe have bought their way out of prison. The FBI has given us that information. Will you take office as soon as you can to stop him?' I said, 'Hal, let me call you back in a few minutes, about 10 or 15 minutes,' and I put down the phone.

"I did that for two reasons: First, I wanted some time to think about it, and second I wanted to make sure it was him. This was long before caller ID. I knew Hal Hardin, I was acquainted with him, but I didn't know him well. I knew him by reputation more than personally. I knew he was a well-respected Democratic lawyer in town who had been appointed by Governor Blanton to a judgeship, and appointed by President Carter as US attorney, and that he was a straight shooter. And I knew that this was an absolutely extraordinary telephone call and extraordinary request for him to make.

"So I dialed back and asked to speak to him, and I said, 'Hal, I would like to see if you could again say to me what you just said,' and he did. When I finished that call, I determined it was Hal. He had said the same thing twice, and I knew down deep in my gut that, as much as I hated it, I was going to have to do it."

Satisfied now that this was not a hoax, nor a prank caller possibly stirred by the rising level of public news coverage about Blanton, Alexander immediately phoned Ingram, who was at his desk in the Crestmoor Road transition office, a few blocks away. (At about this time, Winstead departed the Hobbs Road office with Gene Roberts, returning him to the airport across town for his afternoon flight back to Chattanooga.)

"He hung up with Hal and called me," Ingram recalls. "He told me what Hal had said, and he told me to come over. So I went from Crestmoor over to Hobbs." When Ingram arrived, Donelson was in the room with Alexander.

DONELSON, SIXTY-TWO, WAS ALREADY a legend in Tennessee politics—a distinguished Memphis attorney and a towering figure in the state's Republican Party. He would later become a law partner of Senator Howard Baker.

Politically savvy, Ivy League–educated, charming, and broadly experienced, Donelson had been a member of the Memphis City Council, the chairman of Tennesseans for Eisenhower, and one of a handful of Tennesseans (including Baker and Dunn) credited with the birth of the modern Republican Party in Tennessee. Donelson was a noticeably senior hand in Alexander's core team of advisers, most of the others being in their twenties and thirties. For Alexander, remembering his own experience in the Nixon White House, Donelson was the sort of senior éminence grise that Arthur Burns and Bryce Harlow had been to President Nixon—savvy, broad-gauged men of deep experience and wisdom of the wider world.

By this Wednesday morning, Donelson had already been announced as Alexander's first cabinet appointee. He would run the state Department of

Finance and Administration, meaning he would be the first among equals on the new cabinet. Donelson was more than qualified for the new position; he had become a celebrated tax attorney and a longtime advocate of tax reform—supporting enactment of a state income tax, which inevitably put him at odds with most of his party's elected leaders, including at times Alexander.

"He was my first appointment," Alexander explained later. "The reason was that I was trying to restore confidence in state government, so I wasn't just asking who might be available to serve in the cabinet, but who might be the very best person I could recruit to serve in each job. I started with Lewie because he was one of the most distinguished attorneys in the state. He had helped build the Memphis Republican Party since the 1950s. He was a sixth-generation descendent of Andrew Jackson's wife, Rachel.

"No one in the state represented a family with a thread that ran longer in a more distinguished way through Tennessee history. What Lewie always said was that, when I met with him in November, not only would I make him the commissioner of the Department of Finance and Administration, but he would be, in effect, the chief operating officer of state government. My message to him was, 'Lewie, you run the state, and I'll be the governor,' and that's the way we did it."

Donelson also had other qualifications in the form of working connections to the top Democratic leaders in the Tennessee General Assembly. At this time, Alexander did not know House Speaker Ned McWherter and Lieutenant Governor John Wilder, speaker of the state senate—but Donelson did. He had been McWherter's lawyer, in fact, assisting him with business and tax matters over several years. He also knew Wilder and from time to time had assisted him behind the scenes with lining up Republican votes on legislative issues.

Even with his impressive election victory, Alexander knew that as a new Republican governor he was wading into problematic waters with the Democratic-controlled legislature. In order to steer successfully, he would need both formal and informal channels of communication with the Democratic leaders, and Donelson could help him navigate his way through both.

INGRAM TOLD ME THAT the information Hardin conveyed in his midday call created an immediate turmoil of thoughts and a need for quick counsel and analysis and, in any event, required a new way of looking at how the rest of the week might unfold. As Hardin persisted during this early phone conversation, Ingram recalled, the magnitude of the implications began to set in.

"There was no enthusiasm for this in our shop," Ingram said. "It was a risky thing. It was a crazy thing. There was the chance that the action would be challenged, that the whole thing would be in contest, and everybody would look like a fool.

"As I recall, Hal was pretty specific in his first conversation with Lamar. He mentioned the early swearing-in in the first conversation. So, we were dealing with the worst case from those early moments, and we didn't want to do it. Didn't think we *should*. Didn't think we *could*. Just didn't *want* to do it," he said.

"It was going to spoil things. It wasn't our problem. And we worried, a little, about being set up—not intentionally, not maliciously by anybody, but worried that we could end up being a fall guy for it."

Alexander remembers that it was clear to him, at this early hour, that he would have to take the oath before Saturday after all, and likely before this day was out. For all the reasons he had felt it should not be done this way—the disruption, the doubts, the "un-American aspects" it suggested, the partisan or public division it might engender—the issue now seemed to him oddly settled. The facts were overwhelming. Any reluctance was now relegated to simple regret.

"I remember telling Tom, later in the day, that this is the kind of thing when a hundred things could go wrong, and ninety-nine of them probably will," Alexander told me. "I spent the next six hours trying to think of everything I could do to keep those ninety-nine things from going wrong."

WITH BOTH DONELSON AND INGRAM now present, and Winstead at his post just outside the closed door of the private office, Alexander phoned Hardin again. The US attorney resumed making his case for moving the swearing-in forward by three days.

"I explained to him," Hardin remembers, "why I had felt compelled to call him—that I was calling not as a federal official but *as a Tennessean*. I then urged him to go ahead and take his office early. I implored him—I used that word—to take office as soon as possible to prevent the releases.

"I explained to him the information that I had, among other things that Governor Blanton was considering the release of Eddie Denton and other individuals that were the target of a federal grand jury investigation. I explained to him that that event—coupled with the information that we had that Denton indeed had paid money to get out of the penitentiary—and that Governor Blanton had recently commuted the terms or pardoned some fifty-two criminals in the middle of the night—that I felt that he had no alternative but to assume the office now. I also told him all evidence indicated Blanton was out of control."

Alexander, in an interview later, said he did not recall Hardin mentioning any prisoner by name.

"He didn't give me any details, just the overall situation that he had learned," Alexander told me. "He just said, 'I need you to take office early.'" He said he told Hardin that he felt he didn't need to know further specifics about the government's investigation, that he recognized the sensitive nature of the FBI's findings.

But he also told Hardin he was not convinced that taking the oath early would be proper or permitted under the state's constitution. He said he believed it was a poor, if not disastrous, precedent to establish in a nation known for peaceful and orderly transitions of power following democratic elections.

"Most Americans don't favor coups, which is what that was," Alexander said later. "This is something you hear about in Latin America, not in the United States. I had always marveled at how the nation stopped to admire the most important transfer of power in the world at the presidential inaugurations. Nothing could stop or tarnish the regular renewal of democracy at inaugurations, not bitter election contests or even an assassination or a presidential resignation. In the United States, the torch is always passed peacefully and with grace. It is a celebration of our right to change governments. It is something that makes us different from a lot of other countries. No matter how bad things had gotten, I could not destroy an inauguration. Surely everyone could wait just three more days."

In the conversation that ensued in the small Hobbs Road office, Donelson told Alexander that the early swearing-in could be accomplished but that "you can't do it without the Democrats." He said McWherter and Wilder must not only be briefed—and quickly—but they should also be persuaded to concur publicly in the decision and also attend any such ceremony.

HARDIN RECALLS THEY DISCUSSED the "legalities of the oath" and other details, but the conversation kept returning to the absence of any precedent.

"I told him that, in my opinion, there was no question, but even assuming there was a question, that it would be better to litigate that at some time in the future, and not worry about it," Hardin told me. "Lamar talked about the fact that Bill Leech, the attorney general, had given an opinion that had thrown the matter up in the air, and that he did not want to do anything that would seem to be improper. He also told me that he would not do anything unless Lieutenant Governor Wilder and Speaker McWherter and Attorney General Bill Leech agreed that this was the course of action, and urged him to go ahead and take the office.

"He did not want to make the move on his own, and he wanted it to be a united front—if, in fact, he was going to do it. I got the feeling that he indeed was going to do it, and after my conversation with him, I felt that there was no question that we were going to have a new governor."

Ingram also remembers three different reservations on Alexander's side as they considered the implications of Hardin's extraordinary call.

"The first emotion," Ingram remembers, "was 'We didn't do all this [campaigning] for two years to do this.' It will just mess everything up. It will spoil the celebration on Saturday. And we got too much to do for that. Then, the second emotions were worrying about it politically. And the third emotions were then about the technicalities, the legalities."

It was the last that prompted Alexander to end the first substantive call with Hardin, with the suggestion that the US attorney now consult the two leaders of the state legislature. Constitutionally, the swearing-in of a new governor is properly the act of the legislative branch, Alexander insisted. He would have to know their opinions about this specific point, whether they would now urge him to take office three days early, and meanwhile he would neither agree to nor recommend such an action himself.

This would initiate another four hours of private discussion, constitutional debate, and protracted negotiations involving the top leadership of Tennessee's state government—with exception of its top-most executive, Governor Ray Blanton. He would not be advised until very late in the day, after the sun had set in fact, and then almost as an afterthought.

Alexander now widened his tight circle of advisers just a bit. He asked Ingram to phone Fred Thompson, the old friend who had been in Nashville earlier in the day but by early afternoon had returned to Washington, DC.

Thompson and Alexander had met in 1968 as young attorneys working in political campaigns. In 1972, when Baker was looking for a Middle Tennessee campaign manager for his reelection effort, Alexander recommended Thompson, then an assistant US attorney. The following year, Baker, then the ranking Republican on the Senate Watergate Committee, offered Alexander the job of minority counsel to the committee. But Alexander, who at that point was living in Nashville with his young family, declined. He suggested that Baker instead consider Thompson, who not only accepted but became a star of the nationally televised committee hearings. (It was Thompson who asked Nixon aide Alexander Butterfield whether the president had secretly tape-recorded conversations in the Oval Office. The answer was yes.)

Thompson had been involved in Alexander's 1978 campaign, and more recently he had been assisting in the transition process of recruiting the executive-level leadership of the new administration, helping to find and vet prospects for various cabinet-level appointments. Most recently, Alexander had phoned Thompson the previous Friday in light of the public suggestions that he might be asked to assume office early. One news report had mentioned an opinion letter from the state attorney general's office, seemingly out of the blue, saying the new governor could be sworn in as early as Tuesday.

"On Monday, I had talked to Fred and asked him to do a little research," Alexander remembered. "It might have been on Friday, when the rumors started, or maybe it was Monday when we heard about the attorney general's opinion. Could there be any basis for this—that the legislature could come to me and say, 'We're going to swear you in early, to stop Blanton from doing these things'? Fred did a little research and got back to us on Monday."

After the second phone conversation with Hardin, Alexander phoned home and told Honey what was happening. For her, it was already a stressful day.

"I was at the house, packing," she said. "We were literally moving that day to the mansion. My whole recollection of the day was that it was very gray, it was raining, Leslee was sick, the movers came, and the house just started getting emptier and colder. We literally ended up having one mattress left for her to lie down on—it was the last thing we moved out of the house."

Relying in part on Thompson's research and also his own understanding of the tradition and rules of transition, Alexander told Hardin he knew that inaugurations were the province of the state legislature, not the incoming governor. It was therefore essential, he said, for Hardin also to inform the two leaders of the state legislature—House Speaker Ned McWherter and the speaker of the state senate, Lieutenant Governor John Wilder. It was clear to Alexander at this point that it was necessary now to have a discussion with McWherter and Wilder so that they could all discuss the new facts together, ideally face to face. At Donelson's suggestion, he also asked Hardin to inform Bill Leech, the state's attorney general.

Alexander then remembered that Wilder, coincidentally, had been scheduled to come to his Hobbs Road office, at 2:45 p.m., for a meeting on another matter. He therefore suggested to Hardin that possibly McWherter and Leech might also be available at that time.

Finally, Hardin remembers, Alexander mentioned one additional invitee. "He suggested that I might bring Chief Judge Joe Henry with me, and let him stay outside until we made the decision, and if we had made the decision to go, we would go at that time," Hardin told me. Henry was the chief justice of the five-member Tennessee Supreme Court. "We discussed the political consequences of such a move, and, again, Lamar reiterated to me that he would do it only if all three leaders [McWherter, Wilder, and Leech] urged him to do it."

At this point, Hardin hung up the phone and sped forward with his assignments, instructing his secretary, Kay Rasmussen, to phone Leech, McWherter, and Wilder as rapidly as possible.

"Kay, get in touch with Bill Leech," he told her. "We're going to have a new governor by sundown."

But within five minutes, she had run into two obstacles that meant delay. She could not reach Leech; his secretary informed her that he was at Baptist Hospital, where his wife was delivering their baby. Further, Wilder and McWherter were at this hour engaged in a meeting of the state's Building Commission.

Hardin phoned Alexander again, telling him these circumstances. Alexander suggested that in Leech's absence, he should try to reach either Bill Koch or Hayes Cooney, telling him "they are familiar with the situation." Cooney was the chief deputy attorney general, Leech's second in command, and Koch, one of six deputy attorneys general ranking just beneath Cooney, had been previously assigned by Leech to act as the liaison between the AG's office and the Alexander transition team.

Koch soon arrived at the Hobbs Road office and joined in the discussion alongside Donelson and Ingram.

"I was lining up every Democrat I could find," Alexander told me later, "to make this as legal, and constitutional, and proper as possible. There was no map. It was like being told your mission is to go through the valley of the shadow of death, and there are ninety-nine chances out of a hundred that you'll be killed. And you know you have to go. You don't want to go, but I was determined to go. If there was any possible safe way to get through that valley, I was determined to do it. So I was trying to think of every possible thing we could do to make this extraordinary event happen in as appropriate a way as possible. Trying to think of everything that could go wrong—to make it accepted by the public, make it have bipartisan support, and launch a new administration.

"The worst thing would have been to have, on top of the Blanton scandal, an unsuccessful, unprecedented, early swearing-in that amounted to an un-American, clumsy coup by a group of people taking office in an unconstitutional way. That was the challenge. Nobody in his right mind would want to even try that, but I didn't have a choice so I had to do it. I didn't think about it very long; it was obvious I had to do it, as soon as I hung up the phone."

At the noon hour, McWherter, Wilder, and Leech were not immediately available for Hardin's calls. All three were together at the downtown Hyatt Hotel, across the street from Legislative Plaza, attending a private luncheon.

They had been invited to a carefully planned VIP briefing by the organizers of the forthcoming 1982 World's Fair, to occur in Knoxville. The fair would require public financial support, and its leaders were counting on an appropriation from Tennessee's state government. They had arranged this luncheon briefing for top officials of the state legislature, including Building Commission members and the state's constitutional officers. These officials, together with the incoming Governor Alexander, would eventually sit in judgment on the exposition's funding request.

The organizer of the Knoxville entourage was Bo Roberts, who had previously been Governor Ellington's top staff member and later a senior administrator at the University of Tennessee. He was now the staff president of the Knoxville International Energy Exposition Incorporated, the non-profit organization formed to develop and promote the fair. The leader of the project was Jake Butcher, the Knoxville banker who had lost the primary to Blanton in 1974 and the general election to Alexander in November, and was now serving as the chairman of the exposition board of directors. This group had arranged the special luncheon, in a private dining room on the Hyatt's mezzanine level, and had brought the project architect along to make the presentation.

"We had brought our model of the World's Fair site," Roberts remembers. "It was to be a major briefing for the constitutional officers and the legislative leadership about the fair—to make sure they had full knowledge. The governor-elect [Alexander] had already had a briefing, well before the primary, and was very supportive. It was a very nice luncheon—prime rib, and I think we probably had wine involved, too. We spent a lot of money, for that time—probably the equivalent of $100 per plate, in 1979 dollars. Altogether we probably had fewer than twenty people in the room. Everybody was seated, getting started with the program."

Apparently, Leech's secretary had been able to get a message to him as the luncheon began, alerting him that the US attorney was trying to reach him on an urgent matter.

"I remember somebody came in and whispered in Bill Leech's ear, and he stepped out," Roberts recalled. "He was gone awhile. He came back in and whispered in the ear of Ned McWherter, and Ned and John also left the room. They were very polite about it, but we kept getting interrupted. Then either Ned or Bill Leech came in and said, 'We really apologize but some of us are going to have to leave.'

"They left the room and were gone. A little air went out of the room when that occurred. They were very nice. We all knew something was going on, but we had no clue what it was—until we found out later in the day. It was on the day of the coup—the day it was happening. Of course we had no idea."

The three men departed through the hotel lobby, walked across Union Street, and walked to the speaker's offices in the Legislative Plaza.

At about 1:30 p.m., Alexander adjourned the small group at his Green Hills office. He asked Donelson to contact McWherter and Wilder directly on his behalf. Donelson had known both men for decades and had been McWherter's attorney previously. Then Alexander left the office for the two-mile drive home.

"I remember Herchel Winstead drove me home for lunch to see Honey and check on the moving," Alexander said. "Herchel rarely said anything to me, without me saying something to him first. But he knew what was happening, and as we got in the car, Herchel said to me, 'You are going to be governor before dark," and I knew he was right.

"So I went home and told Honey what was going on. The rest of the day was almost like a new campaign—and the new campaign was to perfectly execute something that you absolutely, totally, completely did not want to do. But I knew I had to."

By the time Alexander arrived at this hour on Wednesday, the residence on Golf Club Lane was a changed place.

He and his family had lived in this house for almost eight years now, and they knew this would be their final day there. They had bought this two-story brick colonial in 1971 from Kenneth L. Roberts, a prominent Nashville banking executive. (Roberts, in 1966, had run unsuccessfully for US Senate against Alexander's old boss Howard Baker.) Here, the young family had lived through two campaigns for governor and a nearly constant stretch of public life over a five-year period.

When her husband arrived, Honey Alexander was multitasking. She was caring for Leslee, her sick daughter, and also coordinating the crew of moving men who were going from room to room, emptying them of furniture and clothing boxes. Carole Sergent, who with her husband Dr. John Sergent were among the Alexander's closest couple friends, was there assisting her. One truck had departed already with the first load, heading for the official residence on Curtiswood Lane where Carole Martin would oversee the unloading.

"This was the house we had lived in for nearly eight years," Alexander remembers. "The furniture was gone, clothes were packed in boxes, half of the boxes were at the governor's mansion. The house was cold, there was nothing to eat, nothing to wear. Leslee was home sick with a cold, and what was supposed to be happening that day was that the family was supposed to be moving into the governor's mansion.

"I went home more than anything else to tell Honey and explain to her. She was planning to go on over to the governor's mansion with our sick child to move in that day. She was pregnant, sitting there at the house in the cold with Leslee coughing, and not knowing what we were going to do."

ALEXANDER REMEMBERS THE FEELINGS of upheaval and frustration in that first visit home on Wednesday afternoon. At one point, as they talked hurriedly about this awkward twist that their long journey was now taking, the emotion boiled over.

He and Honey sat together in the otherwise empty bedroom of the cold house, and he described what would likely be happening at the end of the day—and where and with whom.

"At one point, talking to Honey, I remember I just slammed my fist into the wall, and I broke the plaster, the plaster in the wall in our bedroom. I was embarrassed that I'd done it, but I guess it was just needing to let off some steam. The pent-up emotion came from the indecision—tiredness, emotion, uncertainty—and no outlet for it. The attorney general himself believed, at this point, it was unconstitutional for me to be sworn in, and we didn't yet know whether the lieutenant governor and the speaker would join me in being sworn in. And there was the extreme outside possibility that the governor would find out about it and surround the capitol with the National Guard or the highway patrol."

It was his right hand that cracked the hard plaster, the hand that had shaken thousands of others over a long campaign, and now the hand was aching. The hand he would shortly be raising, after sundown in a sudden ceremony, at the end of a day that was not supposed to happen.

"Honey later said it was the worst day of her life that day. She said, 'This is going to be more like a funeral.' And we had no idea how it would be received by the people."

CHAPTER 12

The Rise of The Speaker

I've plowed new ground and walked a new road.
—Speaker Ned McWherter, January 17, 1979

IN JANUARY 1969, seven-term congressman Robert A. (Fats) Everett died, and Ned Ray McWherter's career as an elected official began.

Though a generation of years separated them, these two men had much in common and in time knew each other well. Both hailed from rural West Tennessee, Everett from Union City, McWherter from Dresden, twenty-four miles apart in the territory north of Memphis, far west of Nashville, between Jackson and the Mississippi River. Like McWherter, Everett had been born on a farm in this broad flat country, and the congressman and his protégé were both large men physically. (Both stood six feet four inches tall. McWherter weighed 250 pounds, wore a size 52 jacket and a XXXL shirt.) In time, the elder congressman became the young man's first political mentor.

Everett relished his work of meeting and greeting constituents across Obion and Weakley Counties, listening to their stories at courthouse squares and along country roads, responding helpfully to their needs when he could. In Everett's campaigns, the young McWherter served as a driver and informal aide to his role model. While so doing, the young man watched, listened, and learned.

A journalist who frequently interviewed McWherter, Rick Locker, the Nashville bureau chief of the Memphis *Commercial Appeal*, observed in a 1990 retrospective profile that "McWherter fell under Everett's spell, worked in his campaigns, socialized with Everett and his friends and nurtured a passion for politics at Everett's side. Everett was an old-style Southern rural Democrat who placed more emphasis on cutting through red tape for his constituents than on foreign affairs—although he amassed considerable power in Congress."

McWherter already possessed a strong work ethic. Unlike Everett, he did not have a college degree, but he was a savvy and retentive student of life. He had learned early the necessity of hard work, friendships, and loyalty through his upbringing and first jobs.

HE WAS BORN IN PALMERSVILLE, Tennessee, the only child of Lucille Golden Smith and Harmon Ray McWherter. This tiny community was also the birthplace of Pauline LaFon, later Pauline Gore, wife of Senator Albert Gore Sr. and mother of Vice President Albert Gore Jr. When they were girls, Lucille and Pauline walked together to school at the Webb Elementary School in Palmersville.

Harmon and Lucille were sharecroppers who made a hard living on the farm someone else owned. They later opened a hamburger stand in the town of Dresden, and through hard work and strong spirit they grew it into the Dresden City Café, which they owned, and where their son also worked lunch hours as a dishwasher and server while he was in high school.

At Dresden High, McWherter was an active and engaged student. He was cocaptain of the football team, played basketball, served as president of the Future Farmers of America, and was voted Best Looking in his class. After graduation, he wanted a college degree and attempted it four times—once at Murray State University in Kentucky, twice at the University of Tennessee at Martin, and finally at Memphis State University in 1950. He always hoped for a football scholarship—only to be quickly sidelined each time by a recurrent knee injury.

When he was seventeen, in 1948, McWherter joined the Tennessee National Guard and there befriended many of the characters who would figure importantly in his business and political life to come. These fellow guardsmen included, in the early years, his cousin Cayce Pentecost, who would serve on the state's powerful Public Service Commission, regulator of utilities and trucking. McWherter once said "My cousin and close friend Cayce Pentecost and Fats Everett had more influence than any other two people in getting me into politics."

In 1953, McWherter married Bette Jean Beck. They raised two children, Linda and Mike, and separated in 1960. She died in 1973. On a long wall of the library at McWherter's Henry County retreat, called *Riverview*, overlooking the broad Tennessee River and the Ned McWherter Bridge in the distance, there are three oil portraits: Bette, Harmon, and Lucille.

After the final football injury, McWherter departed college for the last time. He returned to Dresden, and took a job at Bay-bee Shoe Company, maker of children's shoes and boots. He later managed Sheffield Shoe Corporation in Alabama. When Sheffield Shoe failed, two businessmen in Martin, Tennessee, bought its equipment and established the Martin Shoe Company, where they hired McWherter as a salesman. He supplied domestic retailers across the eastern United States—his most important early buyer was Dollar

General Stores, based in Scottsville, Kentucky—as well as customers in the Caribbean, including Puerto Rico, the Dominican Republic, and schools on the island nation of Cuba.

In his later years, McWherter did not speak publicly of his early experience in Cuba. His time there was in the immediate pre-Castro years while President Fulgencio Batista was in power and aligned with the United States, but after his political career began, he possibly thought the timeline of the Cuba story might become confused with Castro's regime. Even so, his son Mike McWherter told me that his father often spoke of this experience in the privacy of their home, remembering it fondly, sharing his memory of business arrangements and also the dangers of doing business on the prerevolutionary Cuban frontier.

Always the entrepreneur, the young Tennessean conceived a potential opportunity combining modern domestic shoe manufacturing processes with the need for uniform shoes in the Catholic schools in Cuba's eastern region. Mike McWherter described this early venture for me.

"Dad had the idea to sell shoes to the rural parochial schools, where students dressed alike, and he knew the shoes could be mass produced," he told me. "He arranged with the manufacturer to ship what he ordered into the airport in Havana, and he would transport the shoes to the eastern end of the island. He had to avoid the warring factions along the way. This was in 1959, and you would run into either people loyal to Batista or people fighting with Fidel Castro. Dad said he was advised to keep his money hidden on the way back to Havana, and only have eighty or a hundred dollars in any one place. Of course, eighty dollars was a lot of money in that place at that time."

McWHERTER'S TIME IN LATIN AMERICA was an unlikely biographical detail that he shared with two other participants in the 1979 coup. Apparently none of the three knew in his later years that the others had also spent time there.

All three—McWherter, Hardin, Alexander—had these experiences while in their twenties, although at different times, and in the period spanning the latter years of the Eisenhower administration and the abbreviated presidency of John F. Kennedy. In addition to Hardin's Peace Corps service in Colombia, Alexander spent a six-week period with a group of US college students touring South America. Both Hardin and Alexander later described these times as "formative" periods in their lives.

In November 2000, as a former governor, McWherter visited Cuba on a goodwill trip. He invited his two closest associates, Jim Free and Harlan Mathews, to accompany him, and both accepted. "Ned was very interested in going over to Santiago de Cuba, on the eastern end of the island," Free recalled. "No one goes over there, but he wanted to because of his memories of his visits there as a young man."

OVER THESE FORMATIVE TWO DECADES, McWherter proved to be a shrewd and adroit businessman. He made small initial investments in a trucking business and a beer distributorship and also made savvy if modest early forays in the stock market. Along the way, he also became active in civic and political organizations, and this further extended his circle of friends.

In 1963, he hired Madelyn Bradberry, then nineteen, as his bookkeeper. She was the daughter of friends of McWherter's parents. Her father had died that May, and Madelyn needed work. McWherter hired her on a "three-month trial basis," worried that working together might harm the family friendships. She married George Pritchett later that year and kept the job well past the trial period. When McWherter died in 2011, Madelyn Pritchett had been his business partner for forty-seven years.

The businesses they jointly managed included a number of successful companies. McWherter's Volunteer Distributing Company became the important regional distributor for Anheuser-Busch. Likewise, his Volunteer Express grew from a trucking company serving only the Nashville-Dresden-Milan route into a leading regional freight hauler with thirty locations and more than three hundred employees.

Pentecost and McWherter established the first senior care nursing home in Dresden in 1967. A small roadside monument at a park near Hillview Nursing Home commemorates their mothers, Carrie LaFon Pentecost and Lucille Smith McWherter.

In 1968, McWherter, at age thirty-eight, ran for an open seat in the state's general assembly and won. In January 1969, he took his freshman's seat literally on the back row in the vaulted chamber of the Tennessee house of representatives at Nashville. In short order, however, McWherter would move to the front of that vast room. He also quit the National Guard at this point, retiring with the rank of captain, figuring he would be unable to attend the monthly drills any longer.

Reelected in 1970 and 1972, he became chairman of the Democratic caucus in the state house of representatives. Soon after this, he was named chairman of the powerful Calendar and Rules Committee. This particular panel held sway over rules of procedure and also the flow of bills from the standing committees—either sending them to the house floor for final voting, or to the oblivion of "study committees" (and soon forgotten).

This early step into leadership was an extraordinary rise for such a young member and was made possible by McWherter's careful tending to the support of his fellow Democratic members, especially those from the rural western part of the state. These particular members would form the loyal center of McWherter's political power base for years to come.

McWherter's ascent to speaker, in 1973, came about also because of his style as a quietly moderate tactician within the house—in sharp contrast to the combative, partisan demeanor of the incumbent speaker, Jim McKinney of Nashville. Two related episodes—in starkly different settings—illustrate their contrasting personalities and politics and help explain how McWherter's speakership came to be. The first occurred on a houseboat in the middle of Percy Priest Lake near Nashville, the other over dinner on the twentieth floor of a downtown office building.

Tom Wiseman, then the state treasurer and later US district court judge in Nashville, recalls the day that Representative John Bragg, the Democrat from Murfreesboro, came to his office at the capitol to discuss the speakership, and his worry that McKinney was engaging in some questionable practices. "We made up our minds something had to be done about it, and that Ned could possibly be speaker."

In June 1972, after the legislature had adjourned its session for the year, Bragg hosted a houseboat outing on a sunny afternoon. He was the chairman of the house's Finance, Ways and Means Committee, owing to his appointment by McWherter. His commercial printing company owned a large houseboat, which Bragg kept at Four Corners Marina. Here, Bragg invited McWherter and five others for an afternoon of relaxation on the lake. The guests included two other ranking house members—Representatives Stanley Rogers of Manchester and Cletus McWilliams of Franklin—and McWherter's staff assistant Jim Free. The other two guests were Wiseman and the Secretary of State Gentry Crowell; these two constitutional officers had served with McWherter in the house previously, were loyal to him, and owed their current appointments to the Democratic caucus.

Rogers was especially resentful of McKinney's style. He had recently run athwart McKinney's legislative strong-armed tactics and had seen his own bill to establish a statewide kindergarten program go down in defeat; Rogers had campaigned for this goal, and it was embraced as an administration bill by the Republican governor Winfield Dunn. Because Dunn supported it, McKinney had targeted the kindergarten measure for defeat, and it had been voted down along partisan lines.

This summer afternoon was not a time McWherter would typically be in Nashville. At this point in his career, he did not often visit the capitol between legislative sessions, which typically ran from January to May. He was persuaded to join this particular gathering, however, through a bit of well-intentioned subterfuge. McWherter was told the houseboat outing was to celebrate young Jim Free's birthday. (His birthday is actually January 17.)

Free had first met McWherter while working as a college intern from Middle Tennessee State University. McWherter, then chairman of the Calendar and Rules Committee, entered the meeting room and spoke to Free, who was sitting quietly in the back of the room.

"Do you know what we're supposed to do?" McWherter asked the young intern. "Yes, sir," Free replied, after only one week of orientation in the legislative procedures.

"Then get your pencil and tablet, and come on and follow me," the chairman said.

"And I did," Free told me, "for the rest of his life." When McWherter became speaker in January 1973, he named Free his administrative assistant, in effect his chief of staff. Free was eventually chief clerk of the house, the youngest in the country.

The only other person on the boat that day was Bragg's son Tommy, who was on a brief visit home while on a speaking tour for the US Air Force. The younger Bragg drove the boat while his elders lunched and talked. The main agenda was to persuade McWherter to take on McKinney for the speakership at the next opportunity.

"The boat trip was arranged by several of us—casual, no ties," Rogers told me. "Everybody on the boat wanted Ned to be speaker. We'd all been together for a number of years. There wasn't a nonfriend in the bunch, and we all had a common interest. It was not a rural vs. urban thought process, or conservative vs. liberal. It was just felt that Ned McWherter could do a better job than Jim McKinney had done."

It turned into a long afternoon, Wiseman recalled, "longer than a case of beer."

"Over hot dogs and hamburgers and beer—Budweiser beer, of course, because that's what Ned distributed—they asked Ned to run for house speaker. 'Either you're going to run, or we're all gonna run, and you'll have to pick among us.' Ned got it. He knew they were serious."

Wiseman said the members of the group pledged to "go out and get you the votes" in the house when the time came.

"We all said, 'We've got to do this'—that was the pitch we all made," Wiseman said. "Of course, he worked on it, too. We all hustled our friends in the legislature."

After lengthy discussion, McWherter agreed. Free described this as the moment McWherter "took a step, for the first time, toward running against McKinney."

WORD OF THIS DISCUSSION got around, of course, and the meeting on the houseboat soon came to McKinney's attention. Free recalls a subsequent confrontation. McKinney called and invited McWherter to meet him for dinner at the downtown Nashville City Club. McWherter agreed, but he also took Free along with him.

McWherter was not a confrontational person, his allies at the time recall. His style was the opposite of McKinney's brash, acerbic, vengeful manner. McKinney therefore did not handle McWherter well at this awkward dinner meeting.

"McKinney was not happy that I was there," Free remembers, "and in the conversation he became threatening to Ned, saying there would be repercussions if he persisted in working to be speaker. Anybody who knew Ned McWherter would tell you this was no way to get him to do something. I remember Ned got up and went to the restroom. While he was gone, there was no conversation at all—like a block of ice descended over the table. McKinney and I were both just looking out the window. Then Ned came back to the table and said, 'Well, I've decided I'm going to run.' McKinney became threatening and blustery, and we left. In the car, Ned said to me, 'Free, while I was in the bathroom, I started thinking about McKinney's threats, and it just pissed me off.'"

Both men worked through the fall to line up their votes in the Democratic caucus. When the fifty-one members met in December to elect the next speaker, each representative marked his choice on a blank piece of paper. No names were affixed. The anonymous ballots were collected and taken to a clerk's office just steps away from the house chamber, with one monitor present for each candidate. The count went forward quickly. At the end, before the last piece of paper was unfolded, the tally stood at twenty-five votes for McKinney and twenty-five for McWherter.

The final ballot was opened, and it bore McWherter's name. He had won the caucus election by one vote.

MCWHERTER'S BIOGRAPHER, BILLY STAIR, was his legislative assistant and later served him in the governor's office as the senior policy adviser. He described how the so-called West Tennessee Caucus worked, noting that "in the early 1970s, this group included virtually all the legislators between Memphis and the Tennessee River."

"With few exceptions over the years, the group's members had a remarkable similarity," according to Stair. "All shared an uncompromising fiscal conservatism that was balanced by a legacy of Jacksonian populism. The West Tennesseans also shared a genuinely sophisticated sense of humor, often laced with barnyard language, that could be brutally effective in closed-door political debate. They would bicker among themselves, but usually close ranks in support of a colleague believed to be threatened by Republicans or special interests. McWherter organized the legislators into the West Tennessee Caucus, which met every Tuesday morning in the speaker's office to discuss legislative strategy. . . . Years of camaraderie among the West Tennesseans produced friendships and political loyalties that simply cannot be appreciated by those who were not a part of the group."

State representative John Tanner, later the US congressman from Tennessee's northwestern Eighth District, became a McWherter stalwart soon after his election in 1976. He had known McWherter and his family for years.

"Back in that day," Tanner told me, "the legislature had not yet become so polarized, and basically the conflicts had much more to do with the rural-urban context than it did Democrat and Republican. The West Tennessee Caucus and the East Tennessee rural Republicans worked together. We had to stick together or we'd be overwhelmed by the urban guys."

Representative Jimmy Naifeh, a member of the caucus from Covington, Tennessee, roomed with Tanner during legislative sessions over a ten-year period. In 1987, Naifeh succeeded McWherter as house speaker. He disagrees with Stair's description of the size of the West Tennessee Caucus in the 1970s, but he concurs that the group was nonetheless effective as an organizing force, fostering a solidarity that benefited their party, its legislative goals, and ultimately McWherter's political career.

"He [McWherter] was the one who started it, and it was twelve to twenty-four members at any given time," he told me. "We met together once a week. We did everything together. A lot of other members didn't like it; but, of course, Ned and John [Wilder, the senate speaker] were from West Tennessee, too."

THIS GATHERING POLITICAL POWER in Tennessee also boosted McWherter's influence among national Democrats, most dramatically with two other southern governors who became president, first Jimmy Carter of Georgia and later Bill Clinton of Arkansas. Both Carter and Clinton sought his support in their campaigns and his advice during their respective years in the White House.

In 1974, when Ray Blanton was elected governor in Tennessee, Carter was already traveling across the country building his national campaign. But the Georgia governor courted not his counterpart Blanton but McWherter, who as the preeminent leader in the state legislature became one of Carter's principal supporters in Tennessee and eventually at the 1976 nominating convention in New York. Years later Clinton, though a generation younger, would be even closer to McWherter. In his 2004 autobiography, *My Life*, Clinton recalled McWherter's role his own 1996 campaign, describing the Tennessean as "a huge bear of a man who was the only person I ever heard call the vice president 'Albert.'

"Ned Ray," Clinton added, "was worth so many votes that I didn't care what he called Al, or me for that matter."

McWherter died in April 2011. In a final profile, journalist Bruce Dobie described McWherter's death as the end of "the age of the rural South Democrat."

"McWherter's honesty and straightforwardness inspired a loyalty among staff and supporters that made him an incredibly magnanimous force. Tragically, against the steady advance of the Republican Party across the South, the Democratic Party that he led has mostly vanished. He was a man to be taken utterly seriously, but he could also be an absolute riot. In the end, one remembers him flying down a two-lane road to yet another campaign speech, his so-called 'Redneck Express' barreling through exhausted little towns filled with falling-down barns, and the little old ladies serving fresh lemonade from hardware store washtubs, and the old farmers grinning from under their hats, and McWherter standing up to the patient and forgotten crowd and telling them that he was one of them."

CHAPTER 13

The Cosmos of the Lieutenant Governor

Let the senate be the senate.
   —John S. Wilder

HE WAS THE LONGEST-SERVING lieutenant governor in America, a lawyer by training and a cotton gin owner, lender, farmer, and pilot also. Yet to most who knew John Wilder—politicians, journalists, and friends—he was, underneath it all, an enigma.

His law office was on the town square in Somerville, Tennessee, east of Memphis, but the farm where he lived, which had been in his family since the 1880s, was in an unincorporated community called Longtown. This home, together with the Braden Methodist Church, up the road, where he taught Sunday school for fifty years, was the true center of his life outside of politics.

In Longtown, Wilder lived with his beloved family: his wife, Marcelle, and his sons, Shelton and David. Here, on land he owned, stretching over six thousand acres, he managed a cotton gin and farm supply business. At one time, Wilder's Longtown Supply Company, founded in 1887, was the largest cotton gin in Tennessee.

Wilder was a quiet, courtly, deliberate man. He was sparing and measured in his words and at times could also seem cryptic in his statements. Jim Travis, a television news reporter and former anchor for the ABC affiliate in Nashville, recalled Wilder's speaking style—simple declarative sentences, in measured cadences—and remembered he often referred to himself as "the speaker" rather than "I" in the customary first-person.

"He would say, 'the speaker feels,' or 'the speaker believes,' referring to himself," Travis told me. "I was always taught to never trust a politician who refers to himself in the third person, like they were disembodied from their own actions."

Wilder was also a private man. He was reserved with details about his own life, even with his family, according to his son Shelton. He had served in the US Army during World War II, but the son told me he did not remember his father ever telling stories from his military service.

"He never really talked much about the army. When the war was over, he came home and ran the cotton gin, the farm, and the lending business, financing people to make their crops. He started law school, at the University of Memphis, the day my brother, David, was born, in 1947. He went to school at night, for ten years, and passed the bar in 1958."

He called himself a "Jeffersonian Democrat," even kept collections of Thomas Jefferson quotes on his desk, and his politics was fiercely local. One of the Jefferson quotes that Wilder saved at his desk and shared with visitors: "The democracy will cease to exist when you take away from those who are willing to work and give to those who would not." He reared his sons to appreciate an honest day's work.

"Our dad was how you saw him," Shelton Wilder remembered. "He was what he was—not a lot of pretense about him. He expected his children to work hard, and he required it. When I was ten years old, they put me in the field to chop hay in the pasture. Dad always felt everybody had to contribute and do what they could. He taught my brother and me that we were expected to work. He was a good father."

OVER HIS LONG POLITICAL CAREER, Wilder won and held office in his home district without any apparent alignment with the major statewide machines of his day. His family and closest political allies confirm that he had no connections to, or benefits from, the vestiges of the old Crump-McKellar machine and its Clement-Ellington heirs, nor of the Kefauver-Browning progressives. He remained independent of all these and charted his own course.

In Nashville, Wilder survived in his leadership office by keeping a generally low profile, by maintaining a conservative voting record on issues, and when leadership votes came up every other January, by cutting deals with his core of senate allies.

The Wilder allies in the thirty-three-member state senate were a hybrid coalition of Democrats and Republican members. By assembling at least seventeen of these every two years—employing a rewards system using his power to appoint the chairs of all standing committees—Wilder was able to hang on to his speakership longer than any other state legislator in America.

Paul G. Summers was a native of Wilder's Fayette County and a lawyer in Somerville. At one time, his law office was across the courthouse square from Wilder's office, and he knew the Wilder family well. He told me his father, Paul Reeves Summers, a judge on the state appellate court, was probably Wilder's closest friend and confidant during their lifetimes. The son was Wilder's campaign manager in 1980 and 1984. (He became an appeals court judge himself, later district attorney, and would serve as the state's attorney general from 1999 to 2006.)

Summers the son said Wilder carefully kept a running tally of which senators were loyal to him and his leadership. Frequently, he would phone them and sometimes travel to visit with them in their home districts to isolate and resolve any problems, to smooth over any rough patches, and to cement loyalties.

"Every morning when he got up and drank his first cup of coffee, and breathed his first breath, every day when he was driving down the road, every moment when he was flying *Jaybird*, every day he was pounding that gavel, he always thought about seventeen," Summers said. "He had seventeen votes on his mind 24/7 for forty years.

"We'd be driving down the road, and he'd look over at me and say, 'Paul, I think I got twenty-one right now.' I don't care what they say about Curtis Person [a veteran Republican state senator from Memphis]. I'm gonna appoint Curtis Person chairman of the Judiciary Committee; he's gonna vote for me.' He talked about it all the time."

David Wilder, Shelton's brother, remembers that his father made leadership appointments in proportion to the two parties' representation in the senate.

"He never made a deal with Republicans or Democrats to be speaker," David explained. "He worked with *individuals* to get their support. When some of the Democrats, who decided to throw my daddy out, told him he should not share any leadership positions with the opposing party, my daddy said he would not do that. He said they would get a third, in line with their proportion in the senate. That was his legacy—just one man's way of doing things."

In any event, one important perk of hanging on to his speakership, year after year, was that it afforded Wilder a virtually permanent seat for himself on the powerful state Building Commission. This influential body, which includes the governor and both speakers and others, sits in judgment on all significant government construction proposals ranging from armories to highway projects to state college dormitories.

Wilder was also commonly addressed as Governor Wilder because historically in Tennessee, the senate speaker is accorded the unofficial but revered title of Lieutenant Governor. This title does not appear in the state's constitution. It is traditionally conferred on the senate speaker because he is first in the line of succession, should anything ever happen to incapacitate the sitting governor.

"**He was very complex,**" former senator Tom Garland, of Greeneville, told me. "I don't know if anyone truly knew John Wilder. Marcelle, his wife, was the closest—both of them very spiritual. He read the Bible and prayed with her every morning, at the breakfast table; they kept an apartment in Nashville, down the hill from the capitol.

"John always said, 'Let the senate be the senate'—the way he looked at it was, there were thirty-three senators, and his job was to preside, not control. John didn't tell anyone how to vote, but he 'courted' some of them how to vote. He didn't push it. If it was an issue he really wanted, he might come to committee meetings, and it was impressive to see him walk through that door. You knew it was something important. You knew he was there for a purpose, not just to listen to debate—he was coming in there to influence. If it was something he was strongly in favor of or opposed to, he might actually cast a vote but that was very unusual.

"Most of the time, he let it flow. The house was different; McWherter and his group ran it all. Wilder, on the other hand, saw himself as more the presiding officer."

The reporters in the capitol hill press corps were often amused by Wilder—his taciturn manner and courtly nature, his odd sense of humor, and his fondness for speaking at length about the alignment of nature and humankind. In speeches and interviews, he would frequently comment that this or that proposal was "not in tune with the Cosmos."

"When John would talk about the 'Cosmos' everybody would laugh," Garland recalled, "but there was a side of him that was seeking a better understanding of things—the bigger picture. I'm not sure anyone really knew John."

Senator Douglas Henry, the veteran chairman of the Senate Finance Committee, may have known Wilder the longest and best. But even he acknowledged that his friend of many years "could be very cryptic at times."

"It wasn't too easy understanding what John was saying sometimes," Henry recalled. "Some said he was nuts, but he wasn't. He was very smart. Yes, he would say, 'Let the senate be the senate,' and I believe he simply felt that the institution of the senate was more important than any one member. That's what he believed. That's what he stood for. He was a Methodist; he believed in the higher order of things, which he called the Cosmos, some superior scheme of things outside ourselves."

Wilder was an avid pilot, a bicyclist, and a hiker.

"Wilder was an athletic nut," his longtime associate Leonard Bradley told me. "He rode a bike ten miles a day, rain or shine."

"I went on a hiking trip once with Senator Ben Atchley and Senator Garland," Bradley remembered. "Next week, Wilder called me and said, 'Leonard, I heard you took Senator Garland and Senator Atchley backpacking. You always told me you would take *me* backpacking.' I called his secretary, and next weekend we went."

Their destination was in the mountains of western North Carolina, just beyond the Tennessee line. Wilder offered to fly his own plane, *Jaybird*, to Nashville, pick up Bradley, and land again at Cherokee Aviation at Knoxville's McGhee-Tyson Airport. They would go by car over the state line. Wilder had his own idea about ground transportation, too.

> WILDER: I'll get a state trooper to take us.
> BRADLEY: But, Governor, we're going to North Carolina.
> WILDER: It's OK. He knows the way.
> BRADLEY: He may have to wait several hours for us.
> WILDER: He's used to waiting several hours, anyway.

They met at state hangar, where Wilder kept his plane while in Nashville, and off they went, Wilder at the controls. At one point en route to Knoxville, Bradley remembers Wilder asking him to take the controls:

> WILDER: Here, you fly *Jaybird* for a while. I want to take a nap.
> BRADLEY: I don't know how to fly.
> WILDER: You just look at this needle . . .

"I flew the thing for fifteen minutes," Bradley told me. "It was on automatic pilot. He landed us at Cherokee Aviation, and, sure enough, the trooper was waiting there and drove us over into North Carolina. We came back on Sunday. Not a word was said, by either of us, about politics and government. We talked a lot about the Cosmos, of course."

REPRESENTATIVE JIMMY NAIFEH, a Democrat from Covington, Tennessee, was another frequent passenger on *Jaybird* when Wilder was the pilot on flights between Fayette County and Nashville. Speaking at Wilder's memorial service in January 2010, Naifeh told of a flight "one night in a raging monsoon," according to Jackson Baker's report in the *Memphis Flyer*.

"Fearing that Wilder intended to land the plane in the grassy field near his Fayette County homestead in Longtown, a nervous Naifeh hopefully suggested that they continue on just a tad further to a bona fide structured airfield at Arlington. Wilder, as Naifeh noted, would on some occasions do just that. But not this time. As Naifeh recounted, pilot Wilder said, in the playfully broken English that he often spoke, "Uh uh, Jimmy, *Jaybird* want to go home!" And so they splashed down in what amounted to a marsh, throwing hunks of grass and torrents of water everywhere. But getting there, after all, in one piece."

BRADLEY RECALLED LONG CONVERSATIONS about business, agriculture, and soil conservation.

"We talked about chemistry. He had a degree in chemistry from UT, which he turned into a fertilizer business, and agriculture. In his factory, he would analyze soil that farmers would bring to him. There was some sort of analyzer he had that was tied to a fertilizer manufacturer in Chicago. Somehow this machine would analyze the chemical composition of the soil the farmer brought, and then the analysis would come back, and he would make fertilizer that was tailored to the farmer's soil and whatever he was trying to grow."

Wilder served as director of the Soil Conservation District, and eventually he became chairman of the National Association of Conservation Districts.

HE COULD KEEP PEOPLE GUESSING and often left news reporters scratching their heads. M. Lee Smith was publisher of the *Tennessee Journal*, a closely read weekly political newsletter in the capital city. He was one who called Wilder an "enigma."

"He was just an unusual person, to the say the least," Smith said. "He had strange reactions to things. He was always pleasant, always a gentlemen, but he was unpredictable about a lot of things."

Travis, the television news reporter, also recalled a scene when Wilder walked out of the senate chamber—stung by a remark that he took as an affront and a challenge to his character.

"It was a debate about abortion," Travis remembered, "and two senators were debating across the chamber, when one of them challenged Wilder on some point of procedure. Wilder was hurt by the remark, really cut to the quick. I remember him leaving the chamber, with an odd expression on his face. I bolted out of the TV press box at the side of the chamber and followed him to his office, and shut the door. He was literally in tears. He just talked his way through it with me."

Nelson Biddle worked for both Blanton and Wilder. In the governor's office, he had been the policy and legislative coordinator—meaning he was the administration's lobbyist—until the summer of 1976, when he managed Wilder's senate reelection campaign. When the campaign ended, Wilder hired Biddle to be his top assistant. This positioned Biddle as the closest observer of the lieutenant governor and his way of managing the upper chamber.

"The nature of Wilder was that he was a stickler for the rules," Biddle told me. "You could not get him to deviate, as speaker of the senate. Over the years he wanted to deliberate on everything. That's the way he ran the senate, as a deliberative body."

THROUGHOUT HIS LONG POLITICAL LIFE, Wilder largely kept his own counsel and steered by his own independent lights. Of all his associates in business, politics, and government, his most trusted friends were probably Lewis Donelson, the Memphis lawyer and tax policy guru, and Paul R. Summers, who knew Wilder over many years of working together in Fayette County.

"He was a very thoughtful person," Donelson said of Wilder. "He thought things through. He was very smart. He knew that senate like the back of his hand—knew what he could do and not do."

The Summers family hailed from a tiny community called Yum Yum, a few miles from the Wilders in Longtown. Summers earned his law degree from Cumberland University in Lebanon, Tennessee, and also owned a Gulf Oil distributorship, which did business with Wilder's Longtown Gin and Supply Company. He became a general sessions judge in 1960, a chancery court judge in 1972. Three years later, he was named executive secretary to the Tennessee Supreme Court. In 1977, Governor Blanton appointed him to the Tennessee court of appeals, from which he retired in 1982.

The Wilder sons knew the Summers family well. Paul R. was called Big Paul by the Wilder children, Shelton Wilder told me. They called the son Paul Garvin.

Over many years, Judge Summers, according to his son, would sit for long hours with John Wilder whenever they were both back home in Fayette County, and they would talk over business, the economy, and politics.

IN THE DAYS FOLLOWING THE 1979 COUP, he said, it is likely that Big Paul was one of the very few people that Wilder took into his confidence about his decision and his feelings about the event. What was said is lost to history.

Three years later, Alexander, recognizing the special family relationship, obliged when Wilder asked him to consider appointing Paul Garvin Summers to be the new district attorney for the West Tennessee District that included Fayette County.

After the elder Summers' death, Wilder sponsored a senate resolution in the 2004 legislative session honoring the memory of his old friend.

CHAPTER 14

The Dance

Why can't somebody make up his mind?
　　—Honey Alexander, January 17, 1979

ONLY A DOZEN PEOPLE were now aware of the secret deliberations going on across Nashville—over landlines and in private rooms downtown and in suburban Green Hills—hurried conversations that, at first, were awkward and halting.

Except for McWherter and Wilder, who had worked together in the legislative halls for years, all the principals in this emerging coup were simply unaccustomed to working together, nor to speaking to each other at all, let alone collaborating in private about Governor Blanton and what seemed to be the rising velocity of madness.

In reality, it was more of a dance, with the principals taking the measure of each other through the quickening afternoon. This dance played out over four long hours, the pressure ever building, and with no one eager to take the visible lead. Even so, this tiny handful of senior leaders were now discussing the shape of a solution.

In their second phone conversation, Alexander's immediate response to Hardin had been that before proceeding further in any way, the US attorney should consult the two top leaders of the state legislature, Speaker McWherter and Lieutenant Governor Wilder, and also Bill Leech, the state attorney general.

"Lamar told me to call Tom Ingram, his deputy, and to coordinate the matter with him," Hardin said. "He told me Tom would be standing by at the Hobbs Road office. I reached Tom, and we talked about who should be brought into the conversation."

This set in motion a series of calls and conversations that would dominate the afternoon. For Hardin, sitting at his desk at the federal building, this was an anxious round of calls to make.

POLITICALLY, TENNESSEE'S STATE GOVERNMENT, in its executive and legislative branches, was still in the firm control of the Democratic Party and its duly elected officials, and at the legislature, the power centered in the offices of McWherter and Wilder. In Tennessee, the thirty-three members of the state senate and the ninety-nine members of the house of representatives elect their two presiding officers, called the speaker in both chambers. In the senate, the title of Lieutenant Governor is also bestowed on the senate speaker, and under the state's constitution, this person is first in the line of succession if the sitting governor is removed, resigns, or dies. The house speaker is the second in line.

Wilder and McWherter also shared rural West Tennessee roots with Governor Blanton. They had served with him in the legislature in the early years and had supported him in his past campaigns. No one, other than Blanton himself, ranked higher in the Democratic Party in Tennessee. (The junior US senator, Jim Sasser, the former state Democratic Party chairman, was at this time only midway through his first term in Washington.)

McWherter in particular had accumulated power and become the very center of influence in the Democratic-majority legislature. His informal authority derived, in particular, from his influence over fundraising for local Democratic legislative races across the state, eclipsing and eventually usurping that function which had traditionally been performed by the state party's official apparatus. McWherter had now consolidated this fundraising in his own office. His desk and the office chairs surrounding it had become the undisputed main venue for countless legislative strategy sessions. And all of this, in turn, had given rise to a growing aura of legislative independence relative to the Democratic governor.

HARDIN NOW DIALED SENATE SPEAKER John Wilder, and his next call would be to McWherter. By this time, apparently, both speakers had returned with Leech to their offices from the World's Fair briefing at the Hyatt.

Hardin remembers speaking with Wilder only briefly at first, giving him essentially the same information that he had shared with Alexander, and they discussed Alexander's insistence that both speakers be promptly briefed and become involved in planning what should be done in view of the alarming new information. Hardin said he recalls that Wilder was quiet and noncommittal in this initial conversation. He told the US attorney that McWherter had been in the Building Commission meeting earlier and that he would "send somebody after him or try to set up a conference telephone call." Wilder then asked his longtime assistant, Maxine Roberts, to locate McWherter.

"Wilder kept saying that he would support Lamar and said he would help him in any way that he could," Hardin remembered. "He advised me that he could not get the legislature back in session. He talked quite a bit about the political aspect of the move, and he said that he could not urge Lamar to do it, he felt, but that if Lamar did do it that he would back him at that point. He also stated that he thought it would be politically expedient for Ned to go along, in his opinion, and that the political repercussions would be favorable and not unfavorable."

AFTER WHAT HARDIN REMEMBERS as "long pauses on the phone," he finally heard McWherter's voice. Hardin now repeated his facts to both men.

"I explained to them the situation we were in, and what Lamar had said, and at this point they both insisted that they could *not* urge him to do it, but if in fact he did do it, they would stand behind him. Wilder said that he did not think that Leech should be involved in it, because Leech might have a 'conflict of interest' because he would have to represent the administration, whether it was the Blanton administration or the Alexander administration, and that might cause a conflict. I explained to him that, in my opinion, I did not think that was correct."

McWherter spoke up. He said he and Wilder would support the early swearing-in, but could not proactively recommend it.

"We will concur in the action," he said. "We will not advocate it." Wilder then made a comment, which Hardin paraphrased from memory, that "their intent was not to water down the impact of the oath taking early, but that this had to be their decision."

This two-part stance would remain the two speakers' position for most of the next three hours. It would not be acceptable to Alexander.

IN THE BEGINNING, TENNESSEE was merely the westernmost county of North Carolina, where Jackson was born. The state government of Carolina did not cede this western portion to the new federal government until 1789. At that point, this new jurisdiction between the Appalachian Mountains and the Mississippi River was officially called "the Territory of the United States, South of the River Ohio," for this was how it appeared on the early hand-drawn maps of the young country. Seven years later, Congress approved the new constitution that the territorial governor, John Sevier, had delivered on horseback to the nation's capital, and Tennessee thus became the sixteenth state of the Union.

As in many other states in the new country, Tennessee's name derived from an ancient Native American word. Early European explorers in Appalachia had visited a Cherokee village, in the foothills of this region, called *Tanasi* or *Tenase*, variant spellings of the same indigenous spoken name for the river now called the Little Tennessee. In even deeper human time, the Cherokee word *Tanasqui* meant "the place where the river bends." On maps of this region, the river meanders from north to sound and over eons has carved a distinct horseshoe route at the point of the ancient settlement.

Over these hills and through this extended river valley the Cherokee had routed the Creek in early times. In the middle 1700s, colonial commander John Sevier had in turn fought and routed the Cherokee. Their larger portion vanished in the 1830s, displaced by authority of President Andrew Jackson's Indian Removal Act of 1830. This act, enforced throughout the South, was the genesis of the Trail of Tears. Its staging grounds, called concentration camps, were situated in the Appalachian foothills. The exodus, in great sadness, lead across the length of Tennessee to Oklahoma where the Eastern Band of the Cherokee nation remains headquartered today.

The first state capital was established at Jonesborough, in the remote eastern mountains, and in 1818, the young state's western boundary was fixed far away west at the Mississippi River. (In 1826, after two more interim sites, the capital was moved permanently to Nashville.) Tennessee's laws were mostly copied from North Carolina's, but the topography of this newest state appears in reverse. Tennessee's terrain actually mirrors that of North Carolina, both beginning at a border in high country, descending both west and east through piedmont to plantation flatland, and on to the far water boundary.

The two states together, from the Mississippi to the Atlantic Ocean, span a distance of 939 miles—the distance from New Orleans to Detroit. Johnson City, in eastern Tennessee, is closer to Toronto than to Memphis.

The earliest constitution of this expansive new state was adopted in 1796. According to historian J. G. M. Ramsey, President Thomas Jefferson remarked that he thought Tennessee's constitution was the "least imperfect and most republican of the state constitutions." It granted the right to vote to all freemen, white and black, who were twenty-one or older.

Over all this time, across two ensuing centuries, while Tennessee's state constitution has been amended many times since its adoption, its instructions about swearing in a new governor have never changed. Yet this became the heart of the issue that was hastily, but deeply, debated by the powers that be through the afternoon of January 17.

By this afternoon, on the suddenly urgent question of how soon a newly elected governor could be sworn into office, there were already two opposing interpretations—both originating, to Bill Leech's consternation, in his own office.

THE LEGISLATURE HEARS FROM the attorney general most often in the form of written opinion letters, answering questions of constitutionality or legal interpretation that members have posed, usually for the purpose of moving a proposed piece of legislation forward in the general assembly. In practice, such an opinion would have the force of law, unless its finding were later overturned or modified by a court.

During the 1970s, the most active practitioner of the "opinion letter" maneuver was state senator Victor Ashe II, a pugnacious Republican from the party's stronghold in Knoxville. Ashe was quick to pick a political fight and visibly pleased when he succeeded in doing so, and he frequently asked the attorney general for multiple "opinions" on a broad diversity of policy or procedural topics. Ashe was bright, analytical, and trained in the law. He was a graduate of Yale (where George W. Bush, the future president, was his roommate and a fellow member of the secretive Skull and Bones society) and the University of Tennessee law school. He had been a young intern for Congressman Bill Brock of Chattanooga and later for Senator Howard Baker.

At twenty-three, Ashe was elected to the state house of representatives. He served there for six years, then announced he was running for a state senate seat held by an entrenched incumbent. But he was not yet thirty years old, the minimum age specified in the Tennessee constitution, and the state's supreme court declared he could not be on the ballot. Ashe thereupon persuaded his mother, Martha Ashe, to run. She won, served briefly, then promptly resigned when her son turned thirty; he was quickly appointed to the vacancy by the Knox County legislative body.

As the youngest state senator, Ashe enjoyed policy debates and was also fond of his partisan role of self-anointed gadfly in the heavily Democratic legislature. Ned McWherter was fond of Ashe, in spite of their partisan differences. According to Wiseman, the speaker once said of the young Knoxville Republican: "Victor is like a mosquito flying around your head—he won't hurt you, but he sure is worrisome."

Ashe would also routinely request opinions from the attorney general's office. Depending on the timing of a given legislature maneuver or his mood, the young senator would announce the opinion he had received, often with an accompanying press release for the capitol hill reporters—always designed to buttress his position on the issue at hand.

The letter he sent in December 1978, following the arrests of Blanton's men, posed a simple-seeming question about the timing of a governor's swearing-in. "Can the Governor-elect be administered the oath of office prior to his inauguration?" The letter did not seem remarkable at the time because it was one more request in a long line of so many. Ashe has even described himself as a "prolific opinion seeker." If it had come from any other member of the legislature, such a question might have set off fireworks. Not this time. Rather, not just yet.

Ashe told me the request was his own idea, and further that he did not collaborate with any others on its content or timing. "I did not discuss the request with Lamar, anyone on his staff, or anyone in the legislature," Ashe told me. Both Alexander and Ingram confirm this.

ONCE ASHE'S REQUEST LETTER arrived at the attorney general's office, it was assigned to a young assistant attorney general named William W. (Tripp) Hunt III, twenty-eight, a graduate of the University of Virginia law school. He had been on the job just two years when Senator Ashe's letter came to his desk.

"When I first went to the office, I started doing criminal appeals, which everybody did first if you went there directly out of law school," he told me. "After that, we moved into the civil division and specialized. One of my specialties was campaign finance, political questions, government ethics, lobbying, that general area. That's how I got involved in this.

"Senator Ashe knew the system. An opinion request from him was not unusual," Hunt told me. He also remembers that his research on this particular request did not require much time.

The constitution clearly specifies how a governor can be removed from office—through impeachment, which can be initiated only by the state legislature—but this was not Ashe's question. Instead, the young senator was asking if there were a difference in meaning between the terms "oath taking" and "inauguration." Could they occur on different dates? Can the oath be administered before inauguration day? If yes, how much earlier?

Hunt quickly found Article VII, Section 5, which provides that the term of office of the governor "shall be computed from the fifteenth of January next after the election of the Governor." In his letter back to Ashe, dated January 3, Hunt responded in the affirmative: Yes, a new governor can be sworn into office at any time after midnight January 15.

Quoting from *Black's Law Dictionary*, Hunt explained that "inauguration" is defined as "the act of installing or inducting into office with formal ceremonies," and he concluded: "Therefore, an inauguration is simply a ceremonial celebration of the induction into office, and does not necessarily involve an oath." In other words, the actual oath may be administered at any point after January 15, and the "inauguration" is the legislatively scheduled ceremony that solemnizes and celebrates the act. Hunt, finally, also offered that the governor-elect need complete "only three constitutional steps" to take office: January 15 must pass. The election must be certified as final. He must take an oath of office.

The matter of the January 20 "inauguration" thus became a secondary issue for the negotiators on Wednesday. Article II, Section 8 of the state constitution states that a new governor's inauguration should occur during a joint session of the legislature. But the traditional January 20 date for inauguration had been set for Saturday by the new legislature in its recent organizing session, currently in recess; on that Saturday, both houses of the new general assembly would reconvene. This fact, together with the belief that "oath taking" was not the same as "inauguration" and could therefore occur any time after midnight January 15, meant the section did not pose any obstacle to an early swearing-in. Therefore, the Article II, Section 8 question did not play further into the dance on this Wednesday afternoon. (The question would be cited later, however, by at least one of the attorneys representing prisoners whose releases by Blanton were blocked by Alexander's team. This view was rejected by the local courts hearing those cases.)

The reply letter to Ashe appeared over Tripp Hunt's typed name, not Leech's, and it bore no one's signature.

Leech's journey on this question consumed the better part of two days. The first discussion, internal to his office, was on Tuesday, when Leech was still in Washington, DC. He had phoned Hayes Cooney, his chief deputy, for a routine update on office activities, and Cooney alerted him to the new public controversy over the January 3 opinion letter. Leech instructed Cooney to summon Hunt to his office, and within minutes, a three-person conversation ensued over the speakerphone on Cooney's desk.

"Leech was upset with me because of that opinion," Hunt told me. "He never really forgave me because he didn't like being forced into the position he was, though he eventually came to grant that I was correct in that opinion. It was reviewed by the chief deputy and also by Leech. They found nothing wrong with it, and it was issued. A lot of the opinions weren't signed by General Leech at that time. It was not uncommon. Later, they were all signed by the attorney general. Perhaps this is what lead to that."

Leech wanted a second letter issued immediately, superseding the first reply to Ashe. Hunt says he was asked to prepare this second letter. He refused, so Cooney wrote it.

"He [Leech] wasn't too happy," Hunt said. "He wanted me to draft a second opinion, stating you had to do it on the twentieth. I said I could not do it, because that was not the law. So, next thing I knew, they drafted that [second] opinion. I don't remember if they asked me to sign it or not. I wouldn't have signed it."

The new opinion letter appeared over two signatures, Leech's and Cooney's. This new letter stated that a court might hold that the governor's oath taking and the inauguration were meant to be the same thing, that the founders intended them to occur at the same time.

"Joe Henry even called Leech later and said my first opinion was the correct one," Hunt told me. "When you look at the law, they just don't have a date specific for a new governor to take the oath. Nobody had ever thought about it before, but certainly nobody thought a governor would be up all night selling pardons, either. Leech was a Democrat, and he certainly didn't enjoy doing this to another Democrat. In the end, he did it, and that speaks well of him that he ultimately stood by my opinion."

In any case, the new opinion letter placed a cloud over what Hunt had felt was his clear reading of the state's constitution, and made the official view of the attorney general's office rather less conclusive. But this new measure of ambiguity was only temporary. By the following afternoon, this nuance that Leech and Cooney had quickly injected would be dismissed.

ALEXANDER MEANWHILE INSISTED on Tuesday that hurrying up the inauguration—whatever the reason—was "inappropriate."

"In the most fundamental way, in American government, that's not how we change power," he said. "That might be how you change power in a Latin American junta—but I don't just want to pick on Latin American—in many other countries in the world. In my mind, what's special about America is that we have these big fights about elections, and then the power passes peacefully, to the winner . . . and we hand it over. That was in my mind. That fundamentally is the reason I didn't want to do it.

"George Washington said: 'What is most important of this grand experiment, the United States? Not the election of the first president, but the election of its *second* president. The peaceful transition of power is what will separate this country from every other country in the world.'

"Second, there were all sorts of practical problems with how does one go about this? And, third, I knew enough to know the inaugural ceremony is a legislative ceremony. So what I was saying on Monday and Tuesday was that unless the legislature decides that it wants to do this, it would be inappropriate for me to assume the office.

"I figured that would take care of it because I thought there wasn't any way in the world a Democratic legislature was going to swear in a Republican governor three days early to oust a Democratic governor."

For Alexander, in addition to his chief concerns of law, tradition, and appearances, the day's developments also manifested a loss of control.

His 1978 campaign had been a model of careful planning, research, coordination, tone, and timing. The most dramatic and public example of that prior calm and precision was his thousand-mile-plus "walk across the state" that had been three months in the making. Less visible were the internal plans and procedures for fundraising, developing the daily message from the campaign trail, growing the effectiveness of the political operation, careful scheduling, and dealing with news media.

Now, there were external currents bringing new circumstances and other politicians into play, and all this was accelerating as the day wore on. New facts and other personalities seemed to be overtaking, if not overwhelming, the planning of the new administration. Shared decision making in a divided government would come soon enough, he knew—with a new Republican governor but both houses of the legislature still firmly in Democratic control—but must it begin this early? And all this new complexity was, to say the least, threatening to disrupt the festive reunions and parties and pomp of a hard-won inauguration weekend. A layer of gloom thus settled over everything, matching the look and feel of the depressive winter weather outside.

As the day advanced, Hardin had a growing sense that time was running frightfully short for effective action.

FOR MCWHERTER OR WILDER, the possibility of an early swearing-in was not a new subject. McWherter had already phoned Hardin and had mentioned—"really only implied," according to Hardin—that he would be available to assist with any corrective action toward Blanton and to stop the stream of prisoner releases. "I just want you to know I'm here if you need me," he told the US attorney.

"He spoke very slowly—it was brief but very powerful," Hardin recalled. "I hung up the phone and just looked at it, thinking 'Wow!'"

On the previous Friday, January 12, McWherter had even mentioned the idea of an early swearing-in to a *Tennessean* reporter, and his comments were published on Saturday. This prompted phone calls from Alexander, on Monday morning, to Wilder and McWherter, when he stated, "It is totally inappropriate for me to assume power wholly on my own initiative."

The three men did not know, at this point, what Monday evening would bring. It was, in Alexander's words, "a real bombshell." When news media reported on Tuesday morning that Blanton had pardoned Humphreys and released fifty-one other convicted felons, the stakes got dramatically higher for the political leaders.

"That was a dramatic, huge event," Alexander remembered, "and it just turned the state upside down. By Tuesday morning, we were suddenly in the middle of a real changed situation."

SEIGENTHALER REMEMBERS RECEIVING a guarded call on Tuesday from Jim Kennedy, McWherter's top staff assistant, seeming to feel out the editor, prospectively, on what the newspaper's reaction might be to an accelerated change of governors.

Kennedy had succeeded Jim Free as McWherter's top staffer and closest adviser. Born in Schenectady, New York, Kennedy had moved to Tennessee as a child when his father was transferred by the railroad. During college at the University of Tennessee, he worked at the *Knoxville News-Sentinel*. After graduation, he moved to Nashville for a job as press officer for the Tennessee Democratic Party, where he met McWherter.

"John, the speaker wanted me to check in with you about what's going on," Seigenthaler remembers Kennedy saying. "There's some talk about possibly swearing Alexander in early, and Ned just wondered what you might think of that."

"I told him I didn't have any particular feeling about it, one way or the other, but it would be extraordinary and a news event and we would certainly cover it. I thought, at the time, that Ned had Kennedy call me trying to feel me out about whether the *Tennessean* would take their heads off the next morning for doing such a thing."

Seigenthaler said he made no commitment to Kennedy on Tuesday, but the two agreed to stay in touch as the week progressed.

IN A RETROSPECTIVE FORUM at Vanderbilt in April 2012, which was moderated by Seigenthaler, Alexander described his predicament on January 17, 1979, as "being in a high-class pickle." He said he was not reluctant to take the oath early but, rather, resigned to the fact that it was necessary in order to prevent a larger wrong.

"I had to think about how this is a total anathema to our system of government. It's a coup. It's like a banana republic would do. In the peaceful transfer of power—I had watched it in Washington, I had seen Johnson and Nixon and Kennedy and Eisenhower—we had seen those huge contests and then just a peaceful transfer of power. And now we were going to interrupt that, and I knew this was not the way things were supposed to be and that we should do everything we could do to avoid that, but we were not going to be able to.

"I thought that if I knew that, then surely most every other Tennessean knew that, too, and they would not like the idea of a coup. Even if they liked me and did not like Blanton, they wouldn't like the idea of a coup. So, I spent the rest of that afternoon trying to get myself out of that pickle—negotiating, dealing with many different things, any of which might have stopped the process, but knowing all along that it was most certainly going to happen. And all of my efforts were to make sure that it happened as well as it possibly could."

NOBODY WANTED TO DO THIS.

Hardin remembers that Wilder, a lawyer himself, was particularly reluctant throughout the afternoon on Wednesday. Initially, the lieutenant governor even cautioned against involving Leech, worrying that the attorney general, in his capacity as the state government's top lawyer, might eventually have to defend whatever actions were taken. In that event, Wilder argued, Leech would be compromised, conflicted and would effectively be unavailable to represent the administration.

Hardin replied that it would be the attorney general's duty to represent whichever governor and administration might be holding office at the time a complaint were brought forward, and that in this instance, Leech would be called on to represent Alexander, not Blanton, when that day came.

Wilder later also objected to the involvement of Joe Henry, the chief justice, saying he would be conflicted if a legal challenge were filed. Henry, Wilder argued, would have to recuse himself in that case. By this time, of course, Leech himself was in the conversation, and he reminded Wilder that "judges recuse themselves all the time."

Wilder then said he felt it would be inappropriate for Chief Justice Henry to administer the oath—that if the action were appealed, Henry would be "in a position of embarrassment."

"I explained to him that I'm sure Joe Henry would recuse himself, and that would not present any problems, that judges normally recused themselves," Hardin recalled. "I felt that by Joe Henry administering the oath, that Joe Henry would be putting a stamp of approval on the act, meaning the legality of the act."

Alexander insisted that Henry, as chief justice, should participate in the ceremony in order to duplicate as much as possible the traditional legislative oath-taking ceremony. Hardin phoned Henry, and so did Donelson.

"I exchanged pleasantries with him," Hardin said, "and then told him that I wanted to meet him at 3:15 in the afternoon. I did not say where, but he assumed it would be in his office. My idea was that after the meeting at 2:45 if we had reached a decision by 3:10 or 3:15, I would call Henry and have him come to Hobbs Road." (This 2:45 meeting never occurred. By this time, McWherter and Wilder had determined they should not participate in such a private meeting at a remote location.)

Alexander asked Donelson to talk to the chief justice as soon as possible, believing that Henry's participation by administering the oath, would be essential to the success of the coup.

"That was very important to me. The most important point in the ceremony is when the chief justice says, 'Raise your right hand and repeat after me . . .' That few minutes of repeating the oath with your hand raised, with your hand on the Bible and the chief justice in his robes, that symbolizes the peaceful transition of power that Americans expect. If he weren't there, it seemed to me it would be very hard to persuade the people of Tennessee that we had done something that was appropriate. So I pushed pretty hard for him to do it, though I knew he was sick. I greatly appreciated him doing it."

HARDIN PLACED HIS PHONE in its cradle, then buzzed Joe Brown, his deputy.

"I told Joe Brown to get all the information that he had on Eddie Denton and give it to me, and also to have the FBI check back on the latest information," Hardin recalled. (In one tape-recorded interview, a plan to release triple-murderer Denton had been described as "hotter than the Humphreys case—it would make Humphreys look like Peter Pan.") "I told Joe also to be careful that I did not have any grand jury information, because I didn't want an unintentional disclosure of such information to Lamar."

By this time, Leech was returning Hardin's call, responding to the earlier phone message. Together, he and Hardin now established a second conference call with McWherter and Wilder, and the four men again reviewed the investigative information. Wilder suggested that Leech and Hardin should now meet and discuss next steps, and that he and McWherter would return to the Building Commission meeting "as if nothing had happened."

LEECH AND HARDIN DISCUSSED where best to meet.

They agreed they should avoid appearing in either of their offices, as reporters were likely to confront them there. Hardin suggested meeting at his own home because it was in town—Leech's residence being fifty miles away in rural Maury County—but Leech then remembered that he had taken a room at the Sheraton Hotel on Broadway in order to be near Donna at Baptist Hospital. He had stayed there for part of the night before, in fact, between visits to the hospital. They agreed to meet at the Sheraton, located diagonally across the street from the federal building.

At this point, Leech informed Hardin that McWherter and Wilder had decided they should not meet Alexander at his private Green Hills area office "because of the Tennessee Sunshine Law," the open meetings statute that McWherter had championed early in his legislative career.

"We had discussed that previously, and I had told Wilder that this is just another reason why I was not fond of that law," Hardin told me. "We concluded that there would be no violation of the Sunshine Law if Leech and I meet, because he is specifically exempt by statute. Wilder and McWherter were also concerned about their relationship with the capitol press corps. Apparently they had a very good working relationship [with the statehouse reporters] and did not want to do anything that would jeopardize that.

"They were very concerned about the secrecies of the matter. We also discussed the situation—that if we give too much advance notice, that Governor Blanton could possibly go ahead and sign the commutations and the pardons—and all of this would be an effort in futility.

"We also discussed among ourselves the way it could be carried out, that we could give the press advanced notice fifteen minutes before the act, and move swiftly and do it."

Before Hardin left his office for the Sheraton across the street, Joe Brown handed him a copy of the list of thirteen.

"This was the list that Trooper Fred Taylor had told us, on videotape, that they intended to commute or pardon and that there had been payoffs made," Hardin said. "This same list apparently was found when FBI agents on December 15 went to Eddie Sisk's office. I put this information into a folder, and I walked out my backdoor and around by Judge Morton's courtroom, and took the stairs to the sixth floor to avoid any reporters.

"I noticed, as I was walking down the stairs, my legs were a little shaky," Hardin said, "because I knew full well at that time exactly what was going to happen, and I realized that I could easily be making one of the most important decisions that I had ever made—and I could easily wind up being the scapegoat. I went in the tunnel underneath the federal courthouse [where my car was parked], opened the door [to] the tunnel partially, and looked around to make sure no one was there, and I walked hurriedly to my car. I took three or four evasive turns to make sure the media was not following me, pulled into the basement of the Sheraton."

THEY MET IN ROOM 416. Two other lawyers would soon join them.

"Leech and I discussed it and came to a mutual conclusion that there was no other way but have Lamar sworn in that day," Hardin said. "Leech advised me that he had the authority to speak for Wilder and McWherter. We then called Lamar and advised him."

Part of the "dance" throughout the afternoon was an unsettledness on the question of which partner would take the lead.

Alexander insisted throughout the afternoon that McWherter and Wilder announce jointly with him that they believed the early oath taking was proper, and also that they appear with him at the swearing-in. He told me later he was convinced by Hardin, together with Leech's earlier comments on Blanton's power to pardon, that the early swearing-in was the right thing to do, but that it was important for the bipartisan leaders to be seen as having come to the same decision jointly—a detail that McWherter and especially Wilder were resisting.

"I knew from the moment I put the phone down the second time that I would be sworn in as governor before the day was over," he told me. "My decision was not whether to be sworn in early, but how to do it with minimum damage. It was immediately clear that I would have to do it, because of the risk that Governor Blanton might release more dangerous offenders, including perhaps James Earl Ray. And it was well known that as the day wore on, Blanton would often drink and do irrational things. And I could not ignore such an extraordinary call from a respected United States attorney."

Alexander, who was envisioning a joint statement that described a joint decision, described this exchange with Leech early in the afternoon:

Leech: They said they would be glad to back you up.

Alexander: Under no circumstances! We will have to do it together.

"I may have even asked them to *invite* me to do it, but they didn't want to do that, and I don't blame them for that," he told me. "I mean, this was an extraordinary enough act, and Wilder was very reluctant. He was Blanton's state senator—I mean, they are all over there from the same neck of the woods."

Alexander was adamant. "I could hear Lamar's voice as it was raised, insisting that they encourage him to make the move," Hardin told me. "Bill then handed the phone to me, and I discussed the situation with Lamar, and he asked us to get back in touch with Wilder and McWherter and see if we could get them to publicly urge him to do this."

It was apparently at about this time that Donelson reached the two speakers by phone. In an interview, Donelson recalled that McWherter told him simply, "I'm for it," but did not commit that he would also be present at the early oath taking.

McWherter said nothing more. After a pause, Donelson broke the silence saying, "But, Ned, I want you to be there." He remembers that McWherter then agreed. Donelson said his call to Wilder was even briefer.

Hardin said he learned from Leech that McWherter and Wilder had now agreed to "urge Lamar to take the office" and that both would appear with him at an oath-taking ceremony at the end of the day.

Alexander, remembering the dual opinion letters that had emanated from Leech's office, now put the question squarely to the attorney general: "I said, 'Bill, I'm not going to do this unless you tell me it's legal and constitutional.' And he told me it was legal and constitutional. And I asked him to stand with me when I was sworn in."

Cooney and Koch arrived in room 416 at about this time.

"We got a call from Leech, who was already over at the hotel room, that we need to come over there. Cooney and I get in the car, and we drive over to the Sheraton and go down the ramp to the underground garage. Leech had given us a room number. We were taking great steps to come in without being seen. We ran into somebody in the lobby and worried that our cover was going to get blown. When we got to the room, Leech and Hardin are already there."

Cooney, a Vanderbilt law school graduate, had been a fixture in the AG's office and was well known to state government leaders. Koch, born in Honolulu, was also a graduate of Vanderbilt law school and by this time was already a veteran in the attorney general's office. He had been the first law clerk employed there, during his second year of law school, and though his plan had been to return to Hawaii and practice law in his home state, he moved his legal residence to Tennessee and remained on the attorney general's staff in Nashville.

Hardin, Cooney, and Koch all remember the conference in room 416 lasted over two hours. Throughout, the four lawyers would either pace about the tiny room—sleeves rolled up, ties pulled down, hands jammed into pants pockets—or alternate between sitting at the one small table near the window, or on one of the twin beds. (There were only two chairs at the table.) Leech smoking, Hardin running fingers through his hair. The scene looked more like a frenetic campaign headquarters than a hotel sleeping room.

"Leech began the discussion," Koch remembers. "He said he'd gotten some information from Hardin, and turns it over to Hardin. He tells us his information. At this point we have Tripp Hunt's opinion and also Leech's letter of several days later. The tenor of the meeting is that an early swearing-in is *not* going to happen unless Leech gets comfortable with the idea. We went thru the statute and the constitution. We discussed how the election result had already been certified.

The first part of the meeting, Koch recalled, was "getting Leech to a point where he could firmly come down on one side or the other."

"Hardin hadn't done much research, but he was pushing pretty hard on the early swearing-in being the only way." Koch remembers. "Cooney and I were pretty comfortable that the law permitted that. So it was mainly a matter of having a discussion with the boss. It was a vigorous and lively give and take. Leech had a lot of questions—questions that had already been asked but were being asked again. The 'swearing-in early' moves from hypothetical to real."

Hardin recalled that McWherter seemed more willing to move forward with the early swearing-in, meaning the ouster of Blanton, and that Wilder was more cautious and expressed more reservations. On a surviving piece of hotel notepaper, Hardin scrawled this note:

"Ned on one side. John on the other."

CHAPTER 15

The Decision

He could clear out the prisons.
—Deputy Attorney General Bill Koch in a 2012 interview

THE FINAL DECISION INVOLVED reaching an agreement on two inter-connected points—the legal or constitutional basis for the extraordinary action, and a consensus on who would been seen as having initiated it.

Leech had become the central facilitator, managing the essential communications over the one telephone in room 416, where he and the other lawyers were working together. In Koch's recollection, this process—getting the two legislative leaders and Alexander together on the main issues—was "arduous."

"It was like handling Jell-O—very fluid, moving around," Koch told me. "Part of it was a trust question. They all wanted to make sure how it would happen—so they could know that the path they were going to walk down did not lead to a cliff. We all knew there was not going to be a hue and cry about 'power grabbing' or abuse of office. All the newspapers were roundly castigating Blanton. There was not a serious concern that there was going to be a groundswell of reaction to this, other than relief.

"Lamar was not an early adopter of this idea. Neither was Wilder or McWherter. It was mainly a matter of getting them to the point of 'Let's all go together, at the same time.' Lamar wanted to have all the details in place and understood."

BUT THE LONGER THE CONVERSATION went on, the more definitive Leech became, "more certain in the correctness of his position, that he could defend it if it were challenged," in Koch's words.

"All of this hinged on Leech satisfying the speakers and Alexander that he could unequivocally endorse the legality and the advisability of this action—that it was the right thing to do, and that it was legal. They all knew that if this were going to happen, they didn't need any Monday morning quarterbacking," Koch said. "This was really the last option. Part of the discussion was 'Is there anything to do other than this?' Hardin's position was that there was nothing else. And the legal answer was 'No, not if he [Blanton] was preparing legal documents to grant pardons.' Under our system, any pardon document the governor signs is not reviewable by a court. A governor's act of clemency under our constitution cannot be reversed; the legislature can't reverse it. There is no recourse."

Through the afternoon the discussion in room 416 was intense, searching, exhaustive. The four lawyers alternately paced, sat, stood. Hardin would run his fingers through his hair, Leech would light one cigarette after another. Koch remembers the room was "fairly tense."

"There had certainly been no occasion in Tennessee's history where a governor had been sworn in early," Koch told me. "We couldn't find another factual event where this had been done anywhere in the country. It just hadn't happened, so we knew we were now operating beyond clear black-and-white precedent. So the question is, can you extrapolate an answer from the facts you have.

"The state constitution provided for swearing-in a new governor, but it didn't dictate the time, manner, and circumstance in which it can happen. So, you take the facts you know and come up with the most sensible answer that honors whatever you think the constitution and the statutes envisioned. Constitutions are not always written in exquisite detail. They set out general principles. Statutes get more specific but sometimes aren't. We were simply trying to decide whether given the law we had, would the law support what Hardin was telling us needed to be done, or wouldn't it. It was not like someone could 'open the envelope' and have the answer. We had to make that decision on our own."

They discussed whether Blanton's pardon, once signed, might still be held invalid if the actual document were not physically delivered. They were unsettled on this point, but Koch said the attorneys were unanimous in believing that "once Blanton issued pardon documents and they were delivered, there was nothing we could do about them. He could clear out the prisons."

FINALLY, BETWEEN 4:00 AND 4:30 P.M., the four lawyers agreed that bringing Alexander into office early could be successfully defended if legally challenged in court.

"We all came to the conclusion that they could defend it if it became necessary," Hardin remembers. Koch said, "Once things settled down, it turned from 'Can we?' to 'How we . . .' We talked about 'What would Governor Blanton do?' and 'We need an oath of office' and "The constitutional officers have to be told . . .""

The next task was to get McWherter and Wilder to agree that the early swearing-in was legal and that they would recommend it to Alexander.

"There were calls to Wilder and McWherter. At this point, the speakers and Alexander were not ready to commit, so there had to be some cajoling and discussion. Finally, the speakers and Alexander were ready to go," Koch said.

"And they wanted to do it that day."

THE WORK NOW SHIFTED to working out logistics for the swearing-in ceremony.

While Donelson had spoken to Chief Justice Henry earlier in the afternoon about administering the oath of office, the consensus and the details were not known at that time. Also, it was important for all the participants to arrive at the court building no later than 5:45 p.m., in order for the ceremony to occur at about 6:00 p.m.

Cooney and Koch were dispatched to find the chief justice and nail down his participation. Leech agreed to coordinate with the two speakers about time and place.

Finally, because of the legal and political complexity of what had been decided, the words that these officials would use in the next ninety minutes now took on special importance. Alexander told Leech he would take the lead on crafting a joint statement. Leech agreed that when he received the draft he would discuss the words with the two legislative leaders.

At about 4:30 p.m., Nashville time, Alexander made two phone calls—one to Chattanooga, the other to Washington, DC.

The first call was to Gene Roberts, whom he had seen just four hours earlier in Nashville. Roberts was now back at his own desk at Chattanooga's city hall, in a routine end-of-day meeting with Ron Eberhardt, his public information officer.

"I was having my regular meeting with Gene, and the call came in on his private line," Eberhardt told me. "He answered it, and I only heard one end of the conversation." Throughout this brief call, Roberts maintained eye contact with Eberhardt and showed no visible reaction to what he was hearing.

"When the call ended, he said, 'Well that was the governor-elect,' and he passed the information on to me. The crux of the conversation was that Lamar was communicating to Gene that Blanton had this stack of pardons and paroles on his desk, that the US attorney was afraid he was going to sign them, and that the speaker of the house and the lieutenant governor had asked him to be sworn in early to prevent these documents from being signed and becoming irrevocable."

Roberts then related to Eberhardt even more sobering words—that Alexander was concerned about the security of the capitol building. He said Alexander was considering a contingency plan to deploy a sufficient number of state troopers tonight to "encircle" the capitol grounds. The purpose of this tactic, if it were deemed necessary in the next two hours, would be to prevent any evidence from being spirited away by Blanton's people.

"It was the most incredulous call I'd ever heard about," Eberhardt remembered. "Gene said Alexander had told him it was going to be the job of the Tennessee Highway Patrol to encircle the entire capitol hill complex, not letting anyone in or anyone out, and they couldn't take anything out with them except their coats and pocketbooks, so as not to sneak any evidence out." He said Roberts related this exchange on the call:

ALEXANDER: Gene, do we have about fifty loyal troopers?
ROBERTS: Yes, I think we do.

At this point, Roberts was still the city police and fire commissioner in Chattanooga—and not yet in formal control of the highway patrol. His appointment to the state position had been announced in late December, but he would not be sworn in until Saturday.

"I had tried to think of all the things that could go wrong," Alexander remembered, "and there were two things—either of which could make a laughingstock of our state. One was that Governor Blanton would find out and, since he's the commander-in-chief of the National Guard, he could order them to encircle the capitol and we'd have two governors at once. Or, the second might be that the highway patrol might do the same thing. The governor can use the highway patrol for extraordinary things. Governor Clement used the highway patrol to integrate the schools in Clinton, and earlier governors had used the highway patrol to break strikes and deal with the coal miners in Jellico.

"Those two things worried me. I knew the troopers were among the most politically sensitive state employees, and they would be looking to the new administration even before the inauguration; in fact, a few were already assigned to me. I wanted to be sure, when I sent Lewie and Koch to secure the capitol, that there would be somebody there to help them.

"For the National Guard, I sent Tom Ingram to talk to Carl Wallace [the current state adjutant general, originally appointed by Blanton] and make sure he didn't take any order from the governor that afternoon. Carl wanted to keep his job. He was a Democrat."

ALEXANDER NOW PHONED DOUG BAILEY, the political consultant in Washington, DC.

By this afternoon, Bailey had become more than a political consultant to Alexander. He would spend the next eight years coming to Nashville on a regular basis, meeting with Alexander and helping him communicate his programs to the public as clearly as possible.

They discussed now the scenario that had emerged through the afternoon, and the shape of the ceremony that would occur at 6:00 p.m. Alexander asked Bailey to help him finish up the wording for the public statement he would read at the ceremony, incorporating his notes from the last call with Leech.

"What I had first asked the speakers to do was 'Ask me to do it' since they were the legislative leaders and this (swearing in a new governor) was a legislative matter," Alexander remembers. "What they said to me next was 'You go ahead, and we'll support you.' I said I'm not going to do that. What we finally agreed was that we'd do it together. In the statement that I wrote, and that Leech cleared with them, we agreed we would do this together—not a matter of me stepping out and them backing me up, which they first asked me to do, but we would do it together.

"That was actually the beginning of an extraordinarily good working relationship over the next eight years, especially with McWherter. That was the first thing we ever worked on together, and we never worked on anything that was more difficult. We found a way to do it that respected where he was and where I was, and demonstrated unity to the people of Tennessee, and doing things in a constitutional way."

JOE HENRY WAS AT HIS Nashville apartment, at the Capitol Towers, recuperating from recent heart surgery. He had returned to work at his court office. Koch was assigned to secure Henry's agreement to administer the oath.

"Cooney and I go back to our office [on James Robertson Parkway]," Koch remembered. "We're a block and a half from Henry's apartment. I call Henry. He's at Capitol Towers, convalescing from heart surgery. Rather than entertain company there, he says, 'I'll get dressed and meet you at my office,' meaning his office at the court building."

Shortly before 5:00 p.m., Koch met Henry in his chambers, on the third floor of the Tennessee Supreme Court building, and informed him of the day's developments.

At this point, memories differ on Henry's initial reaction.

Cooney told me that Henry "was convinced it just had to be done—and it had to be done promptly." Alexander recalls that Henry "agreed immediately to do it," but he did not speak to the chief justice directly that day, communicating instead through Donelson first and Koch later in the afternoon. Hardin remembers Henry being reluctant but never refused.

Donelson remembers that he met with Henry in the judge's chambers. "I didn't want to ask Chief Justice Joe Henry over the telephone. I asked if I could come see him. I went down to the supreme court building, and we talked." He recalled this exchange at Henry's desk, behind the closed door:

HENRY: Lewie, this is a very serious matter.
DONELSON: Yes, it is, but I've given it a whole lot of consideration. We've

talked to the FBI, and there are going to be some more pardons.

Everybody's going to have a black eye.

HENRY: You're right.

However, it was Koch who met with the chief justice last and is the only survivor of that conversation. (Henry died the next year.) Koch told me in our interview:

"Henry said, 'I don't want to do it. I'm not sure it's legal.' He basically asks all the same questions we've been through at the hotel. I advised him that if he was unwilling to administer the oath today, another judge will be found. At that point, he reluctantly agreed to do it."

AT ABOUT 4:30 P.M.—as the die was now cast and the weighty issues of procedure and law seemed settled, and after Cooney and Koch had departed—Leech called the Sheraton's room service. He ordered two packs of cigarettes and a six-pack of beer. These were delivered shortly to room 416.

When he offered Hardin a beer, the US attorney declined, reminding his old friend that he never drank alcohol in the month of January—a personal, private memorial to a vow he had made as a young man in his Peace Corps days. The two old friends continued to talk. Hardin remembers they reflected on the implications of the afternoon's discussion, how odd the situation was, how important the rule of law.

"We realized the significance of the moment," Hardin told me. "I asked, 'Where is the government?' I said to Bill I felt like we were a government in exile in this room."

"Hal," Leech replied, "at this precise moment we *are* the government. The *only* government."

All the discussions between the three groups—Alexander in his Hobbs Road office, the two speakers at Legislative Plaza, the government lawyers in their hotel hideaway—were accomplished by telephone with only Donelson and Leech acting as the principal intermediaries. Leech conferred as he went with Hardin, Cooney, and Koch, as did Donelson with Alexander and Ingram. Donelson, Koch, and Cooney also visited with Chief Justice Henry at different times in the afternoon.

Hardin and Leech did not see Alexander all day. They communicated with him only by telephone. In fact, the principals in the coup were never present in the same room that day until they met at the supreme court building at the end of the afternoon, and Hardin chose not to attend that final event.

"IT WAS PROBABLY THE MOST DRAMATIC, dynamic day I've ever spent in my life," Tom Ingram remembers. "It made election day look like a piker, because the pressure was on from noon that day really through the afternoon to the time they swore him in. It was phenomenal. You just felt it. I can still feel it.

"It was only when everybody in Wilder's office clearly concurred that it had to be done—and that they would stand there with Lamar—did he seriously consider it. He would not have done it without that huge, enthusiastic, strong commitment of support. . . . We weren't going to go out there and do it by ourselves. It was going to have to be something that we were just virtually left with no choice but to do, not for lack of courage or anything of that sort, but it was just a radical thought. For it to look unilateral or overly aggressive or greedy or premature on Lamar's part was unacceptable politically."

ONCE HE HAD AGREED to administer the oath in the extraordinary ceremony, Henry kept his own counsel through the rest of the afternoon. Henry's widow told Hardin years later that the chief justice did not share with her that afternoon what he was about to do.

He also did not confer with any his brethren on the supreme court that afternoon, according to one of his colleagues, Associate Justice Robert Cooper. In fact, Cooper remembers that when he learned what had happened on the television news later that night, he disagreed with Henry's action—thinking it to be not only unprecedented but not permitted by the state's constitution.

"Wilder, McWherter, and Chief Justice Joe Henry—really [none] of them had the power to terminate Blanton's power," Cooper told me in an interview on his ninety-first birthday, thirty-two years after the coup. "The only group of people who can remove a governor is the legislature, by impeachment. We [other justices on the court] didn't say anything about it publicly. He'd already done it. We only said to him, the next day, 'You just be sure you do it right on Saturday, just as though there hadn't been anything done on Wednesday.' Joe felt it was the right thing to do, and we didn't criticize him."

Had they conferred on Wednesday, without a formal request before the court, possibly two or more of the justices might have determined that this was only a political dispute between the other two branches of government. But they did not confer, and Hardin's information was in any case overwhelming. By this time if they had brought Leech into the deliberation, it is likely he would have persuaded them that the early oath taking was the only means of preventing a public safety emergency.

ALEXANDER'S PREFERENCE FOR THE Democratic leadership of the legislature to appear prominently at such an unprecedented ceremony also extended to Hardin, who had initiated the request in the first place. Hardin resisted. He told me Henry advised him not to go.

"Lamar gave Bill Leech certain conditions that would have to be met before he would agree to do it," Hardin remembered. "Bill wrote down those conditions. One of them bothered me—that I would have to appear with Lamar at the swearing-in. I just did not feel comfortable doing that, mainly because of my US government position. Joe Henry also said that it was not good for me to do, and I did not want to give the appearance that this matter was political. And also, because we had an investigation going on, I did not feel that it would be proper for me to participate in any publicity on the matter."

Ultimately, Hardin did not attend.

Honey Alexander said the final word came when her husband returned home for the second time on Wednesday afternoon. She still did not feel prepared. Far from it.

"When Lamar called and said, 'We might be doing this,' I said, 'We can't! I don't have any clothes, you don't have any clothes, the children don't have any clothes. I can't do this.' The clothes were literally packed in wardrobes and gone by the time he called. I had saved back a dress to wear to Jackson that night, and I don't even think I had stockings. And I had seen the Bible. I had thought, you know, things can get so confusing and I know this is important to Lamar, for Saturday, so I'm going to keep this so I know where it is."

This was the Bible that her husband's great-grandparents had used when they married in 1869 and had been given to him by his cousin Hazel Brickell Curtis. Honey had separated it from the packing process earlier in the day, and it was now one of their few possessions remaining in the house.

ALEXANDER PHONED HIS WIFE "SEVERAL TIMES" through the early afternoon.

"It was very uncertain, really, until the very end," she remembers. "Lamar was saying, 'This might be happening. I'm talking to McWherter and these other people.' At one point, he said, 'It looks like it might happen, but I don't know when. I don't know where.' I remember there was an undercurrent of worry about what Blanton might do.

"I wondered 'Why can't somebody make up his mind?' And literally until Lamar arrived home, the second time, and said, 'We're going,' I wasn't sure whether it was going to happen or not. . . . It was such a painful day. He was very emotional, and he's not an emotional person."

Lamar Alexander routinely joined in the music making with his Alexander's Washboard Band on the campaign trail in 1978. Here, pictured singing with Terry Tabors, the candidate plays the washboard as his trombone awaits.

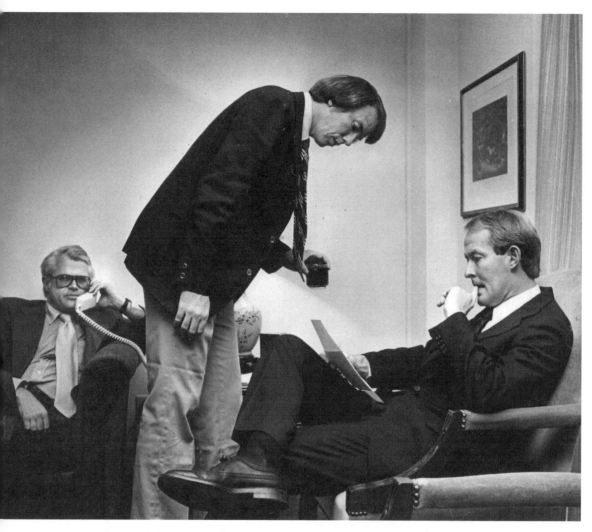

Election night 1978. Tom Ingram, campaign manager, and Alexander discuss victory remarks in a suite at the Opryland Hotel. Seated at left is political consultant Doug Bailey.

Opposite: After his victory in November 1978, Alexander received a congratulatory telegram from Governor Ray Blanton and also this envelope, containing a key to the governor's office.

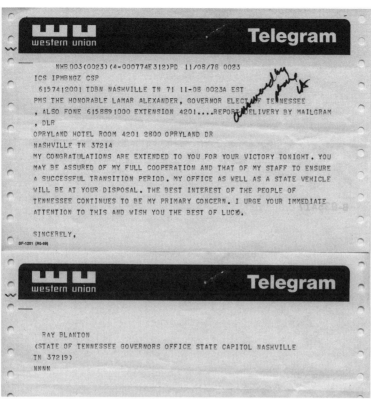

NHB 003 (0023) (4-000774E312) PD 11/08/78 0023
ICS IPMBNGZ CSP
6157412001 IDBN NASHVILLE TN 71 11-08 0023A EST
PMS THE HONORABLE LAMAR ALEXANDER, GOVERNOR ELECT OF TENNESSEE
, ALSO FONE 6158891000 EXTENSION 4201....REPORT DELIVERY BY MAILGRAM
, DLR
OPRYLAND HOTEL ROOM 4201 2800 OPRYLAND DR
NASHVILLE TN 37214
MY CONGRATULATIONS ARE EXTENDED TO YOU FOR YOUR VICTORY TONIGHT. YOU
MAY BE ASSURED OF MY FULL COOPERATION AND THAT OF MY STAFF TO ENSURE
A SUCCESSFUL TRANSITION PERIOD. MY OFFICE AS WELL AS A STATE VEHICLE
WILL BE AT YOUR DISPOSAL. THE BEST INTEREST OF THE PEOPLE OF
TENNESSEE CONTINUES TO BE MY PRIMARY CONCERN. I URGE YOUR IMMEDIATE
ATTENTION TO THIS AND WISH YOU THE BEST OF LUCK.

SINCERELY,
SF-1201 (R5-69)

RAY BLANTON
(STATE OF TENNESSEE GOVERNORS OFFICE STATE CAPITOL NASHVILLE
TN 37219)
NNNN

R. Blanton
Adamsville, Tennessee 38310

Governor's Office
State of Tennessee
State Capitol Building
Nashville, Tennessee 37219

Supreme court justices William Harbison, left, and Joe Henry are seated next to Judge Paul R. Summers at a 1977 legislative hearing. Photo by Gerald Holly.

Governor Ray Blanton, after the public controversy began over his pledge to pardon double-murderer Roger Humphreys, son of a political friend in East Tennessee.

Opposite, top: Wilder congratulates Blanton on his final State of the State address to a joint session of the Tennessee General Assembly, on January 10, 1979. House Speaker Ned McWherter stands to Wilder's left. Seven nights later, Blanton would be removed from office.

Opposite, bottom: Blanton, hands raised, acknowledges the applause of senators and representatives following his final State of the State address, on January 10, 1979. This standing ovation would be his last.

Tennessee attorney general Bill Leech walks to a meeting on January 18, 1979, the day after the coup. In the rear is reporter Fred Travis, Nashville correspondent for the *Chattanooga Times*. Photo by Gerald Holly.

C. Hayes Cooney was the chief deputy attorney general, Leech's number 2.

William C. Koch was one of six deputy attorneys general on Leech's staff. He had been assigned by Leech to serve as liaison with the incoming governor-elect Lamar Alexander. Photo by Billy Kingsley.

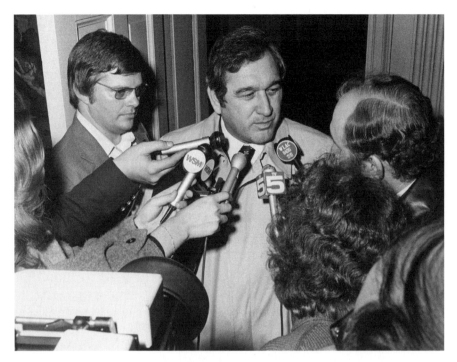

Blanton stops in the doorway of his office to talk with news reporters, minutes after signing his name to fifty-two clemency documents, including the commutation for Roger Humphreys, on January 15, 1979. At left is Blanton's press secretary, Jim Gilchrist.

No longer the state's first lady, Betty Blanton stands beside her husband on the front porch of their new private residence as he answers reporters' questions, following his removal from office.

With Honey Alexander holding the family Bible, Alexander takes the oath of office on January 17, 1979, administered by Chief Justice Joe Henry. The Alexander children, Drew, Leslee, and Kathryn, are at center facing the Bible, and McWherter, Leech, and Secretary of State Gentry Crowell are seen in the rear. Photo by J. T. Phillips.

Alexander takes reporters' questions following the early swearing-in ceremony.
Photo by Nancy Rhoda.

This editorial page cartoon by Sandy Campbell ran on Thursday morning, January 18, 1979, showing Tennessee's state capitol tower at night with both the state flag and Alexander's red-and-black plaid shirt against a full moon. Campbell, who had drawn another cartoon for Thursday earlier in the day, was asked for a replacement after the newspaper learned the early swearing-in was occurring late Wednesday.

Following the coup, Ned McWherter, John Wilder, and Lamar Alexander worked well together for the next eight years. Alexander said the three of them developed a mutual respect through their extraordinary experience of January 17, 1979. Afterward, they held bipartisan leadership meetings every Tuesday morning the legislature was in session.

McWherter greets President Bill Clinton and Vice President Al Gore Jr. at a reception at the Tennessee executive residence.

CHAPTER 16

The Yellow-Dog Chief Justice

The last one to the car is a Republican.
 —Joe Henry, remark to his children

THE CHIEF JUSTICE OF THE Tennessee Supreme Court was recovering from a heart attack, at his downtown Nashville apartment, when his call came.

He did not like the idea of an early swearing-in. He resisted it as a departure from inaugural tradition. It was also contrary to his personal constitution to help any Republican get into any office early, a mortal sin against his civic religion as a faithful Democrat.

There was no Democrat with a more colorful political history than Joseph W. Henry. His career had been shaped by politics, by his service in World War II, and by his love of the law as an honorable profession. He founded his law firm in Pulaski, Tennessee, in 1941 and eventually became the only attorney to serve as president of both the state bar association and the Tennessee Trial Lawyers Association.

Henry served with distinction in the US Army in World War II and afterward was elected in 1948 to a term in the Tennessee legislature from Giles County. From 1953 to 1959, he served as the state's adjutant general, or commander of the Tennessee National Guard, by appointment of his friend Governor Frank G. Clement.

Two decades later, in January 1979, another Democratic governor, Ray Blanton, was in deep trouble. Henry would play a part in the end of Blanton's story.

In the early days, Joe Henry had been a close adviser and confidante to Governor Clement, the charismatic young "boy governor" and favorite of the powerful Crump-McKellar machine in its heyday.

Clement, with Henry's help, had a brief walk on the national stage at the 1956 Democratic National Convention when the young governor, seen as rising star by some in the national party, was invited to give the keynote address at the Chicago nominating convention. In preparation for the big event, Joe Henry had helped him craft the words.

The words were harsh—full of righteous fury—and became famous. In the televised speech, broadcast on black-and-white screens statewide and across America, the handsome Clement accused the Eisenhower administration of being the "party of privilege and pillage" with a "sordid record of broken promises and unredeemed pledges." At that point, he was just getting warmed up. Clement excoriated the Republican ticket, calling Eisenhower "the most available front . . . for a discredited, defunct party," and denounced Vice President Richard Nixon as the "Vice Hatchet Man" and the "most intemperate political individual in the history of modern American politics." A former prosecutor and FBI agent, Clement accused the Republican Party of "aggravated assault and battery upon the political and economic bodies of the forgotten farm folk of America." At one memorable point, he roared, with echoes of the fire and brimstone of the southern evangelists:

"How long, O how long, America, shall we continue to condone the conduct of an administration that cuts back the strength and size of our military establishment, . . . a cutback so severe that an army chief of staff has reported to us that he felt he had been called on to destroy rather than build a military establishment."

Today the speech is remembered with mixed opinions, even (or especially) among older Tennessee Democrats. One celebrated journalist with a national readership, sportswriter Red Smith, criticized Clement's convention performance: "For volume, endurance and unflagging pace, no sports figure could have matched the bull-throated boy wonder of the cornpone belt." Smith suggested that the next day's headlines should read: "The Democratic Party smote the Republicans with the jawbone of an ass." At a time when the national party recognized Tennessee politicians on the order of Senators Estes Kefauver and Albert Gore, this was hardly the public reception for which the Clement team had hoped. The young governor's identification with national politics proceeded no further.

Henry had assisted his governor with these words and, like most in the Clement circle, believed the performance had been electrifying for the party. After all, this was the kind of rare political opportunity if not triumph that elated the boss and boosted one's own sense of ambition and entitlement. Henry was known to have his eye on a state supreme court seat at this early period, but it was not to be. As the story goes, Henry in fact believed he had the appointment in the bag for the combination of his qualifications and, not least, his service to Clement, but when he took the call from the governor, it was more a courtesy call to an old friend. Clement informed him he had selected another lawyer instead. Henry hung up the phone and remarked famously to an associate: "I have been bit in the ass by my own dog."

His elder son, Joseph W. Henry Jr., also a lawyer in Pulaski, told me the break with Clement was bitter.

"He had a promise from Frank Clement," the son told me, "that when there was an opening on the supreme court, Clement would appoint him. Clement didn't do it, and that caused a rift between the Clement family and the Henry family. My father said that spot had been promised to him; Clement appointed someone else and said, at the time, that there will be another time. According to my father, the spot was his. It was promised to him. My father awoke one morning to a phone call from someone telling him Clement had appointed someone else. My father was drinking at that time and stayed mad at him [Clement] for a long time."

"It turned out to be the best thing that ever happened to him," Joe Jr. added. "He went on to form the Tennessee Trial Lawyers Association. He was the first really rural lawyer to be president of the Tennessee Bar Association. Most of the really good things that happened to him in his life happened after that thing with Clement. If Frank Clement had made good on his promise, my dad would have been on the supreme court for a very long time, but I don't know if he would have turned out to be as effective as he did. I don't know if he would have been ready that soon. By the time he went on the court in 1974, he had all the experience and the discipline. He was also more of a character in 1974 than he was in '64. He was 'larger than life' at that point."

A son of Governor Clement, Judge Frank G. Clement Jr., told me he remembers that his father balked on the judicial appointment for Henry because of his drinking, "which was ironic because my father had his own problem with alcohol."

Two years before the 1956 convention in Chicago, however, Clement appointed Henry adjutant general of the Tennessee National Guard. Both men served in the guard, officially the state's militia, as did Ned McWherter and many other political leaders across the state. (Long after his last term as governor, Clement was an officer in the guard until his death in an automobile accident in 1968.) In 1956, Clement dispatched National Guard troops to Clinton, Tennessee, to quell rioting sparked by court-ordered school integration; General Joe Henry famously rode Patton-like into town in his military tank—his helmeted head appearing above the turret—carrying in his holsters two silver-plated, stag-handled pistols. His sidearms were not fired on this day, but his photo in battle gear ran in *Life* magazine.

"He looked for all the world like a southern George Patton," Joe Jr. told me. "He was an event guy. He sort of lived for moments like that. I think he loved the military more than most anything. When the war broke out, he made a very disciplined decision to be the best soldier he could be. He went overseas and became a battlefield leader for an all-black group—he commanded a platoon in Italy. He entered as an enlisted man; when he left the war he was a major. He got the Bronze Star for bravery. I heard him say, many times, that of all his military positions, he was proudest of his infantry badge."

THE SON ALSO REMEMBERS the father as a proud Democrat, exuberant and joyful in advocating the party line and the Democratic ticket.

Like Silliman Evans Sr., Joe Sr. was steeped in the Democratic politics of the New Deal and was likewise a battle-tested survivor of rough-and-tumble campaigns that pitted the Crump-McKellar machine and its candidates (including Clement) against progressives like Browning, Kefauver, and Gore. Henry wrote speeches for Senator McKellar, as well as for Clement.

"I remember when our family would go somewhere, and my brother Bob and I would run to the car, instead of saying, 'last one in the car is a rotten egg,' our dad said, 'last one in is a *Republican*.' We grew up thinking a Republican, at best, was akin to a rotten egg."

A 1971 speech at a Democratic Party rally in Johnson City was typical of Henry's fiery partisan rhetoric.

It was eight months after Dunn had taken office that Henry lamented the recent loss of both the governor's office and also the US Senate seat long held by Albert Gore Sr. He said Democrats had grown lethargic and "victimized by stale and ineffectual party leadership." He quickly mentioned it had been half a century since the last Republican governor in Tennessee, and then declared "the 50-year plague of political locusts struck again" with Dunn's election.

"To the governor's office came a genial gentleman, an utter stranger to the art and science of government, accompanied by an agglomeration and conglomeration of inexperienced, inept, lean and patronage hungry individuals whose primary specialty, we learn, was 'staff re-organization,' a literal translation of which simply means firing Democrats and hiring Republicans." Henry called Tennessee's new Republican Senator, Bill Brock, "a political pigmy" whose candidacy "validates the age-old adage that every tad-pole wants to be a frog."

The true blame for these outcomes, he said, lay not with the Republicans but with Democrats themselves.

"We stand scarred and riven by the ploughshares of political primaries," he said. "Our wounds are self-inflicted as, slowly but surely down through the years, we have committed ourselves to a course calculated to culminate in defeat and disaster. . . . I am talking tonight of truth and consequences, and am telling it like it is, and complete candor compels the admission that a succession of what has been called 'leap-frog' government left us without fresh and new leadership. I do not sail under false colors and, therefore, readily admit that I was a part and parcel of the 'leap frog' regimes and have no apologies therefor."

He used the occasion to push a number of election law reforms including compulsory voter registration by party, to prevent further "cross-over voting," which he defined as "the obnoxious practice of Republicans slinking into our primaries and influencing their outcome only to oppose our nominees."

"Regardless of how we nominate in 1972, or thereafter, the Democrats of Tennessee must be prompted and motivated by one, overriding, pragmatic purpose—to elect Democrats. . . . I submit to you that it is the solemn duty of every Democrat to dedicate himself to a revitalization of democracy in Tennessee and to purpose in his heart to do his bit to the end that we relegate the Republican Party to the secondary role in Tennessee which it has known so long and which it so rightly deserves."

The Henrys in southern Middle Tennessee were allied with the McWherters in rural West Tennessee, and the two families were close over many years. When Ned McWherter's son Mike was in law school, Joe Henry Sr. gave the young man a clerkship in his own court offices.

IN AUGUST 1974, Henry was part of a statewide judicial election that placed five Democratic judges on the five-member Tennessee Supreme Court. This had begun the year before, in 1973, when both Republican and Democratic politicians and lawyers began considering the upcoming expiration of terms on the high court.

For Democrats, the looming vacancies were problematic. With a Republican now governor, Dunn could be expected to pack the court. (Democrats also feared this would, in turn, "de-Pack" the attorney general's office, as a Republican majority on the court would be expected to oust the incumbent David Pack, a Democrat.) Also, as Democrats saw it, the development of a new selection method was also less about justice and court decisions than the politics of the state Building Commission. In Tennessee, the court selects the state attorney general, who at this time was ex officio a voting member of the Building Commission, which controlled the funding and timing of significant construction projects. Democrats feared that a Republican court would tip the balance and swing the commission's decisions the wrong way on important projects.

The state Democratic Party chairman, Jim Sasser, shortly announced that his executive committee would establish the Judicial Selection Commission. This group soon recommended eight candidates, and Sasser's executive committee selected five: William H. D. Fones of Memphis (the lone incumbent), William Harbison of Nashville, Chancellor Ray Brock, appeals court judge Robert Cooper of Chattanooga, and Henry.

The chief strategist behind the scenes, according to Cooper, was Ned McWherter. The five candidates ran a low-budget, low-volume campaign with no aggressive fundraising. ("We ran it on a shoestring," Cooper remembered.) They visited radio stations and newspaper editorial boards, sometimes individually but often as a group. Their media adviser was Tom Seigenthaler, owner of a public relations business in Nashville and brother of John, the *Tennessean* editor. They toured the state in a rented motor home, driven by Tom's nephew John Michael Seigenthaler, then eighteen years old and out of school for the summer. On the sides of the bus were large banners that promised "A Great Supreme Court!"

"McWherter organized this for us," Cooper told me. "He became our advance man. We enjoyed him very much. In the motor home, with the airconditioning going out every now and then, we figured that if the five of us could get along without any ill tempers, we could work together as a court."

The five men were mostly reserved in their joint public appearances. They understood that a judge soliciting votes could come off as unseemly, and in any case, they knew the ethical rules governing the judiciary. Those rules prohibit a judge or a candidate for a judgeship from rendering an opinion—for example, on the constitutionality of the death penalty—prior to a formal proceeding. For these reasons, at their campaign stops it was normally Henry who seemed most at ease on the stump, having come most directly from a tradition of partisan combat. He was buoyant, upbeat, even joyful in the campaign process, seeming to draw energy from audiences large and small. The stylistic differences created occasional friction among the candidates, and their young driver recalled one testy scene at a campaign stop in Paris, near the Tennessee River in West Tennessee.

The local operative had assembled a dinner audience to meet the candidates and raise campaign money for their slate. John Michael Seigenthaler remembers that Harbison, a distinguished jurist who was generally shy in public, became particularly nervous when the host concluded his introductions and announced the guests would shortly be asked to make campaign contributions.

"Joe got up and told the crowd why they were running," Seigenthaler said. "The local person in charge of the event then got up and said, 'OK, gentlemen, it's time to get out your checkbooks.' It was getting to be a little like an auction. You could see the faces of these judges; Harbison didn't like it, and he told me to go tell Joe to stop it. He said, 'Tell Joe this has to stop now—knock it off, or I'm leaving.' In the end, Joe called a halt to it—and said to the guy, 'You do this later,' and we got out of there.

"They all got along surprisingly well, but it was kind of like walking on a tightrope," he said. "You had Joe, who was very political, but you also had some respectable legal minds, like Justice Fones, who was so mild mannered and not a political animal really. They were all a little bit uncomfortable with the idea of running. It was not a comfortable place for them to be—except for Joe, who liked it. It was like they didn't know what they were doing riding around in a bus, being in a campaign. Joe was kind of in charge.

Henry certainly stood apart for his ringing rhetoric and lyrical language. "I have a strong conviction," he said in a standard line, "that justice is man's greatest interest on Earth—that justice is the same whether owed by one man to four million Tennesseans or by four million people to one man—that justice is the aim of free government and the key to liberty under the rule of law—that liberty will be pursued until it is obtained, or until liberty is lost in the pursuit."

They largely downplayed their partisan natures, depending on the audience, and they were successful. This unofficial "Democratic slate" was elected in the August primary.

Legal scholar Carl A. Pierce has written: "When the victorious Democrats assembled in Nashville to take their oaths of office, it was clear that this was a new Court. Only Justice Fones was a carryover, and he had been on the Court only a year." Fones was fifty-six; the only new member who was older was Henry, at fifty-seven. Justice Fones was named chief justice because of his seniority, having served on the previous court.

The five soon modernized many aspects of Tennessee law and procedure, at a time of national turmoil and challenge over the issues of religion, free speech, obscenity, openness in government, and gender equality. Fones recalled in an interview in 1995: "Those of us on the '74 court felt we had to make up for a hundred years of not bringing the law up to date."

Henry became known among lawyers and scholars for the colorful flourishes of prose in his written opinions, so reminiscent of his fulminations as the party leader on the campaign trail. On this modern court, he was also willing to join his fellow justices in making the occasional breaks with tradition when the constitution and the facts dictated, recognizing that times had changed.

He seemed to sum up his own recognition of this new paradigm in an early decision by the new court. In a 1975 opinion, in an early gender-equality case, Justice Henry wrote:

"We live in a new day."

CHAPTER 17

The Arrival

It was a cold, dreary, dark night . . . and all the press and all the cameras were following us down the street. It was almost like someone making a movie.
—Ned McWherter

LARRY DAUGHTREY THOUGHT he had it figured out at 2:00 p.m. In fact the decision had not been made by then, but he wasn't wrong.

More than just a "nose for news," Daughtrey, a native of Abilene, Texas, had a roster of sources that ran deep and long in the capitol and legislative offices. He had, by now, been a reporter for the morning *Tennessean* for sixteen years, beginning with his undergraduate days as a Grantland Rice Scholar at Vanderbilt University. (He and Alexander were classmates. Daughtrey was the campus correspondent for the *Tennessean*, Alexander for the *Nashville Banner*, and both would graduate in 1962.)

Seigenthaler had hired him full-time in 1962, and in 1965, Daughtrey was half of the two-reporter team, with Bill Kovach, that had busted up the practice of secret committee meetings in the legislature. (After the pair entered two so-called executive sessions of standing committees and refused to leave, the legislature enacted a law specifically banning the *Tennessean* from such meetings. The US district court, in *Kovach v. Maddux*, swiftly declared that act unconstitutional.) When Kovach departed for the *New York Times*, Daughtrey became newspaper's top state government reporter.

"I'd been told that whatever was going to happen was going to happen at the supreme court," he said. "I went over early in the afternoon and looked around, and there wasn't anything there. I went to Joe Henry's office. Henry and I were buddies going back to the National Guard in the '60s. I walked into his office, and his desk was absolutely clear except for a miniature bottle of Jack Daniels, and one of the *Tennessee Code* books that was open. In the old days, I could read upside down, and what he had opened the book on his desk to was the oath of office. I knew then, and he knew he had let out the secret."

He then returned to Legislative Plaza, and as far as he was concerned, his suspicions were confirmed.

"Wilder was walking around most of the day and was like the cat that swallowed the canary," Daughtrey said. "Of course, the speaker [McWherter] didn't say anything, except, 'Don't go home, don't go home.' That's when I called Seigenthaler. I said, 'They're getting ready to kick Blanton out.' Of course, John always wanted to be in the know."

Peggy Reisser, the young *Banner* reporter, was in the capitol making a final round of stops at various offices before departing for the day. On the ground floor, in the legal counsel's office, she observed an unusual level of activity for a late afternoon.

"I recall a flurry, a lot of papers being mimeographed in some of those ground floor offices," she said. "I went back upstairs, and somebody—I don't remember who—said, 'Something's going to happen. They're going to swear in Lamar.' I went downstairs, to the Legislative Plaza."

There, in the corridor outside McWherter's office suite, the number of reporters had begun to grow. By 5:00 p.m., at least three other reporters in the regular capitol hill press corps had by now received phone calls from sources who seemed knowledgeable. Bill (Rocky) Rawlins, the veteran Associated Press reporter, was at his bureau office when he received a tip that an announcement would be made, relating to Governor Blanton. He typed out a quick bulletin and then got into his car and drove to the plaza.

Other reporters for the *Banner* and *Tennessean* also responded, as did Duren Cheek, the chief of United Press International's Nashville office and another senior member of the capitol press corps, and reporter-camera teams from the two of the city's three network TV affiliates.

All of these gathered outside the speaker's office at 1 Legislative Plaza, waiting and watching, but no one was available to talk, at least no one in any official capacity. They saw no one go in the door to McWherter's office, and nobody came out.

The door was closed, in fact, and this alone was unusual.

McWherter had cultivated a reputation for openness and for largely unrestricted access for news reporters to his meetings. In the early 1970s, at about the time he became speaker, the legislature had adopted the Tennessee Sunshine Law, making any decision-making meeting open to the public, including news media; the Tennessee Press Association had printed pocket-sized copies of this simply worded act, on yellow cardstock to suggest the sunshine. McWherter had subsequently gone beyond the letter of this law, however, and made it known that any meeting in his office could be attended by any news reporter; this included the informal leadership discussions that were not technically decision-making meetings.

With the passage of time, this open-door policy had become so widely known and understood and acknowledged that by the end of the decade, not many reporters went to the trouble. It had become routine, uneventful, and generally unproductive to attend McWherter's meetings, and so for any enterprising reporter looking for the unusual, the speaker's open door just wasn't fun anymore.

Today was different. On this late afternoon, the doors to 1 Legislative Plaza were shut. There was secrecy in the air, and a sense that new strategy might be afoot—all sharpened by the turmoil surrounding Blanton and the heightened talk of what might be done about it.

Reporters in the corridor were alert for any sign or movement. The regular local members of the capitol hill press corps were milling around in the hallway—Fox and Reisser for the *Nashville Banner*; Daughtrey and Doug Hall for the *Tennessean*; Mark McNeely for the *Knoxville News-Sentinel*; Cheek and Fred Sedahl for the UPI; Rawlins for the Associated Press; Lee Smith; Fred Travis of the *Chattanooga Times*; Denise LeClair, reporter for the ABC affiliate, Channel 2; Hank Allison for the CBS affiliate, Channel 5; Anne Marie Deer with WKDA-AM; and a few others. There were at least two national reporters, including Howell Raines from the *New York Times'* Atlanta bureau, and Eleanor Randolph of the *Chicago Tribune*. Two TV cameramen were also standing by.

"We knew something was going on—and that there was a possibility there might be an early swearing-in," the *Tennessean* reporter Hall told me. "We weren't getting much information but had some sense—probably from McWherter's office—that we shouldn't go anywhere. Jim Kennedy [McWherter's top staff assistant] was running all over the place, but people weren't talking so everybody was suspicious. Howell Raines was here for the *New York Times*, and Eleanor Randolph for the *Chicago Tribune*. They were in town covering the whole fall-out from the Roger Humphreys pardon, covering the Blanton story. Then we got word that this was going to happen."

Hall thought he heard someone mention that whatever was coming would be happening upstairs in the War Memorial Building auditorium. He mentioned this to Raines, Randolph, and Smith, and the four of them made a dash for the plaza elevator—only to realize, suddenly, that they were in the wrong location. They were also, strangely, trapped inside.

"We got a bad tip, from somebody, that it was going to happen in the War Memorial auditorium, so we went over there," Hall said. That building, with a spacious auditorium, is connected to the plaza by an elevator that opens into the War Memorial lobby, one floor above where the mass of reporters now stood. "We go in, but then we couldn't get out. It was after-hours, the building was locked. Of course, this was before cell phones, so there was no way to call anyone for help."

Smith remembers: "We couldn't get out of the building, we kept running into locked doors. We finally got outside, and burst into the supreme court chamber—and there was nobody in the room. About that time, Ramsey Leathers [the court clerk] came in the rear door."

They were now in the right place, but early. It would be twenty more minutes before the scene in the courtroom would begin to take shape.

Back in the Legislative Plaza, inside the speaker's office, there was also nervousness, as top officials of two branches of state government conferred for one last time about whether and how to force a power shift in the third branch. This conversation group was small: Speaker McWherter, Lieutenant Governor Wilder, Attorney General Bill Leech, Gentry Crowell, and McWherter's top aide, Jim Kennedy. McWherter and Wilder listened as Leech reviewed the information he had from the federal authorities and explained again the legal basis for what he was now recommending.

At this moment, Wilder's office was empty except for his new aide, Nelson Biddle.

"There were a bunch of meetings going on," he remembers. "Wilder had hinted to me what was going to happen. It was all very hush-hush. Wilder clued me in, just because I had worked for Blanton for four years, and he didn't want me to be taken by surprise. He didn't want me to say anything; we just didn't know where or when or how.

"The bad part about it was that when the word was given, to put the whole plan in motion, I was in Wilder's office by myself, and a call comes in, and it's Governor Blanton. He asked me, 'Nelson, what's going on?' I lied to him and said, 'I don't know, Governor.' At that time, it was being implemented, late in the afternoon. I didn't have a conversation with Blanton about it—I didn't know what to say—but obviously someone had told him that something was fixing to go down, so he called Wilder's office.

"I've always regretted lying to him," Biddle told me. "It still bothers me. I wish I'd hung up the phone. He had been very good to me."

Shortly after this, Wilder returned to his office.

AT 5:25, REPORTERS IN THE HALLWAY saw the door to McWherter's suite swing open. The entourage from the speaker's office emerged, wearing raincoats, in a consensus of somber silence.

LeClair phoned her newsroom and spoke to Jim Travis, who had been pulling double duty on the Blanton beat—covering developments for both the local station and also transmitting updates to New York for inclusion in the network's own coverage of the expanding story in Tennessee. Travis had returned to the station only minutes before LeClair called in.

"We had just gotten back to the station. I had a network producer with me from ABC News," Travis remembered. "We had just finished a piece on the commutations, and it had just aired on ABC's five o'clock feed. Just as it aired, I was working on another local story, and right about that time I got a call from Denise, at the speaker's office, saying, 'You've got to get down here with a truck.'"

"Where you going?" UPI reporter Fred Sedahl asked McWherter.

"Just come on," the speaker replied. "Go with us."

The group moved deliberately toward the north end of the corridor, then paused outside Wilder's office. His door opened, and the lieutenant governor appeared, wearing a trench coat.

This particular group of state officials, often jocular, was not so on this late afternoon. Making no further comment to reporters, McWherter, Wilder, Crowell, and Leech strode with their aides past the cafeteria, to the escalator that rises to street level at the north end of the subterranean plaza. At the top landing, a marble corridor leads one way to the capitol building elevators and, in the opposite direction, to the double doors opening onto Charlotte Avenue. The group, now in single file on the escalator as it reached the upper corridor, quickly exited to the street one by one.

Outside, in the chill of the late afternoon, each person in order turned right on the east-west sidewalk and moved the brisk half-block to the supreme court building on the corner across Seventh Avenue. What had been a single file of officials and reporters, as they cleared the door, now formed a spontaneous cluster around the two speakers moving west on the tree-lined sidewalk. Some of the reporters shouted questions, others moved in silence, the glow of three television cameras illuminating the legislative leaders in a cocoon of eerie light.

"I remember that walk, from the Legislative Plaza across the street, everybody trying to write and talk," Peggy Reisser remembered. "David [Fox] almost walked into one of those trees on the sidewalk. There was a lot of talking and questions on the street."

McWherter later remembered this as "probably the longest walk I've ever taken in Nashville."

"It was a cold, dreary, dark night," he told me. "It had already turned dark. And all the press and all the cameras were following us down the street. It was almost like someone making a movie. But it was a responsibility I thought we needed to do, and we did it."

When they entered the front door of the court building, someone directed McWherter, Wilder, Crowell, Leech, and Kennedy to a rear corridor. This brought them to the court's robing room.

ALEXANDER AND HIS FAMILY arrived with Tom Ingram, by car, entering the same building from the rear, on the west side opposite the front door the speakers were approaching.

Winstead was behind the wheel. He had transported Alexander and Ingram from the Hobbs Road office to the family residence on Golf Club Lane. At home, Alexander had changed clothes. The closets were empty, their contents having been moved to the official residence. Honey Alexander, scrambling to get the family ready, had reached personal assistant Carole Martin there by phone.

"Carole, you've got to get them to take a box of clothes off the truck," she said. "Lamar needs a suit and a shirt." Carole quickly complied, but the moving crew did not; they "balked," she said, until Trooper Robbie Bell came to her assistance, telling them, "Do as she asks."

Martin quickly went through the boxes and found a suit and shirt, but she could find no necktie, belt, or shoes. Before she could depart to make the delivery, the phone rang again. Honey Alexander had one more request. She asked Martin to stop en route and buy a pair of maternity pantyhose. All this Martin then delivered to the otherwise nearly empty Alexander residence. Alexander borrowed a belt and tie from Ingram (Donelson later remembered that the borrowed necktie was his), and he wore the brown shoes he had had on during the day. For Leslee, Honey borrowed a dress from her neighbor Sara Hardison.

Honey remembers the end of the afternoon as a swirl—unsettled, sick, and sad.

"I was sad. I was exhausted—we'd had a full week of activities. This, tonight, was the last of the series of inaugural events across the state, in Jackson. I was five months pregnant, and I had these little children to transition to a new thing. I was exhausted and not feeling well—I had a cold, too. One child sick. It was just cold and horrible."

On the ride from the Green Hills residence to the court building, the family rode through light rain in silence, the parents and three small children all cramped together in the rear seat. Also in the back seat, in Honey's lap, was the large Alexander family Bible. In a second car, Carole Martin rode with Trooper Hugh Hayes. It was rush hour, but they were heading into town now, in the opposite direction of the outbound traffic.

"There wasn't any chatter at all," Winstead remembered. "They were just quiet."

Once downtown, the two black sedans turned off of Charlotte Avenue and paused as the heavy metal door on the west side of the supreme court building slowly rose. The cars now moved quietly into the basement garage. Bill Koch and Lewie Donelson were standing there, awaiting their arrival.

Koch had been designated by Leech, his boss, to serve as a liaison with the governor-elect, and in the three months since the November election, he had already assisted in preparing some policy initiatives relating to Alexander's campaign pledges about criminal justice. Alexander had asked Koch to meet him at the court building when the time came this afternoon. Koch now motioned to Winstead to pull his vehicle into the first empty parking space on the left. The second car followed, turning it into an adjacent space. The metal door closed behind them.

Few words were spoken as they exited the cars. Honey Alexander carried the family Bible. Alexander had placed a bookmark at his father, Andy's, favorite verse. (He would use this same Bible for the oath taking this evening, and again on Saturday.)

"For some unknown reason, Honey had held back the family Bible. Almost everything else had been sent to the mansion—her clothes, the children's clothes, most of my clothes—but she had kept it back, or we never would have been able to find it. This was the Bible that had been used at the wedding of my great-grandparents in 1869. So, Honey produced the Bible, for which I was eternally grateful. What that permitted me to do was open it to my father's favorite verse, which was II Timothy 2:15. ['Study to show thyself approved unto God, a workman that needeth not to be ashamed, rightly dividing the word of truth.'] That was very important to me."

At this point, in the dim light of the underground garage, Alexander stood for a few moments with Koch, Donelson, and Ingram, and they discussed details of their contingency plan. Here, decisions were made on the spot in rapid succession.

Alexander instructed the three men to be ready—as soon as the swearing-in was completed—to "secure the capitol." They should go there immediately following the ceremony. No one they might find still there should be permitted to leave with anything but their personal property—no official papers or other documents of any type were to be removed.

They also discussed what should be done tonight about the prisoners that Blanton reprieved on Monday but who were still behind bars. Koch suggested that any further releases should be stopped, in any cases where the actual clemency paperwork had not yet been delivered. Alexander agreed with this approach, and he instructed Koch to inform Commissioner Murray Henderson immediately of this policy as soon as the swearing-in was completed.

Finally, with Honey Alexander standing nearby with the children and holding the family Bible, Alexander also asked Donelson to be ready to say a brief prayer once the oath was administered.

KOCH NOW GUIDED THE GROUP to a tiny, wood-paneled, private elevator reserved for judges. But in this cramped compartment, measuring just four feet square, it took two trips for the group to reach the third floor.

In the first load, Koch accompanied Alexander, Ingram, and Donelson up to the third floor, bypassing the public lobby on the first floor, avoiding the gathering knot of reporters who were beginning to arrive. The rest of the Alexander family followed with Carole Martin.

Once upstairs, Koch lead them down the long corridor to the opposite end of the floor and into the office suite of Chief Justice Joe Henry, who greeted them with a smile.

Henry's office was simply furnished. His law books lined the shelves along three walls. His desk was clear, but for two items. One was the statute book that Daughtrey had seen earlier in the afternoon, still laid open to the page containing the oath of office for a new governor. The other object was the miniature bottle of Jack Daniels whiskey. It was a commonplace on Henry's desk, a souvenir of sorts, and it was most definitely not for drinking. It was a tiny memorial, he often told visitors, to his years of hard drinking followed by his latter years of hard-won sobriety. It sat unopened but visible. Henry greeted the new guests.

"This is certainly unprecedented," he said to Alexander.

Only one other person was in Henry's office when this group arrived. Alexander's press officer, Debby Patterson, Columbia native and public relations executive, had served as the press officer for the campaign. Around 4:30 p.m., Ingram had phoned her with two terse instructions: He asked her to contact the other campaign and transition staff members and tell them to "go immediately to the supreme court building downtown." Once that was done, she was to go there herself and proceed quickly upstairs to Chief Justice Henry's private office.

INGRAM HAD ALSO PHONED at least two others, a Democrat and a Republican. These were the lawyers John Jay Hooker and Lew Conner, who, in very different ways, had helped to bring about this strange event.

Hooker had kept the Humphreys affair alive in the news throughout the preceding year, consistently railing at Blanton, and more recently had gone to chancery court in an attempt to restrain Blanton from permitting any further clemencies unless he had personally signed his name. Hooker had succeeded on the latter, securing a chancellor's ruling that clemencies were invalid unless signed by the governor himself.

Conner and Alexander had first met when they were fellow students at Vanderbilt University, and they later became law partners in Nashville through a merger of two firms in 1971. Conner had been a key fundraiser and close adviser to Alexander in both the 1974 and 1978 campaigns. (Near the end of the 1974 campaign, Conner and five others cosigned a loan of $38,000 to make a last-minute purchase of TV advertising—$25,000 of which was not ultimately paid off until the 1978 campaign.) Lew and his wife, Ashley, together with John and Carole Sergent and also Robert and Marcia Echols, were now among the Alexanders' closest couple friends.

"Tom called me at my office down at the bottom of the hill toward the end of the afternoon, maybe 4:15 or so," Conner told me, "and he said, 'Get up here, right now. Lamar's going to be sworn in early.'"

INGRAM: Are you wearing a necktie?
CONNER: Yes.
INGRAM: Good, we may need it.

"They never used my necktie," Conner said. "I just hung up the phone and beat it straight up the hill."

Patterson reached as many staffers as she could, but at the late hour, some could not be contacted. (There were neither cell phones nor pagers in Nashville at this point.) Using her desk telephone and dialing numbers quickly, she reached as many as she could and to those communicated only the time and location—no other substance, not a word about the purpose.

By 5:30 p.m., some two dozen Alexander staff members had arrived in the supreme court building lobby. Patterson herself was now upstairs.

"Tom and Lamar and Bill [Koch] came in Justice Henry's office almost immediately after I got there," she remembered. "Tom told me what was about to happen. He said, 'You ought to go downstairs, because the reporters will be here any minute.' I went down and stood in the lobby beside the big front doors, and at that point people just kind of rushed in—McWherter, Wilder, a bunch of reporters, Bill Leech, who I'd known all my life. I went into the robing room with Bill Leech and stood there with Lamar and Honey and the kids. I hadn't been in the robing room before."

Alexander did not know Henry well at this point, though he was aware of the recent heart attack and was appreciative of the jurist's attention and participation on this winter afternoon. The two men exchanged greetings and a few words about the oath that Henry would administer shortly.

"We need to go downstairs now," Koch said. He led them onto the private judges' elevator adjacent to Henry's office. It was a quick ride down to the first floor, and then a few steps further into the robing room.

THIS ROOM TODAY STILL APPEARS much as it did in 1979. The robing room is the private space where the five justices of the state's supreme court have their final moments of preparation before holding court in the adjacent public chamber. It is a quiet sanctuary that certainly most Tennesseans have never glimpsed, and that in fact most employees in the court building itself have never entered. In truth, it is nondescript.

A conference table sits in the middle of the high-ceilinged room, and arrayed around the four colorless walls are sundry cabinets, chairs, and a few items of office equipment. It is said to have changed little in décor or furnishings over the past half century. On this late afternoon in January 1979, a black rotary telephone sat on a side table.

When McWherter, Wilder, Leech, Crowell, and Kennedy entered the room, Alexander and his family were already present, together with Henry, Ingram, Koch, Lewis Donelson, and Patterson. Fifteen people were now in the room. No one sat. The chairs remained empty. Carole Martin, who was helping tend to the Alexander children, remembers a solemn atmosphere.

"Nobody sat," she told me. "It was like a funeral. We acknowledged each other with our eyes—no speaking."

Both McWherter and Alexander, in interviews years later, remembered this scene and a final brief exchange. It was the first time they had come face to face all day, after hours of communicating through intermediaries and one telephone call.

ALEXANDER: Are you comfortable with this?
McWHERTER: No, but I'm going on the same advice you're going on.

McWherter explained later: "I had a great deal of respect for Bill Leech and for Hal Hardin. I didn't want to do it. I was not comfortable doing it. But there are some things in government you have to do where you don't have a high confidence level, and I thought it was our responsibility. I feel like [Lieutenant] Governor Wilder felt the same thing, but I've never really discussed it with him since then.

"As I remember it," he continued, "we were all standing. I remembered that Ray could get mean, and I knew it. I said, just jokingly, to someone that he [Blanton] appoints the adjutant general and he's in charge of the National Guard, and he could have us arrested for trying to overthrow his power. We'd better get on with this and get out of here.'

"Someone said, 'He wouldn't,' and I said, 'He *could*, he *would*, and he *might*.' That was true. He could've had us arrested."

HENRY WAS IN HIS BLACK ROBE, and it seemed he would speak first with a word of orientation and instruction. But Alexander spoke first, giving the small group a rundown of how the next few minutes were to unfold.

There was no need now to review the issues of corruption and crime that had given rise to this emergency proceeding, nor the constitutional issue about how to resolve it, nor the consensus conclusion that had been reached about resolving it all on this particular day. By now, this was well understood by all in the room but the three children.

Alexander would be "governor-elect" for only a few moments longer. He now described the simple sequence they would go through in the next room. They would enter and form into a group before the assembled press corps, and he would read the brief statement he had in his hand—the statement that had been fully vetted by all the participants over the past two hours. Henry would then administer the oath, Alexander would make a brief further comment, and then recognize McWherter and Wilder for their remarks, and then Donelson would be called on to offer a prayer. Alexander said, finally, that he anticipated there would be many questions from reporters, and it was agreed the principals would stand together and give answers for as long as that took.

"I was trying to make sure that this extraordinary event—which I hated to do—went as well as it possibly could," Alexander told me. "So from the time of the second call to Hal Hardin, all the way up to the stage managing the presence, to the statement, I wanted to make absolutely sure that when I gave that statement following the swearing-in that I was clear to everybody about what was going on."

ALEXANDER THEN TURNED TO the door leading to the court chamber. There was a shuffling of feet as the group began forming into a single file to walk into the adjacent courtroom. Koch and Patterson departed for the lobby, entering the courtroom from the public door off the lobby entrance.

But at that moment, McWherter spoke, stopping the movement.

"Has anybody told Governor Blanton?" he asked. "Someone should call him and tell him what we're about to do. I don't feel comfortable doing this and not saying anything to him about it."

At this point, recollections of how Blanton was told differ slightly, though all agree it was Leech who told him. Alexander, in a separate interview years later, said it had already been agreed that Leech would give Blanton the word though not until moments before the ceremony was to occur.

"It was pretty obvious that the person to tell him was Bill Leech," Alexander remembered, and that the proper moment for the call was "just before the swearing-in, because of the fear, whether justified or not, [that] he might sign more commutations."

But McWherter said he remembered that "they all turned to me and said, 'Well, you'll have to do that.' I asked Jim Kennedy to call out there."

Kennedy glanced at his pocket calendar, found the number for Blanton at his new private residence, and walked to the table with the black rotary phone. McWherter shifted with him, standing next to Leech. Kennedy picked up the receiver and dialed. Betty Blanton, the governor's wife, answered.

"Mrs. Blanton, this is Jim Kennedy," he said. "Speaker McWherter is calling for Governor Blanton." After a few seconds, Blanton came on the line. Kennedy handed the phone to his boss. McWherter quickly said: "Governor, Bill Leech is here, and he has something he needs to tell you."

In either version, McWherter extended his arm and handed the phone to the attorney general. Leech gave Blanton a quick summation of what was now in progress, and as he spoke, McWherter and the rest of the entourage exited the robing room.

"Governor Blanton," said Leech, "I wanted to let you know that in a few minutes Lamar Alexander will take the oath of office, and he will be the new governor of Tennessee." When McWherter was interviewed later, he said he remembered hearing Blanton exclaim, "The hell, you say!" Recounting the brief conversation later for Mark McNeely, capitol bureau chief for the *Knoxville News-Sentinel*, Leech said that Blanton paused and then replied, "This hurts me very deeply, Bill. I hate to go out of office like this, but I accept it, and I acknowledge your message."

As Leech and Blanton exchanged these words, the others were filing out of the robing room through the narrow passage leading up three steps to the open courtroom. They walked in silence, and great dignity, emerging into a glare of TV camera lights and the flash of still cameras. A breathless anticipation descended on the larger room—the feel of something important about to happen.

"I worried," Honey Alexander remembered, "about things like, 'Have we called Lamar's mother yet?'"

THE LOCAL CBS AFFILIATE, WTVF-Channel 5, had interrupted its regular broadcast a few minutes before 6:00 p.m. This was the Nashville station's first remote live broadcast, and for the first time in anyone's memory, the local affiliate had broken into the hallowed *CBS Evening News with Walter Cronkite* with coverage of the coup in Nashville.

WTVF is headquartered on James Robertson Parkway, at the foot of capitol hill, and from his anchor desk on the lower level of this building, the anchorman Chris Clark was now on camera telling viewers what they were about to witness. The satellite-equipped truck was parked outside the supreme court building up the hill. The station would continue its live coverage for over an hour, alternating shots from Clark's anchor desk to reporters Hank Allison and Dave Caylor on the scene.

Then the image on the screen shifted, showing the interior of the courtroom on the hill. Allison, whispering into his own microphone, was now giving the names of state officials as he saw them enter the supreme court chamber, one by one.

CHAPTER 18

The Oath

Let Justice Be Done Though the Heavens May Fall
  —Motto on the Seal of the Tennessee Supreme Court

"**The scene inside the court chamber** struck me as something out of *All the King's Men*," Howell Raines told me, "with all the dramatic personae arrayed as if in a scene from a novel or stage play about Southern politics. I remember being impressed with how McWherter and Alexander handled themselves."

The Alexanders with their three young children reached the center of the room first, Honey Alexander carrying the oversized family Bible in her arms, seeming to lean backward to counterbalance its heft. Once inside the courtroom, Alexander seemed clearly interested in guiding the two legislative leaders to positions of prominence so that they would appear within the camera frames, then Leech, then Crowell. Honey stood to Lamar's immediate left side in this view, with their son, Drew, and daughters, Leslee and Kathryn, gathered in front of her and Justice Henry to the right.

"It was not an event, like many today, that was manufactured for television," Alexander said in an interview twenty-six years later. "I can still feel it. It was an electric experience for me. Some of the people there didn't know why they were there, or what they were about to see. Suddenly out of the back door appeared me with my family, and these other leaders. It started at 5:56, and it was over eight minutes later."

Only moments before this, news reporters and photographers had been denied early access to the court chamber. They had been held in the building's ornate lobby, called the Hall of Justice, with the double doors leading to the courtroom closed tight. The lobby is thirty-two feet square, its ceiling sixteen feet high, the floor and walls made of marble. Finally, at about ten minutes before the hour, those doors opened. In the rush, these journalists and other guests stepped over the bronze, marble, and terrazzo of the Court's large circular seal, six feet across, inlaid in the center of the lobby floor. The visitors in their haste doubtless did not pause to read the inscription of the Court's Latin motto, but it too helped set the tone for the extraordinary evening: *Fiat Justitia Ruat Coelum* ("Let Justice Be Done Though the Heavens May Fall").

Once inside, there was pushing and nudging among the reporters and photographers, typical of impromptu news conferences, as they maneuvered for position in front of the officials. In the surviving videotape of the event, the flash attachment on Nancy Rhoda's still camera momentarily blocks the view of the Channel 5 videographer. Radio reporters Anne Marie Deer and Allen Williams pushed in with their audiocassette recorders, extending their handheld microphones forward. Other reporters filled in around these.

One reporter was, by choice, still outside the courtroom, standing in a small corridor across the lobby.

The UPI's Duren Cheek held the receiver of the one payphone in the lobby, while his colleague Fred Sedahl was now posted inside the court chamber to take notes for the wire service. Their plan was to keep this one landline to themselves, swapping off as one and then the other entered the courtroom to observe the proceedings and interview the principals as soon as possible afterward. Their principal competitor, the AP's Rawlins, thus did not have telephone access to his own bureau.

"We had hung out in the lobby for a few minutes—it might have been twenty minutes—and then we were ushered into the court chamber," Sedahl remembers. "There were fewer than fifty people there—politicians, observers, reporters—there wasn't a huge throng of onlookers. There were a few of Alexander's people there, but not a crowd. It was solemn, a lot of people just whispering. It was not a celebratory kind of scene, but a very quiet and reserved scene."

Jim Travis, reporting for the local ABC affiliate, Channel 2, arrived at this point and joined the growing throng of journalists pushing to the front of the room. Travis remembers his station had acquired remote capability by this time, like its competitor Channel 5, but the equipment was not in place at the supreme court building. He recorded two reports from the scene on videotape, first for the local ABC affiliate and then for the network feed.

He remembered the night:

"We got there just in time, soon enough to squeeze into the half circle around Alexander and his wife holding the Bible. It was like a big circle, and they were in the middle of it. There was a lot of jostling to get in position, so you could get a good shot and hear what was going on.

"It was a palace coup, no question about it. Pretty unique in American politics."

Further back in the courtroom, most of the hastily assembled guests stood, with a few taking seats in the green Naugahyde chairs of the court's gallery.

And, furthest back, in the lobby doorway, stood Bill Koch. This position would enable him to make a quick departure at a designated moment—with instructions that no one but Alexander, Ingram, and Donelson knew at this moment. No one would know, until the predetermined moment arrived.

ALEXANDER SPOKE FIRST, glancing at times at the yellow piece of paper in his hand. This was the handwritten draft that he had composed and then read over the phone to McWherter and Wilder for their approval as a joint statement for the public.

"I've been authorized by the lieutenant governor and the speaker of the house to make this statement on behalf of the three of us. The United States Attorney for the Middle District of Tennessee informed each of us today that he has substantial reason to believe that Governor Blanton is about to release one or more persons from prison who are targets of the United States investigation into alleged payoffs for pardons and commutations of sentences," he said. "That information, taken with other information of the last several weeks, causes each of us to believe that it is in the best interests of the people of Tennessee for the governor-elect to assume that office immediately.

"We believe that the taking of the oath should be done publicly and with each of us present. The state attorney general has assured each of us that in his opinion the assumption of the office in these circumstances is constitutionally valid."

Reporters and photographers continued to jostle. Leslee's cough accelerated. In the videotape of the event, McWherter, standing directly behind Alexander, is seen keeping his eyes focused forward. Crowell, the secretary of state, who had attested to the fifty-two clemencies two nights before, is seen keeping his gaze fixed on Alexander.

"These are not very happy days for Tennessee," he continued. "This is not a happy day for me. I believe, though, that we have been responsible, and that we have kept the faith of the people by this decision. We seek the people's wisdom. If we hear the people's wisdom, our days of agony can soon go forward to days of pride. I ask for the prayers of the people."

He then turned to his left and looked to Henry. "Mr. Chief Justice, I am ready to take the oath of office."

Honey, with tears in her eyes, held the large Bible steady. Henry administered the oath. Leslee Alexander coughed. Her sister, Kathryn, placed her own hand on the Bible, as Drew stood next to his father.

Alexander raised the same right hand that he had smashed into the bedroom wall earlier in the afternoon, cracking the plaster of the old house, and now took the oath of office.

"I, Lamar Alexander, do solemnly swear that I will perform with fidelity the duties of the office of governor of the State of Tennessee, to which I have been elected and which I am about to assume, that I will support the Constitution of the State of Tennessee and the Constitution of the United States, so help me God."

Blanton's term was now over.

Henry extended his hand to the new governor, and Alexander shook it. Honey Alexander closed the large family Bible and held it to her chest. Donelson, standing off-camera behind Wilder, now was heard saying, as previously instructed, "Let us pray." This momentarily caused Alexander and the other officials to stand in semidarkness as the television cameras turned their lights toward Donelson who, with his eyes closed, offered a brief benediction. Radio reporter Eddie Parker, who had been standing in front of Donelson, now pivoted and held his microphone in Donelson's direction and also bowed his head.

When the prayer ended, a few muffled amens were heard in the room.

REPORTERS AND CAMERA LIGHTS immediately turned back to Alexander. The television screen, which had displayed a graphic identifying him as "Lamar Alexander, Governor Elect," now read "Gov. Lamar Alexander."

In his first words as governor, he now described what would be happening in the following hours and days. For the next three days and three nights, no handbook had yet been written.

"Number one," he said, "I have asked Fred Thompson to return from Washington, where he is today, and he will back by 6:30 tonight, to serve as special counsel to me and be in charge for me of all matters relating to pardons and paroles and commutations." (At this moment, Thompson was still in the air returning to Nashville and was unaware that this was the specific assignment that awaited him.) Alexander continued:

"I have asked the attorney general to inform the secretary of state, who is here, and the commissioner of correction of this event, and of what the effective date of any documents for the release of any prisoners might be. I am asking, and will ask the attorney general to also inform the commissioner of correction that after this point he is not to release anyone from the state prison without a properly executed document with my signature.

"I want to ensure those who are in our state prisons that they will be treated fairly and in an orderly basis, without any interruption in the orderly processing of those matters which properly should come before the parole board or the governor.

"Next, I will take steps to secure what files need to be secured in connection with these circumstances. Next, I am asking each person who is now a part of government—the commissioners and the staff, the people who work with them and the like—to continue what they're doing, to perform their duties as they would have if this event had not happened today. And in all other respects the government will operate, and the government will change on Saturday as was planned.

"Next I ought to assure those persons who are planning to come to Nashville on Saturday that it is my recommendation to the lieutenant governor and the speaker that the events continue just as we had planned them.

"And, finally, I would like to express to the lieutenant governor and the speaker and the attorney general my respect and appreciation for their acting as I expected them to, and as you would have expected them to, in a spirit of leadership and a spirit that would serve the interests of every Tennessean."

Following this, Wilder and McWherter congratulated Alexander and shook his hand, then the two speakers made brief statements.

"This is an unprecedented event," Wilder said. "It's a time when those of us who are in this position must act responsibly, and I believe we have. I think it's significant that our system continues to work. It's a sound system of government. It's stood many tests. It's continued to stand those tests, and this state is going to move forward in the arena of what should be tomorrow."

McWherter: "After advising with the attorney general, the legal counsel of the state of Tennessee, I feel this action appropriate and at this time under the present circumstances, it is in the best interests of all the people of the state of Tennessee. Governor Alexander, I support you in taking the oath."

At this point, the formal comments ended and the principals and Alexander's family now stepped up onto the courtroom's raised dais, where the justices preside during court sessions, elevated about two feet above the main floor. This movement set off more jostling among reporters. Several stumbled and stepped over power cables strewn in disarray on the courtroom floor, while some of the radio reporters had to untangle their microphone cords.

In this shifted position, radio reporter Allen Williams and two other broadcast journalists now had further difficulty reaching their handheld microphones close enough to function. Honey Alexander, standing next to her husband and still dabbing tears from her eyes, helpfully took the mikes from the anxious reporters. At one point, while holding her daughter Kathryn in the crook of her right arm, she also held four microphones in position with her left hand.

"They kept shoving the microphones up there, and there weren't rules, so I wound up holding a whole slew of microphones for everybody," she recalled. "It had not been planned out. I guess if we had another coup we could probably plan it a little better."

This in effect became a news conference, and the news reporters began learning the details. Alexander, resting his forearms on his son, Drew's, shoulders, recounted the day's developments, telling how the unusual situation had unfolded. He explained that the "new information" delivered by Hardin at midday had persuaded him and the two speakers that action must be taken immediately.

"What was different for me today was two things," the new governor said. "One was specific information from the US attorney, which he called me about. The second was an assurance from the attorney general, himself, which he had not been able to give before, that the assumption of office under these circumstances would be valid."

A rapid series of questions followed this.

Q: With only three days left in Governor Blanton's term, why was it so imperative that you take office now?

A: The US Attorney for the Middle District of Tennessee called me at noon and said that he had substantial reason to believe that Governor Blanton was about to let out of the state prisons one or more persons who were the targets of a grand jury investigation into alleged payoffs in connection with pardons and paroles. With that information, I concluded immediately, as I suppose the speaker and lieutenant governor must have too, that that was new and specific information that demanded that I act if I could.

Q: Will you move into the governor's office tomorrow morning and take charge?

A: I doubt it. I'm going to continue my schedule, which is already planned. I'm going to make sure that papers which need to be secured in the governor's office are secured, or any other place in state government, but I expect to continue as I'd planned—to move in and be open for business on Monday in the governor's office, which is when I had planned to do so.

Q: Where are you headed tonight, sir?

A: I'm going to Jackson, a little late. There's a sixth in a series of receptions that we had planned across the state. There've been several thousand people at each one of them, and I'm going to drive down there after this because it looks like I can't fly because of the weather.

Q: Would you be embarrassed by Mr. Blanton's attendance at the inauguration on Saturday?

A: I haven't thought about that.

Q: Governor, are you going to ask the help of the FBI securing the files at the state capitol tonight, or have you made that request?

A: I haven't made that request and doubt that that will be necessary.

Q: What steps *are* you taking to secure the files?

A: I don't think that will be elaborate. I have asked Tom Ingram, who is now the deputy to the governor, to take what action needs to be taken with the appropriate officials to secure the files.

Q: Are there any indications that Mr. Blanton might resist this?

A: I have not talked with Governor Blanton, and I have no idea what his attitude is.

Q: Do you plan to talk to him tonight?

A: No.

Q: Will he be on the podium with you on Saturday?

A: I think we'll just think about that tomorrow. I think it's up to me and the legislature, and we'll just have to talk about that.

CHAPTER 19

The Scramble

I think it will be recorded that Ray Blanton was his own worst enemy.
—John Jay Hooker

THE DEED WAS DONE.

The officials stepped down from the dais, and the courtroom quickly erupted in noise and more movement. Reporters swarmed McWherter, Wilder, and Secretary of State Gentry Crowell, asking them more questions. The UPI's Fred Sedahl rushed out of the room to the one payphone across the lobby.

"I just hope and pray we did the right thing," McWherter told them in a muted voice, his face serious, somber, and contemplative. "I've plowed new ground and walked a new road. It made you about half sick, but you had to do what you think is responsible."

Hank Allison, who had narrated the run-up to the live broadcast for his station, found John Jay Hooker in the crush. Hooker had lead the short-lived petition campaign to stop Blanton's pardon of Humphreys and also had gone to court to challenge other clemencies after it came to light that a Blanton staff member had signed the governor's name to commutations.

"You've been so involved in this," the reporter said. "You've fought this Humphreys case every step of the way. What's your feeling tonight?"

"I think it's, in many ways, a very sad moment for Tennessee, but in other ways it's a great moment," Hooker replied. "Leadership brings out the best in people, and I believe that the leadership we've seen here tonight, on the part of Lamar Alexander and on the part of the Democrats—Ned McWherter and Lieutenant Governor Wilder, and the attorney general of Tennessee— they've come together and made a decision. They decided to transfer the power of government to prevent the wrongs that have taken place from happening any further."

"When history looks at the Blanton administration, how will it be recognized?"

"I think it will be recorded that Ray Blanton was his own worst enemy. I think he brought it on himself. There was no other viable choice. I think the United States attorney today did what he had to do, and when they heard from the United States attorney, Lamar Alexander and the rest did what they had to do."

Allison's colleague Dave Caylor, the Channel 5 reporter, asked Wilder to comment:

"It had to happen," he replied.

"We had to do what we did do. We wished we had not had to do it, but when the United States district attorney called myself and Mr. McWherter and Governor Alexander and advised us that he had certain information that lead him to believe that a number of people were going to be pardoned or commuted shortly, we had no choice so we acted. . . . Those of us in this position must act responsibly, and I think we have."

In another interview, Wilder called the event "a ceremonial impeachment" that Blanton himself had, regrettably, made necessary.

IN THE CHANNEL 5 STUDIO, there was a pause in the broadcast for a commercial break, and this gave Chris Clark a moment to take a breath and ready himself for the continued live coverage. Clark had promised viewers they would stay with the story until 7:00 p.m.

During this off-the-air break, Clark chatted with two producers off-camera. In a surviving videotape of this out-take, one producer asked aloud:

"Does Ray Blanton have any recourse? Can he do anything? Is he powerless to do anything?"

Another voice: "What if he's already signed some papers, before 5:55?"

Clark replied, "Alexander has issued an order."

They decided to route these question to Allison and Caylor, their reporters up the hill, who could put them to Gentry Crowell, the secretary of state. Crowell had attended the Monday night signing session in Blanton's office. If there were other last-minute commutations, they reasoned, Crowell should know.

STILL INSIDE THE SUPREME COURT building, Allison followed McWherter to the lobby, where there was more room to maneuver with a microphone, camera, and lights. He asked the speaker to describe how he felt, as a leader in the Democratic Party, having now sworn in a Republican governor.

"I don't wish to be indiscrete, Mr. Speaker, but you are of the 'other party' than the man just sworn in as governor, the man whose ouster as governor was felt needed by you and other members of your own party. Could you comment on that?"

The speaker looked tired, his eyeglasses fogged. He gave a long answer, essentially repeating the agreed-on public statement.

"As Governor Alexander said a few minutes ago, at noon today after consulting with the attorney general, our legal counsel of the state of Tennessee, and the information that's been made available to me—like governor Alexander, and Lieutenant Governor Wilder—I felt it appropriate, and under the circumstances, that Governor Alexander take the oath," he said.

"And I might point out that Governor Blanton's term could expire on January 15, and that I thought it would be in the best interests of the citizens of our state and of Tennessee that Governor Alexander take the oath, and I support the governor in taking the oath."

Allison bore in. "OK, a good answer, but you really finessed my question there. Do you care to address that at this point?"

The strain of the long day was on the speaker's face, his broad shoulders looking slumped from fatigue beneath his camel-color sport coat. He had just participated in ousting a sitting governor of his own political party, his friend from the early years, from hardscrabble roots like his own, in the same rural region—and all of that had come to this.

"Repeat your question," McWherter replied.

"The man you just swore in is a Republican," the reporter repeated. "You are a Democrat, and most of the people who participated in the decision to swear him in early are Democrats. The man—"

McWherter, seeming impatient, cut him off.

"Let me say to you," McWherter said. "First, I'm a Tennessean. I think this is in the interest of Tennessee, regardless of the party."

"Thank you very much, sir."

One of the Alexander staffers who had been hastily summoned with the rest to the court building was Susan Richardson Williams, a native of Savannah, Tennessee, just miles from Blanton's hometown of Adamsville.

She had been the political director of the Tennessee Republican Party before joining Alexander's transition team in November 1978. She had the perspective of a longtime political combatant who knew McWherter well as a lifelong Democrat. She told me she sincerely admired him, nonetheless, for his selfless leadership on this one day in 1979.

"I would say that was the most important political decision he [McWherter] ever had to make," Williams said. "I also think that's why so many Republicans came to respect him so much. He knew where Blanton had come from and appreciated what he had accomplished—sort of a 'country boy made good' sort of thing. And yet he had to do this thing, because it was the right thing to do."

In a narrow corridor across the dim lobby, the UPI's Sedahl had dashed quickly out of the courtroom and found Cheek, who was still in possession of the solitary payphone. These two reporters quickly compared notes, using cigarette lighters to illuminate the pages of their notebooks.

Cheek then handed Sedahl the phone, quickly crossed the lobby, and entered the court chamber himself for follow-up interviews. Sedahl dictated additional copy to Tom Humphrey at the UPI bureau office. As Sedahl finished this call, Cheek returned to where he stood and took the telephone receiver from Sedahl's hand.

Cheek turned his back to the lobby. He calmly unscrewed the mouthpiece of the telephone handset and removed the transmitter element. This disabled the phone, rendering it useless by anyone else. He then reattached the mouthpiece and returned the receiver to its cradle on the wall. The two reporters now left the building.

When the AP's Rawlins picked up the same phone to call his own bureau office, the device was dead. He probably heard a dial tone, but certainly no one could hear him.

WHILE THIS WAS HAPPENING DOWNTOWN, at the Tennessee State Prison six miles to the west, a US marshal approached the guard station at the front entrance. The visitor presented a subpoena for Eddie Dallas Denton, the convicted triple-murderer.

More precisely, it was a writ of *habeas corpus ad testificandum* that US district judge Tom Wiseman had signed that morning, at Hardin's request. The document being served this evening required the warden to be prepared to present Denton before the federal grand jury. Practically, it meant that the warden could not release Denton, his availability to testify now being required by the powers that be. It required the state of Tennessee to present a prisoner who was in its custody. When served, the warden knew he had to present the prisoner to the grand jury at a designated time and place.

"When Joe [Brown] and I talked early on the morning of the seventeenth," Hardin told me, "I found out that Denton apparently was going to get out, and I typed an order for Judge Wiseman to sign, in order to produce him [Denton] in front of the grand jury. The marshals served it at the prison at precisely the time—5:56 p.m. as I recall—that the governor was being sworn in."

Now, no matter how many times Denton had been discussed by Blanton's agents, no matter the appearance of his name on documents prepared by the governor's men to give him freedom, nor the shady terms of his release mentioned in taped conversations in Memphis, Mr. Denton would not be leaving the penitentiary for a while.

PATTERSON, IN HER HURRIED, late-afternoon calls to the Alexander staff, had not been able to reach everyone.

Most of these men and women had worked tirelessly over a twelve- to fifteen-month period, to help put Alexander into position to raise his hand and take the oath in January 1979. But, like most Tennesseans, several of these learned from television or radio broadcasts that evening that the strange event had occurred, because of the intense secrecy that had been required through the day.

Francis Guess, who would become a member of Alexander's cabinet on the following Saturday, was on the upper level at 100 Oaks Mall in south Nashville, when he observed other shoppers clustered around a public television set. Curious about the commotion, he stepped closer and saw Alexander take the oath—on the TV screen.

Janice Mashburn, later a deputy press secretary, was still a reporter at the *Jackson Sun* newspaper. She was in the newsroom when word of the early swearing-in came over the newswires. Her city would now be the site of the new governor's first public appearance later in the evening.

Bill and Julia Gibbons, husband and wife who would join Alexander's policy-planning staff the following week, were still at home in midtown Memphis, packing for their move to Nashville.

In Knoxville, John King also was still at home, thinking about his own swearing-in the following Saturday with the other new cabinet members. He would become the head of the Tennessee Department of Revenue.

"I was not aware of the possibility of the early swearing-in," King told me. "I didn't have a clue. My reaction was one of surprise, but a degree of relief that things had been put to an end as far as a continuing saga of bad news. I was just glad to see it happen."

Molly Weaver, the young campaign aide who had traveled to sixty counties with Honey Alexander and who had organized the plane flyover at Neyland Stadium in the fall, was also still at home in Knoxville. She was packing her suitcase for the upcoming weekend in Nashville.

"I had the TV on and they broke into the TV coverage," she remembered. "I was getting my things together to go over to Nashville for the inaugural. It was a Wednesday night, and we had already had the Knoxville reception on Tuesday, the night before, at the UT student center. I remember being surprised and relieved, but also disappointed. This event had taken place that changed everything. It was cold and rainy and changed to snow that night."

In Nashville, at Baptist Hospital, where the long day had begun for Bill and Donna Leech with the birth of their son, another birth was near.

Faye Head, a volunteer in the Alexander campaign and transition office, was also in bed in the labor room, unable to make the drive downtown after Patterson called her in the late afternoon. Instead, she heard the ceremony on a bedside radio. Her son Robert was born three hours later.

The radio news reporter Randall Dickerson had worked at WLAC-AM only since August (1978). Like most news reporters in town, he was then a member of the local chapter of the Society of Professional Journalists (formerly Sigma Delta Chi). This trade group met monthly, and its January meeting was scheduled this same Wednesday evening. The announced guest speaker was to be Governor Ray Blanton, his last appearance there before leaving office on Saturday. By meeting time, of course, not only was the governor otherwise occupied, but so were most of the Nashville press corps.

"All this came down fairly late in the day," Dickerson told me, "so I went out there to the SPJ meeting—at one of the hotels out near the airport—just to see if Blanton would show, and he did not."

FRANK GIBSON, A STAFF REPORTER at the *Tennessean,* taught a Wednesday night class in basic news writing at the University of Tennessee's downtown Nashville campus, located two blocks from the supreme court building. He was not involved in the Blanton coverage but had learned of the developing story before leaving his desk in the newsroom.

When his journalism students arrived in the classroom, Gibson switched on a television and, as a classroom exercise, instructed the them to "cover" the unfolding story and write up mock news stories about what they saw.

"I don't remember being shocked," Judge Tom Wiseman remembered. "I remember being pleased that it happened. I had voted for Lamar because I knew Jake too well. I knew what he'd done; when I was state treasurer, I watched what he did, building the banking empire."

The covert planning through the afternoon had been shrouded in secrecy, particularly from Blanton himself and his inner circle. Alexander explained later why this was necessary.

"There wasn't any training manual for this," he said. "For example, I thought about how the governor is the commander-in-chief of a ten-thousand-member National Guard, and what if he orders National Guard to surround the capitol? He has the authority to do that; he's the governor. We had already agreed to keep Carl Wallace as the adjutant general, and so I asked Tom Ingram shortly before the swearing-in to let General Wallace know what was going on and to make sure that he didn't get orders from Blanton to stop it.

"The same thing could have happened with the highway patrol. We have had occasions in state history where the commander of the highway patrol was putting them all on a train to go break a strike or open a coal mine, and I can see Blanton ordering the highway patrol—but fortunately Gene Roberts had already been appointed, not confirmed, and I was already working with some of the senior members of the highway patrol. We made sure that Gene knew what was happening and that we had a precaution. Those may seem like bizarre possibilities, but nothing was too bizarre for this afternoon, because the whole thing is bizarre.

"I had a conversation with General Leech months earlier, probably as a result of Blanton's shenanigans with [the board of] pardons and paroles, and I asked him the question: 'Can a governor empty the prisons unilaterally?' He said, 'Yes—under the constitution, the answer is yes.' There was the possibility that Governor Blanton could issue another fifty-two pardons or a hundred pardons or a thousand pardons. There was that outside possibility, if he knew about it."

DAVE CAYLOR QUICKLY FOUND Gentry Crowell, who was also still in the supreme court room. He now put the question to Crowell about whether more commutations might have been in process on this day even as the coup occurred.

> CAYLOR: Had governor Blanton signed any more commutations prior to this ceremony this evening, that you know of?
> CROWELL: I have no knowledge of any additional signings. I have had no request from the governor's office to witness his signature, so I assume that there's been no additional signings.
> CAYLOR: You were not in contact with Governor Blanton this afternoon? He didn't try to call your office?
> CROWELL: I've had no contact, since night before last.

CHAPTER 20

The Long Night

If he comes to the capitol tonight, I won't let him in.
—Lewis R. Donelson

FOR THE NEW GOVERNOR, the day had been long, but the night was far from over. There would now be a round-trip to Jackson, Tennessee—a journey of 240 miles—before he slept.

An unmarked highway patrol car was waiting at the curb outside, as Alexander stepped through the supreme court lobby, accompanied by Winstead, a plainclothes officer and former Marine MP.

"I took all the cautions I could," Winstead told me, recalling the crowded court building lobby. He remembered one tense moment when he used his blocking skills, learned in college basketball. "We walked outside together. We were almost holding arms.

"This one guy with the media kept putting the camera right in my back, and I gave him a little elbow right in the ribs, and he went down to the floor," Winstead said. "You know how, when you play basketball, you give somebody a little nudge with your elbow? That was the first time that night Alexander ever said anything directly to me, and he said to me, 'Be easy with them, Herchel, be easy with them.' He always wanted to be easy with the news media. I didn't like them in the first place."

They got into an unmarked sedan with Ed Beckman, another trooper on the security detail. Beckman had first been posted at the Nashville airport, in the afternoon, assigned to wait at the state hangar for the governor-elect and then fly with him to Jackson. A reception had been scheduled at the home of Wade Thompson, who had remodeled his home for the occasion, and the larger public reception at the civic center downtown.

But the foul weather had now disrupted this plan. Because of poor flying conditions, the new governor would have to travel by car, not plane. The private reception at the Thompson home had to be canceled.

"I was waiting at the airport when they called me," Beckman told me. "I drove down to the supreme court building." Winstead reached for the radio transmitter and advised the highway patrol dispatcher that the trip to Jackson, its specific route already planned, was now underway.

"We stopped one time—on Charlotte Avenue, at a Wendy's, I think—and got him a cheeseburger and something to drink, and we went on, out I-40 west, to Jackson," Winstead said. "He didn't have much to say. I told him, 'We're fixing to take the bridle off of this car,' and we turned it loose. We went down to Jackson pretty fast. We had the state already alerted that we were coming through, so we didn't get stopped or anything."

Alexander remembers only the first few minutes of the ride.

"Herchel and Ed drove me to Jackson, and I can still remember their big figures in the front seat, their shapes—two big men sitting in the front seat of the patrol car. I just laid down in the back seat and went to sleep, totally exhausted."

He slept in the rear seat for the remainder of the two-hour drive.

Within minutes of the final question from reporters, word began circulating that further action was occurring up the hill, inside the capitol building.

"As soon as it was over," Travis said, "the network had me do a piece for *Good Morning America*. I moved to a window, to the right side of the courtroom, and used the curtains as a backdrop for my report. It was about that time we found out they were securing the capitol."

Moments before the reporters' questions began, Koch had slipped out the door of the supreme court gallery and met Donelson and Ingram in the lobby, as they and Alexander had prearranged in the garage downstairs forty-five minutes earlier.

In silence, these three now quickly exited the building through the double glass doors to the street. They walked the half block up Charlotte Avenue to the state capitol's south steps, essentially reversing the route that the two speakers and the press corps had taken one hour before. They were now executing their first instructions from the new governor. Their assignment, from Alexander, was to "secure the capitol" and ensure that no essential documents relating to executive clemencies were taken away this night.

All three said later they did not know at this moment what they might encounter when they arrived at their destination up the hill. There had been speculation, earlier in the day, that Blanton might use his last moments in power to order the capitol police or even the Tennessee National Guard to secure the building for himself. What might he ask the military department to do? Would he try to return to the capitol, and delay any further transition? Alexander had mentioned this as a possibility earlier in the day. It was thus a hurried, anxious hike up the hill.

As they climbed the stone staircase on the south side of the historic hill, the high tower of the capitol building loomed in the darkness. Interior lights were muted but visible through the windows, the structure seeming to grow larger as they drew nearer to it. Once atop the hill, they turned to the right and approached the east door, the one facing the equestrian statue of Andrew Jackson, the door nearest the governor's first-floor office.

Just inside that door, meanwhile, a capitol hill police officer was on evening duty at the reception desk, chatting with Richard Chapman, administrative assistant to finance commissioner Bill Jones. This officer had already gotten the call that the doors were to be locked, but now he saw three men approaching the east door. He turned to Chapman and asked him for guidance in view of the new lockdown order. Recognizing Donelson, having met with him over several weeks during the transition planning at the budget office, Chapman told the officer:

"I think you better let them in."

INGRAM REMEMBERS DONELSON ISSUING instructions once they were inside.

"We met one security guard, and Lewie told him to lock the doors and don't let anybody out," Ingram recalled.

"Who are you?" the guard asked.

"Don't ask any questions," Donelson replied. "Lock the doors, and don't let anybody out."

This guard suggested that he should speak with the head of the highway patrol. This quickly led to a phone call in which Donelson requested that two officers he knew and trusted from the Dunn administration—Paul Lane and Johnny White—be assigned to help him. These two appeared at the capitol within fifteen minutes. Donelson posted Lane at the east door and directed White to begin checking all the doors; he was to "advise anyone present to depart immediately and that they could not take any papers with them."

Ingram now went door-to-door, walking from one office to the next across the marble floor of the capitol's executive level. Most offices were closed, but he found Blanton staffer Ken Lavender "having a party in his office, off the governor's big office, three or four of them." It was not clear whether these people had heard the news as yet, but Ingram calmly asked Lavender to "finish up and leave."

FINANCE COMMISSIONER BILL JONES and a young budget analyst, David Manning, were working late in Jones's office on the opposite end of the capitol's first floor. Jones, as head of the state's Department of Finance and Administration, had been an important leader of the customary transition planning from the old administration to the new. This had put him into almost daily communication with Donelson, who would succeed him on Saturday.

"All of a sudden," Manning remembers, "the security officer came in and said the capitol was locked down. We couldn't leave. So we were sort of captive. We really didn't know what was happening. We went to the press office across the hall and watched it happen on the TV." (At this point, what they were watching was a televised replay of the event down the hill, because the lockdown happened after the swearing-in occurred.)

"Later, Lewie [Donelson] came up. We'd been working with him during the transition because he had already been announced as the new commissioner of finance and administration. He told us what had happened."

This moment was Donelson's first visit to what was now his new office.

JUST DOWN THE HALL, Shorty Freeland was still in the governor's suite.

"I was in my office still doing some work," he wrote in his 2011 memoir. "I heard they were closing the doors and not letting anyone come in and not letting anyone go out except employees. All they could take was their purse or their personal things."

Shorty quickly determined he had a problem—remembering a supply of liquor in his desk drawer.

"My desk drawer held at least eight to 10 bottles of whiskey which I had kept here for the legislators who would want to take a break when they were during session. They'd come down and ask me to sweeten their coffee or something, which I did. Finding that in my office might not have been good."

He heard someone mention that Ingram was in the corridor. The two men had first met early in Blanton's term when Ingram was a reporter for the *Nashville Banner*. More recently, he knew Ingram as Alexander's campaign manager and now the top staff person in the transition. Freeland now found Ingram, who helped escort him out of the building, with the box of booze under his arm.

Betty Nixon, who until tonight had been Blanton's deputy press secretary, was in her car driving home when she heard the news on her radio.

"I drove back to the capitol and parked and went in through the door on the lower level," she said. "Arthur Brandon [an employee on the custodial staff] was there, and he said, 'Don't come in. It's better for you to go home.' And so I did."

Tom Benson, who had been Blanton's commissioner of economic development, heard the news on the radio.

He had vacated his state office in the Rachel Jackson Building soon after the November election and taken up temporary quarters at the Capitol Park Inn.

"I was appointed and served at the pleasure of the governor," Benson said. "After the election, my deputy commissioner took over, and I was available to him by phone. But when I heard it on the radio that night, I didn't go back to the office."

Just one block southwest of the capitol, Gene Blanton was in his new office when he heard the news.

For four years, this tall and mysterious man had had the privilege of a desk in the governor's own suite, on the first floor of the capitol building. Now his office was on the fifth floor of the old National Life and Accident Insurance Company building, at the corner of Union Street and Seventh Avenue. (On this same fifth floor, in 1925, WSM-AM had its early radio studio facilities and broadcast the *Grand Ole Opry* radio program from this location.)

The governor's younger brother now departed this new office and attempted to return to his old desk. He walked the short distance and climbed the steps to the south entrance of the capitol, but he could not enter. That door, and all others, had been locked.

JOHN P. BROWN, a criminal defense attorney in Nashville, was unaware of the dramatic event when his office phone rang. The caller was a former client, whose brother was in the state prison serving time for a second-degree murder conviction.

> CLIENT: What can we do?
> BROWN: About what? What's the matter?
> CLIENT: I just saw on TV. Alexander was sworn in. I've already given somebody $12,000. I need to get my brother out. How do I get him out?

"He wanted his money back or his brother out," Brown said. "There were rumblings around that that could happen, but I said I didn't know anything about it and don't want to know anything."

Brown insisted that he knew nothing about payoffs for clemency. He was later elected to a general sessions court judgeship in Nashville and served fourteen years.

Donelson and Koch moved downstairs next, descending an interior staircase through a door across the corridor from the governor's office. On this lower level, they went directly to Bob Lillard's office, a glass-partitioned enclosure on the south end of the floor. Lillard was preparing to leave, holding some paperwork in his hand, when Donelson entered the room.

This gave rise to a dramatic scene, without precedent. It was the first serious confrontation between the old regime and the new.

Two remarkable and accomplished men, Lillard and Donelson were wizened, savvy, elder veterans of legal and political battles. Both were former members of their respective city councils—Lillard in Nashville, Donelson in Memphis. Physically, they were virtual opposites. One black, one white. Lillard stood over six foot three, Donelson shorter of stature, each an iconic role model in his respective realm for a generation of young lawyers, activists, and politicians. Each, in his speaking style, evoked images of Henry Clay, Henry Ward Beecher, Everett Dirksen. These two now sat down—tense, emotional, but lawyerly—and discussed the situation, quickly but rather thoroughly.

"All I want to do," Lillard said, "is take out twenty-eight more pardons and commutations, for the governor to sign tonight. There they are. You can look at them if you want to."

"Judge Lillard," Donelson said, "I don't want to look at them at all. You can't take any documents away from the capitol tonight, period. And that's the end of that."

At this, Lillard, seventy-one, held up a copy of the state's constitution. He contended that Blanton had a few more hours yet in office. Donelson countered with the rationale that had consumed much of the afternoon, and he offered to call the attorney general's office for clarification. Lillard nodded.

Donelson went to the phone and dialed Hayes Cooney, Leech's chief deputy. Cooney confirmed the final opinion of his office that Alexander could have become governor as early as midnight the previous Monday. Lillard now suggested that if he were prohibited from taking the clemency documents to Blanton, then Blanton could come to the capitol and sign them on premises.

"If he comes to the capitol tonight," Donelson said, "I won't let him in."

This prompted a second telephone call. Lillard dialed up Blanton himself, at his residence, but was told he was in the shower. Lillard hung up the phone and said to Donelson, "I think I've done my duty. I'm going to leave. There is one file I'd like to take with me." Donelson said he examined the document, and it pertained to a DUI case that Lillard was working on personally. Donelson permitted him to take this with him.

"Just as he gets to the door, the phone rings," Donelson recalled. "It was Blanton." After a few brief words of explanation, Lillard handed Donelson the phone. Blanton told Donelson he was planning to come to the capitol.

DONELSON: I won't let you in.
BLANTON: Are you saying I can't come into the capitol?
DONELSON: Yes, sir, that's what I'm saying.
BLANTON: The capitol is a public building. By what authority can you keep me out?

DONELSON: By authority of Governor Alexander. He's the new governor.
I was standing there when General Leech called you and told you
that you were no longer governor.

BLANTON: I haven't finished my full four years. What am I going to say
to the press?

DONELSON: Why don't you just tell them you called me, and I told you
you weren't governor anymore?

THE STATE TROOPER MET FRED THOMPSON at the Nashville airport.

A former assistant US attorney, Thompson was an active volunteer member of Alexander's transition team. He had been in a cabinet appointment discussion in Nashville that morning, but was back in Washington, DC, for an afternoon meeting with his client Westinghouse Corporation.

"I got a call—I don't remember who it was from—just that Lamar wanted me to come back right away," Thompson remembers. "I got the next plane I could. I had no idea what was going on. When I got off the plane in Nashville, I was met at the airport by members of the highway patrol. What I didn't realize was that Lamar had announced what I was going to do.

"The troopers kind of filled me in as to what was going on and took me to the capitol, because it had been cordoned off," he said. "They had essentially taken it over and wouldn't let anybody in or out. I remember how surreal the whole thing was. The lights were on. It was an eerie feeling. It was vacant, except for the troopers. The only other person I remember there was Lewie Donelson, and I remember us in the governor's office."

THE PHONE AT AUBREY HARWELL'S HOME rang insistently. The time was 6:15.

Harwell and Jim Neal, his law partner of fifteen years, had signed on to represent Blanton in December 1978, shortly after Sisk and others had been arrested in connection with the clemency scandal. Neal, the former US attorney and Watergate prosecutor, and Harwell were now among the highest-profile lawyers in the US criminal defense bar. But Blanton, Harwell told me, had quickly become "one of our most difficult clients . . . almost totally unmanageable because of his personality."

Within days of the arrests, Hooker and Thomas H. Shriver, the district attorney for Davidson County, filed a complaint in chancery court asking for a ruling that only the governor himself—not anyone else on his staff—could legally affix the governor's signature to prisoner reprieves and pardons. Chancellor Robert S. Brandt agreed and issued an order of temporary injunction on December 21. This also reinforced questions about other official state documents now bearing the governor's signature that may have been affixed by another person on his staff. The person most often mentioned was Kenneth D. Lavender, a staff assistant.

So the first issue for Neal and Harwell, therefore, was to help Blanton deal with hundreds of documents that he must re-sign if they were to continue in force. For Ray Blanton this required a marathon session of signing his name.

"What I remember most vividly," Harwell told me, "was Christmas Eve and Christmas Day, Blanton signing his name. Blanton's position was 'whoever's signature, it was my judgment' but we told him he had to re-sign every one. So he signs these. He's angry. He gets profane. He didn't understand his signature was crucial."

Blanton was now calling Harwell, at home, and insisting that the attorney come to his home as quickly as possible. The two lived less than a mile apart.

"I went to Blanton's house," Harwell told me.

"He said, 'Goddamn it, is it true what they're doing down there?' His first question was 'What has happened, and where does that leave me?' I said I would do my best to find out."

Then Blanton made a very specific request of his attorney.

BLANTON: I have to get some things out of my desk. It would have been nice if somebody had called me. I need to go to the capitol, and I want you to go with me.

HARWELL: You can't do that. You can't go there. What do you need?

BLANTON: It's a paper, a document. It's in the upper-right drawer of my desk.

"He was hell-bent to get down there to the capitol," Harwell told me. "I knew they weren't going to let him in." Harwell then remembered, from the breaking news bulletins, that Alexander had also announced he was appointing Fred Thompson to serve as a special counsel, to take the lead in sorting out the clemencies Blanton had already issued. Harwell and Thompson were law school classmates at Vanderbilt and had been friends for years.

"At this point, I was not clear about the extent of Fred's role in this," Harwell recalled. "I told Blanton I would try to get hold of Hal Hardin, and failing that I [would] try Bill Leech or Fred Thompson. I called several numbers. I called Bob Lillard's office. Tom Ingram may have answered the phone, as an intermediary in my search for Fred. Fred called me back. He was very accommodating. We danced for a while. He said, 'I'm not sure I can do that.'

"I said there was nothing in the document relative to the investigation,"

Harwell said. "I said my motivation was to avoid getting Betty [Blanton] hurt."

Thompson remembers this phone conversation with Harwell and said he did find an envelope containing a document in the desk drawer. He said he could not, three decades later, remember its contents but did recall that he cleared it for release to Blanton.

Koch saw the document, however. He said it was checked and ultimately removed from the many files that FBI agents would cart away from the governor's office the following day. The envelope and its contents were reviewed, determined to have no value to the FBI investigation, and approved for release to Blanton's counsel.

"The envelope you're talking about was up in the governor's office," Koch told me, "and it had absolutely nothing to do with the FBI investigation. It had to do with the governor's girlfriend."

The envelope was delivered to Harwell the following day.

WHILE THIS WAS OCCURRING, the telephone in Hal Hardin's kitchen rang. It was John Seigenthaler calling, and the conversation that followed was not pleasant. The notion of secrecy was on his mind, too—that there had been too much of it.

Hardin did not attend the swearing-in ceremony, although his presence had been one of Alexander's "conditions" during the afternoon. Alexander had hoped the US attorney would participate in the ceremony, because it would add another prominent Democrat to the scene. Henry had advised Hardin not to come—feeling it was an inappropriate participation in a state matter by an officer of the federal government. At the end of the afternoon, Hardin had decided he would just go home.

When he finally departed room 416 at the Sheraton, he drove the short distance from the hotel garage to another underground parking facility across McGavock Street from the federal building. He walked through a private underground tunnel connecting the garage to the Kefauver Building basement, and he took the private elevator up to his office, which was now closed and with the lights switched off.

In the darkness, he noticed the message light was blinking on his desk phone. He lifted the receiver and heard a recorded message.

"I pushed the button and it was Blanton's security guard," Hardin remembered. "He said, 'Mr. Hardin, the Governor wants to talk to you.' It was like something out of a movie. There was nobody there."

Hardin did not return the call. Instead, he removed the cassette tape from the answering machine, stuck it in his jacket pocket, returned to his car and drove home. His residence at this time was on Glen Leven Drive, just seven houses away from the governor's official residence. When he arrived there, his wife, Pia, and mother-in-law, Mrs. Jack Norman Sr., were standing in the kitchen.

"You're home early," she said.

"Yeah, turn on the TV and watch it."

Together, they watched the dramatic oath-taking ceremony on a small television set. Mrs. Norman then looked at her son-in-law and said, "You did such a good job!"

At that moment, the kitchen phone rang.

"What in the hell have you done?" the editor shouted. "You and your damned secrecy! Is this a damned banana republic coup you're running around here?"

Seigenthaler told me later, in an interview that Hardin attended, that he had been mainly frustrated as the long afternoon wore on that his staff had been unable to get advance word of the swearing-in.

"John just went through the roof," Hardin recalled.

The US attorney's office had yielded no helpful information to date, and Seigenthaler thought he might be able to bait Hardin into giving him the full story now. Feigning anger was his tool of choice.

"We couldn't get a break on the story," Seigenthaler said. "Here I am, sitting there, we're going to get busted in the *Banner* tomorrow afternoon, and I'm trying to shake it loose."

This call didn't yield any new facts, either.

YEARS LATER, IN THE joint interview with Hal Hardin, Seigenthaler reflected on the sequence of events of that day, on his knowledge of statehouse politics at the time, and of McWherter's way of handling problems.

In this interview, Hardin told Seigenthaler about the early call he had received from McWherter offering to assist if the US attorney needed his help. ("General, this is Ned McWherter. I just want to let you know that if you ever need my help, I'm here to help you.") Seigenthaler speculated on McWherter's thinking at the time. Just as Alexander had "stage-managed" the principal officials at the extraordinary ceremony, giving them their instructions in the privacy of the robing room, was it possible McWherter had simply had enough of Blanton's bizarre and reckless behavior in office, which threatened both party unity and, in the end, public safety?

"You have to consider how deeply serious the crimes were, and how imperative it was to get rid of him," Seigenthaler said. "I think Lamar would have wanted to get rid of that, and I think Ned would have wanted to get rid of it, but John [Wilder] less. Everyone was scandalized by it. . . . I do think you could identify Ned McWherter as the architect of Ray Blanton's agony."

McWherter, for his part, would not speak again of this night for many years.

Ken Renner, who was a capitol correspondent for the *Knoxville Journal* from 1980 to 1985, served as McWherter's communications director after the 1986 election.

"He never talked about it much," Renner told me, "but when he did he wasn't sorry for what he did. He would answer questions, but it wasn't something he wanted to spend a lot of time on. I think it was painful for him. He knew Blanton, had campaigned with him, was part of the 'West Tennessee Mafia.' To see it come to that, and how it ended . . . I don't think anyone would feel a terrible amount of pride."

Gene Blanton, the deposed governor's brother, told me McWherter visited Blanton years later. He claimed the speaker "apologized" for assisting in the 1979 coup, but this version is disputed. McWherter had died by the time of this interview and I was unable to put the question to him, but several of his closest associates, including his son, Mike McWherter, and also Billy Stair, insisted that he would not have used that word.

"More likely," Stair suggested, "what he said was that he was sorry that they had *had* to do it."

Harwell, Blanton's attorney, said the former governor told him later that McWherter had come to his home before the end of January and "told him how bad he felt about it."

"That was typical of Ned McWherter," the attorney added. "He did the right thing, but he also had a huge awareness of how others suffered and wanted to support them in that time. He never kicked a man when we was down but tried to help him up."

For all that McWherter and Blanton had in common throughout their lives—region of birth, hardworking youth, Democratic politics—this, Harwell said, was a point of contrast between the two men. Blanton, he said, "had a cavalier indifference to other people."

THE SUPREME COURT LOBBY now emptied rapidly, as reporters fled to file their news stories, and the public scene now shifted to Blanton's home, on Jefferson Davis Drive, in southern Davidson County. Here, reporters began to gather in the front yard, anticipating an appearance and a statement from the suddenly former governor.

Mike Donegan, a radio reporter for WSM-AM, was at home asleep when his telephone rang. It was his station's assignment editor. "Fay Esters called, woke me up, told me what was going on, and said I should go on out to Blanton's home," Donegan remembered.

Pat Nolan, reporter for Channel 5, remembers being dispatched to the residence after someone in the governor's press office sent word that Blanton was at home and might have a statement at some point in the evening. Nolan and his photographer arrived but remained in their car for several minutes, seeing the front door closed and no one yet appearing from inside the house. Rain had begun to fall.

Mike Pigott, staff reporter for the *Nashville Banner,* and Mark McNeely of the *Knoxville News-Sentinel* were also among the first journalists to arrive. Soon after, other news media appeared, and a crowd began to assemble on the rain-soaked front lawn. Nolan remembered standing on the wet lawn and feeling that Blanton was intentionally keeping the reporters waiting.

Suddenly the front door opened. Ray and Betty Blanton stepped onto the porch. Reporters quickly gathered around them. Donegan described the scene:

"It was early evening. It was dark by the time he came out. We were all standing around in the yard. He came out on the porch. I remember Blanton and his wife came out. Somehow Ray Blanton's son wound up with the WKDA news microphone and holding the microphone into his father's face. I had my own microphone, but his son was holding the microphone like he was the reporter."

Anne Marie Deer told me it was the audio recorded by the young Blanton that she used on the air in WKDA newscasts that night and through the next day. In this awkward news conference on his front porch, television lights illuminating the scene through the light mist, Blanton was asked how he learned about the event that put him out of office. He said he had had "no inkling" of what was planned.

"The attorney general called just before it happened, but I had already heard it on Cronkite's show," Blanton told the reporters on his lawn. "There is such a thing as courtesy. I would have the courtesy to tell me. This was not necessary. Why didn't the US attorney call me? I am saddened for the people of Tennessee.

"I thought that was very thin when they started predicting what I might do," he added. "I would have relinquished the office yesterday if they had asked me. We've tried our best. I feel for the new governor and how he was put into this situation."

SANDY CAMPBELL WAS the *Tennessean* editorial cartoonist and a member of the newspaper's editorial board. He was accustomed to finishing his work—filling an honored horizontal space on the editorial page with his handiwork—and leaving the office each day before 6:00 p.m.

Not today.

The morning had unfolded in the normal way. He came to the daily 10:00 a.m. editorial board meeting with a collection of preliminary sketches. When his turn came, he passed these around the table for the editors to consider and discuss. The final decision maker was Seigenthaler, who selected one for publication the next morning. As usual, Campbell returned to the drawing table in his office, and through the early afternoon he executed the final cartoon in detail.

But on this day, at the end of the afternoon, Seigenthaler told Campbell what was happening downtown—the sudden transfer of power at the capitol—and asked his cartoonist to come up with a new drawing for the next day's editorial page. Campbell returned to his drawing table once again and worked into the evening.

As he pondered the situation and considered possible elements for this hurried new drawing, Campbell concluded it would necessarily be a vertical image, not horizontal as the editorial page traditionally required. For this, he had to obtain permission from the editorial board. When they saw his new sketch, they quickly agreed to the formatting change.

In the new cartoon, which ran Thursday morning, Campbell depicted the high tower of the Tennessee state capitol, in the dark of night, with the state flag attached to the halyard in the customary fashion. But tied below it, knotted to the same halyard by the cuff of each sleeve, was Alexander's red-and-black plaid shirt, unfurled against a full moon.

JOHN PARISH WAS ALREADY in Jackson when Alexander arrived with the troopers. The new governor's press secretary met them outside the Jackson civic center. Inside, the people were waiting—now with the added measure of excitement of the news from Nashville they had seen on TV monitors in the building. "The people waited," Beckman remembers. "They stood around 'til we got there."

Parish had arrived at the civic center early "to be sure everything was in order in my home town," and then he drove to the airport to meet Alexander's plane.

"When his plane was seriously late, I suspected that something had gone wrong," Parish wrote in his private memoir. "Lamar was conscientious about being on time, and it was not like him to be late without at least letting someone know."

Parish then got word of what had happened in Nashville, and also that heavy fog had made it unlikely the state plane would be able to fly to Jackson, necessitating a drive of 120 miles.

"That meant he would be seriously late for the public reception, and that he would have to cancel the private reception," Parish wrote. "The latter did not go over very well with the host, who had spent a lot of money preparing his home for the governor's visit. I assured him that we would reschedule it at a later date, but that wasn't completely satisfactory at the time."

In contrast, the reception at the civic center was triumphant.

"I went directly to the civic center to urge people to wait and to apologize for the delay," Parish noted. "My apologies and urging were not necessary;

instead of people leaving, more were arriving after learning of the sensational developments in Nashville."

Though nearly two hours behind schedule, Alexander's arrival in the hall was triumphal. Instead of being one of the last regional thank-you receptions preceding the Saturday inauguration, the event had been transformed into the first public greeting of the new governor. Alexander estimated later that he shook several thousand hands that night.

WHEN THE CEREMONY AT the supreme court ended, Honey and the children departed for their new home, accompanied by Carole Martin. When they arrived, Honey's close friend Carole Sergent was in the kitchen, waiting with a steaming pot of chili for dinner. (While the Blantons lived there, they had continued the tradition at the official residence of using state prisoners as house staff. During the transition period, the Alexanders decided that this practice would be terminated, once the Blantons departed.)

Carole and her husband, Dr. John Sergent, were among the Alexanders' oldest couple friends. The two men had met at Vanderbilt, where Sergent was active in student government and studied medicine, during the time Alexander was editor of the student newspaper. Honey and Carole Sergent met later in Washington, DC, when Lamar brought Honey to dinner with the Sergents one evening. John was then an intern at Johns Hopkins, while Alexander was on Baker's Senate staff.

"Honey told me to go over to the governor's residence and help them unpack," Carole Sergent remembers. "I remember they were coming in later that night, to spend the night. I knew something was going on. She had told me earlier he was going to be sworn in. I was in the bedroom, just trying to get them settled for one night."

After the chili dinner, the children were put to bed, and Carole Martin departed with Trooper Hugh Hayes for her final ride of the day. Her own car was still sitting at the Alexanders' empty residence on Golf Club Lane. From there she drove home.

In the sudden stillness of the Alexander family's new residence, Honey and Carole Sergent sat together in the large kitchen for a few minutes more and reflected on the long day. Then the two friends said good night, and Carole drove home.

Honey climbed the stairs and went to bed. She soon fell asleep.

CHAPTER 21

The White Morning

Sunday, when it snowed, it was like all of it had been washed away.
—Honey Alexander

NEWS OF THE COUP dominated front pages of the next day's newspapers, and still more elected officials spoke their minds.

"It had to be done to stop the insanity of Ray Blanton," said Senator Victor Ashe, the Republican from Knoxville. He described the ousted governor as "an individual who went berserk." Senator Joe Crockett, a Democrat from Nashville: "We kind of feel we've had our own little Watergate. It's a sad time to be a Democrat. I hope the people don't judge the party by the actions of its former leader."

The two days that followed, Thursday and Friday, were full of more quick decisions through an uncharted situation. If there had been "no road map" for the coup itself, this first full day of the accelerated transition was a time unlike any encountered before in American history.

Alexander did not go to the capitol on these two days. He would not sit at his new desk until Monday morning, following the scheduled inauguration on Saturday. Ingram, Donelson, and a few others did arrive early on Thursday to begin reorganizing the office, but on Bill Koch's advice, no official decisions were to be made. The new cabinet officers, who would not be sworn in until Saturday, were cautioned not to visit their new offices until Monday morning and, in any case, were not to transact any government business until after the weekend. This was chiefly to minimize the chances for any legal challenge from outside parties to official acts that might otherwise have been made between Wednesday night and Saturday morning.

In spite of the high volume of television news coverage throughout the night before, at least two members of Blanton's administrative staff at the capitol had not seen or heard the news and arrived for work as normal. For them the day would be most abnormal. They quickly discovered the world was upside down.

ONE OF THESE STATE EMPLOYEES was Lee Lucas. She and her friend Terry Huffman, who worked on the opposite end of the floor in the finance and administration office, normally carpooled to and from their homes in Hendersonville. This morning, neither was aware the coup had occurred.

On Wednesday afternoon, Lucas and Huffman had departed the capitol at about 5:00 p.m. as usual. Once home, Lucas quickly departed to meet her sister Diane, who had offered her an after-hours job assisting with end-of-year inventory at Castner-Knott Company, the retail department store in Hendersonville. Since the inventory work ran into the late evening, Lucas did not see either the 6:00 or 10:00 p.m. local news on television.

"Next morning, Terry and I drove back in to the capitol, and we saw TV trucks parked outside," she said. "I just assumed that was because of the earlier investigation. It wasn't unusual to see TV trucks there. The capitol had already been invaded once by the FBI. Terry parked and we went in. It was about a quarter to eight."

Reporters were in the hallway, clustering around the governor's office.

"I thought, 'Wow, what's going on?' I just assumed I was still working for Blanton, thinking I haven't heard yet from the new administration, but hoping I would hear something. I was mainly just coming in until I was told to do something different. Terry went to her office, on the other end of the first floor, and I went to the reception room. Tom Ingram was there. There were two reporters and a TV camera. I put my purse down at my desk."

INGRAM: Are you Lee Lucas?
LUCAS: Yes.
INGRAM: We need to talk.

He led her behind a pair of double doors, into the space that had been Gene Blanton's unofficial office. Lucas, at this moment, was wondering, "Is this where he tells me to leave? Am I still going to have a job?" This conversation was tense but brief.

"Lamar Alexander was sworn in early," Ingram told her. "They're all gone. He swung his arm in a sweeping motion. "We need you to keep doing what you've been doing as receptionist. Do what you always did. There will be a lot of reporters up here today. You'll have some help."

"He introduced me to Sharon Sinclair," Lucas told me. "I think they knew I could show them what to do with the phones. I cried. He was so kind. I'd been thinking he was going to tell me I didn't have a job anymore. Instead, he was asking me, 'Can you do this. Do you want it?' I said yes.

"It was about eight o'clock now. The last thing Tom said before we went out was 'Remember to say 'Governor *Alexander's* office.' I said, 'Got it. Gov. *Alexander's* office.'"

SHORTY FREELAND, IN HIS memoir *Ray Blanton and I*, remembers returning to his office on Thursday and seeing new faces.

"The next morning I went to work as normal because I knew some of the girls working were scared," he wrote. "I was going to be there to give them some backup, or to let them know I was not afraid of what's going on.

"So I walked into my office, and there was an FBI agent going through my waste basket. I said, 'Sir, I don't have any problem with your doing that, but I might have spit in there last night, and you might get it on your hands.' I didn't, but I just had to say that. He raised his hands up and began to wipe them."

THE WEEKEND AT LAST ARRIVED, with the chill of winter, Saturday morning gray and blustery and cold. The temperature had dropped to thirty-one degrees overnight, and in the reluctant morning light, the leaden sky reflected a muted spirit.

The expansive War Memorial Plaza in Nashville is a granite promenade edged with trees and fountains, and surrounded by history and the memory of celebrations, protests, and presidents. Situated on its west perimeter is the stolid War Memorial Building housing legislative offices, a venerable performance hall, and part of the state museum. To the north, across Charlotte Avenue, stands the state capitol on a hill once called Cedar Knob, the highest natural point in the central city.

To the east, across Sixth Avenue, are two other state office buildings, one named for Rachel Jackson, wife of Old Hickory, the other for President James K. Polk. To the south, across Union Street, stands the Hermitage Hotel, site of the final negotiations in 1920 that made Tennessee the thirty-sixth state to ratify the Nineteenth Amendment to the US Constitution, giving women the right to vote.

On this central plaza, workmen were lining up the last of the folding chairs, all facing a raised platform, as early guests began to arrive at 9:30 a.m., the clock ticking toward 11:00—the time scheduled for the formal inauguration. On the rostrum, dignitaries began to arrive in their topcoats, suits, and hats against the wind.

TV reporter Bob Mueller, who later became anchor for Nashville's ABC affiliate, was working for WTVC-TV in Chattanooga at this time. On Wednesday evening, he had been at his desk in the Chattanooga news room when the early bulletins came in about the extraordinary ceremony that ousted Blanton. Today, three days later, he was in Nashville, on assignment to cover the formal inauguration.

"It was messy weather—raining and cold," he said. "Everything was just gray and somber."

ALEXANDER AND HIS FAMILY now appeared. And legislative leaders, and members of the new governor's cabinet, who would be sworn in following this event. Tennessee's two US senators, Howard Baker and Jim Sasser, appeared—Baker moving courteously about the platform with his camera, taking photographs of the people and scene. Other members of the Tennessee congressional delegation, including the elder congressman Jimmy Quillen, were there. Former governor Dunn appeared on the dais. And two visiting governors, Linwood Holton of Virginia and Cliff Finch of Mississippi. And all these could look up, to their left, and see the south face of the state capitol building towering above, shrouded in the morning mist.

What none of them saw was the former governor. Ray Blanton was not there. He thus became the first governor in the state's history not to attend the swearing-in of his successor. It was his own decision.

ALEXANDER NOW TOOK the formal oath of office for the second time in four days, this time in overcast daylight.

Once more, Honey Alexander held the large family Bible, again opened to II Timothy. Again, Chief Justice Henry administered the same oath. Once more, McWherter, Wilder, and the constitutional officers were in attendance.

"If Wednesday was a sad day for Tennessee," Alexander declared in his inaugural speech, "today is a happy one—for the people and their government are back together again. The pain will stay with us for a while. But today there's room for pride, as well."

The rest of his inaugural address, while hopeful, was somber and earnest about the fundamental challenges of modern government. He made but one reference to the week of outrage and upheaval, asking:

"How can the people and their government stay together with trust and pride? The power of government makes corruption so easy. The size of government makes the people so distant. The computers of government make indifference so likely. The noise of government makes listening so rare. No wonder government becomes the enemy. No wonder pride gives way to resentment or bitterness or fear. No wonder our young people turn away from the profession of public service in dismay and disgust.

"I do not know how much of this we can change. But I know we must try."

When the young governor concluded his remarks, the dignitaries on the rostrum and the people across the crowded plaza—most of them holding umbrellas against the light rain—now gave a great applause. A smile was seen on Honey Alexander's face.

"It was a much happier occasion," she remembers. "We felt like things were a little more under control. People had come from all across the state, family members came from out of state, friends had come, and it was just more of an upbeat event. We have a dear friend who lives in Gulfport, Mississippi, and at the time he arrived, we washed the seafood, and he cooked for us a big wonderful dinner. That helped."

One special guest was the federal judge, John Minor Wisdom, for whom Alexander had worked as a young clerk in New Orleans.

Lew Conner, one of Alexander's oldest friends and his law partner until the election, had been entrusted with the custody of four special couples through the busy weekend, providing them with hospitality, introductions, and ground transportation. The four men had been Alexander's roommates at the New York University law school: Paul Tagliabue, Bill Plunkett, Barney Haynes, and Ross Sandler.

By this time, Haynes had become a distinguished litigator at King and Spalding in Atlanta, Sandler was a senior attorney at the Natural Resources Defense Council (and later the New York City commissioner of transportation), and Plunkett was a lawyer in Westchester County, New York (where he had a young associate named George Pataki, later a three-term governor of New York state). Tagliabue, a Washington lawyer at Covington and Burling, represented the National Football League. (After Tagliabue became commissioner of the NFL, in 1989, the five former roommates would meet for a private party each year the night before the Super Bowl.)

Molly Weaver, the young campaign operative who had arranged for the plane and banner over Neyland Stadium, remembers the official inaugural as subdued, not celebratory.

"The day of the swearing-in was cold and rainy too," she said. "I had maybe gone to Nashville a couple of times in my life. I was amazed at the plaza, and I remember being very disappointed. I was actually disappointed for them—the Alexanders—because they weren't getting to do things the way they had planned.

"It was the first hard lesson—that it's not about the celebratory part of it, it's really about the responsible part of it. We had all been true believers, but it had also been fun. Now it was clear there is a huge responsibility that goes with it."

The remainder of the day was given to swearing in the new cabinet, in a ceremony inside the War Memorial Building auditorium, and to the inaugural parade that lasted three hours. Because of the fitful weather, Honey excused herself at one point, and other dignitaries came and went. Conner and Echols remained on the viewing stand with Alexander through the long afternoon.

"Lamar stood there in that wretched weather for the full three hours and watched ninety-five bands—one from each county—march by," Conner said. "Fully ninety of them played 'Rocky Top' [later designated one of Tennessee's state songs]. It was the coldest I have ever been."

In the evening, three inaugural balls in different venues across the central city featured food, music, and dancing. At each of these, Honey Alexander wore a maternity-tailored gown and danced with the new governor to repeated strains of "The Tennessee Waltz."

On Sunday morning, January 21, Honey Alexander remembers waking to see new fallen snow, all white and even across the broad lawn of the executive residence on Curtiswood Lane. It covered the grass and topped the shrubbery and trees, everything under a quiet blanket of white.

"Sunday, when it snowed, it was like all of it had been washed away," she said. "It was a new day, and it was bright, beautiful. It was clean again. You know, all that gray dirtiness was behind us."

LATER THAT MORNING, the Alexander family, including his parents, Andy and Flo, and their guests gathered at Westminster Presbyterian Church on West End Avenue. The sanctuary was not full, owing to the weather and expectations of standing room only. For this special worship service, the governor's brother-in-law the Reverend William Carl, husband of his sister Jane, delivered the sermon.

"And what did Solomon pray for? 'Give therefore thy servant an understanding heart to govern thy people, that I may discern between good and evil.' . . . How difficult that is to do, even today; for in real life distinction between good and evil is never as clear cut as the good guys and the bad guys or the characters in *Star Wars*. Every area of our lives, whether in politics, business, or the church, is fraught with compromise and gray-area decisions. . . .

"What Solomon prayed for essentially was that he be a good man—something all public officials should covet," Reverend Carl continued. "Lamar's mother told me not long ago that all she has ever prayed for Lamar, since he was a child, was that he be a good man."

Sunday afternoon was devoted to public receptions at the governor's residence. Between 1:00 and 5:00 p.m., an estimated five thousand visitors passed through.

ON THIS SAME SUNDAY morning, Donna Leech finally departed Baptist Hospital, with tiny Will III swaddled in a warm blanket against the biting air. Donna's mother, Sara Babb, of Oak Ridge, had flown into town this morning to help out, so the attorney general's first stop had been at the Nashville airport to pick her up. Later today, he would drive to Charlotte to fetch Katie, now eleven, who had been staying with his mother. She would meet her new brother in the afternoon.

Donna had now been at the hospital for a full week. Bill had visited her often, but usually in the evening after Will had already been removed to the nursery for the night. On one of his visits, Bill brought his daughters Anna and Becca to see the new baby, but their first glimpse of him had also been through the glass of the nursery window. It was not until this Sunday morning—when father, mother, grandmother, and infant finally left the hospital together—that Leech finally held the baby in his own arms for the first time.

The four of them now loaded into the single seat of the gray pickup truck. With Leech behind the wheel, Sara on the passenger side, and Donna in between them holding Will, they headed south. The trip took about an hour. At last, they turned off Highway 247 in Maury County and onto Highway 7, commonly called Santa Fe Pike.

When Leech steered the pickup off the pike, he did not drive up to the house immediately. He stopped at the bottom of the driveway, which on its hillside circuit formed a teardrop or heart shape, the Constitutional Oak standing just inside the point at the bottom of the hill. From this position, they could now see the house through the trees. To their right, they could look across the rolling pasture beyond the rail fence.

Donna remembers how the new snowfall had dusted house, barn, and field, reflecting the late morning sunshine, adding brilliance to the new day. The air was cold and the breeze biting, but to the eye, the scene was as warming as a Christmas card—made warmer still by hearts full of tender emotion, and great expectations for new life. She remembers Bill paused here, where the bundled infant was near the fields and farm for the first time, in view of the hills rising in the distance.

"Welcome home, Will Leech," the father said, aloud, on the white morning.

THE FOLLOWING FRIDAY, January 26, Betty Nixon visited Blanton at his new home on Jefferson Davis Drive. Her purpose was to deliver a few keepsake photos that she had set aside for him while boxing up materials in the press office.

Mrs. Blanton greeted her at the front door—on the same front porch where the immediately former governor, standing with his wife and young son, had held the impromptu session with the reporters on the Wednesday night of the coup—and invited her in. Inside, Nixon observed, Blanton was watching three television sets.

"He had three TVs on and was watching all three channels at the same time," she told me. "I said, 'Why don't you turn those off?'

"But he didn't turn them off. He kept watching."

A DOZEN YEARS AFTER the coup, three men who had shared that day in history now shared a moment of strange serendipity at a father-daughter banquet on a Nashville riverboat.

The three daughters, now classmates in high school, had become best friends. Once they were inside the banquet hall, on board Opryland's *General Jackson* showboat, the grand paddle wheeler on the Cumberland River at Nashville, the girls decided they would sit together for the festive evening.

They proceeded to introduce their dads.

"Not knowing who our daughters' best friends were," Tom Ingram remembered, "they pull all the fathers to the table—and there's Hal Hardin and Eddie Sisk and me at the same table." By this time Hardin was no longer the US attorney, and Sisk had served his sentence.

"And the girls don't know the history. How could they? How quickly the generations move on."

Epilogue

What Became of Them

They never spoke of it after.

Among the principals, there were no further meetings on the subject, ever. In later years, Wilder seemed the least inclined to discuss the coup or to revisit the decision or the day in any form. McWherter did not bring up the subject with the others; in a 2005 interview, he said he had never discussed the coup even with Wilder, whom he knew for forty-three years as legislative colleague, fellow party elder, and friend. Nor did Alexander and Leech, who as governor and attorney general worked together most closely through the early years of the new administration, ever discuss the coup again.

Hardin quickly resumed his work as the US attorney and, two years later, left that post to return to his private law practice in Nashville. Chief Justice Joe Henry, for the remaining months of his life, likewise kept his own counsel about what he had done and why.

There was one attempt at a reunion of sorts, but it was canceled before it happened.

It was to be a private dinner, one year later, at the governor's residence. Only eight people were to attend: the six principals—Alexander, the two speakers, Hardin, Leech and Henry—plus Lewis Donelson and Tom Ingram.

"It was Lamar's idea," Hardin recalled. "He said, 'You know, we all ought to get together while we still remember, and talk about it."

At the time, Alexander instructed his staff not only that the evening would be private but also that if news reporters or others inquired about the gathering, no one should call it an "anniversary" nor use any other term suggesting celebration. Instead, it would simply be described for what it was— the first occasion the small group of participants in the coup had had to come together, out of range of reporters and TV cameras, to reflect quietly together on what had transpired, what they had done, the history they had made.

"I wanted to do it out of curiosity, and maybe for history," Alexander told me. "We all knew what we'd individually done that day—and why—but I don't think any of us knew much about what the others had done."

In short order, all agreed to attend, except Wilder. When he declined, Alexander quickly called the whole thing off—worried that some of the others might then reconsider and stay away also, or that word of the dinner would get around more publicly and its purpose be misreported and misunderstood, or both.

"He [Wilder] was afraid it might look like he was participating in something that was gloating over Ray Blanton's demise," Alexander told me. "He was Ray Blanton's state senator, that was his territory, and he was a cautious man anyway. And so we didn't have the dinner."

Five months later, Joe Henry was dead.

There were a handful of retrospective events over the years involving a few of the surviving participants, mostly organized by the legal communities in Knoxville and Nashville. A public program at Vanderbilt University in April 2012 featured Alexander and Hardin on a panel discussion that also included Fred Thompson and Bill Koch, and Donelson was in the audience. But by this time the other principals in the coup were gone. Bill Leech died in 1996, Wilder in 2010, and McWherter the year after that.

Hal Hardin told me, in 2011, that even he and his old friend Bill Leech never revisited the subject of the coup, did not look back together on how the awkward afternoon had unfolded in room 416 on that cold January day. He also said that over three decades, he and Alexander never reminisced about the extraordinary midday phone call, nor how the decision was finally made just four hours later.

Alexander confirmed this. He told me, in fact, that he had been unaware of many of the specific actions of Hardin and of Leech through that long afternoon of the fateful day, until he read this manuscript.

Nor was it necessary to talk about it.

The decision, though unprecedented, was efficiently transacted. It was a job that needed doing, and the principal officials did it without any excess of review or palaver afterward. Though the final minutes of the transition became suddenly very public, the principals had determined that their decision had to be made in strictest secrecy—lest more prisoners be irretrievably released, lest civil disorder ensue—and possibly this sensitivity continued through later months and years to influence their understanding of the coup. The gravity of the action, and the fact of all the lives it changed, no doubt added to their reticence in discussing it.

Momentous as it was, it even seems in hindsight now as if the coup were one more decision requiring the attention of certain officials, each in his own capacity, each using his best wits and leadership skills, and that they came together for only the moment that the odd transaction required. In that moment, they did their respective duties, as professionals and as politicians, each mindful of his own unique constituency, and then they moved on.

For that matter, the coup was essentially never challenged.

The first challenge might have come from Blanton himself. He was angry and bitter over his ouster, but his own attorneys, Neal and Harwell, advised him to drop it.

"The first question," Harwell remembered, "was whether it was legal for Lamar to be sworn in early. Blanton was raising forty kinds of hell about it that night. Neal and I talked about, 'Should we fight it, or are we better off letting it go? Do we really want to go to war about it?' We didn't want to fight it. We looked at the law, and Neal thought it [the early swearing-in]was legal. He and I, throughout our partnership, would not view things just from a legal basis. Neal would talk about the court of public opinion, and how it was sometimes a cost-benefit analysis.

"When we found out the people who were involved in this—Wilder, McWherter, Leech, Hardin, Lamar, Donelson, Tom Ingram—all of them so respected—even if it had been illegal, our view was, what would be gained by fighting it? You would just piss off people who were already pissed off at you, and what's the benefit? By the time you get the papers filed, my goodness, the real inauguration date would have come and gone."

Others did try. In the months following, a number of the inmates whom Blanton had reprieved on the preceding Monday night—but who, on Alexander's order, were not physically released—went to court seeking their freedom. The closest to a legal challenge to Alexander's early taking of the office came in these proceedings. In criminal court, Nashville attorney Ed Yarbrough, representing convicted armed robber Joseph W. McKenna, argued in part that Alexander had no authority to halt the releases because the early swearing-in was legally groundless. Judge Raymond H. Leathers ruled that McKenna had been legally reprieved by Blanton and ought therefore to be released, but he rejected the argument about the validity of the early swearing-in.

There was never a contrary conclusion by any higher court.

NOR WAS THE COUP ever attacked politically. Doug Bailey, Alexander's campaign consultant, later suggested that any thought of a political challenge would have been blunted by Alexander's soaring public image by this time.

"Nobody ever challenged it," Bailey said. "I do believe Blanton had very few friends by that point—that was clear—but I also believe Lamar had an image that was so unusual and spotless and that he had done this thing—

that maybe most people laughed off, to begin with, but it became an amazing feat—to have walked across the state—no cheating, no nothing—staying in people's homes overnight, and all that. It gave him an aura of 'this is not politics as usual' and by the time this [the coup] happened, there was a degree of trust involved that I have never seen involved in our politics—ever—a sense that if he's doing it, it must be OK."

IN ONE INTERVIEW LATER, Wilder referred to Blanton's removal as "impeachment, Tennessee style" but he said little else about the episode. For the most part, no one asked him to elaborate. After the first weeks following the event, in fact, there were even few interviews with the principals.

In our 2012 interview, Wilder's younger son, David, discussed the significance of the coup in a manner that probably indicated how the lieutenant governor may have felt about the coup in his later years. David Wilder said he believed that it was his father and also McWherter, together with Leech, who bore the largest burden of responsibility for the decision on that January day. As Democrats, these men had the most to lose, he suggested, and therefore showed the most courage.

"Daddy talked about it," he said. "You can imagine how this weighed on him. The Democrats who were in power at that time were the only ones who could allow this to happen. Alexander, not that he wanted to do it, didn't have the authority to do it by himself. All he had to say was yes. Daddy and Ned were being asked to be the judge and jury. If either one of them hadn't agreed, this wouldn't have happened.

"Here were two guys who were Democrats, but who set that totally aside. It had to be horrible for Ned and Daddy to do this, to allow the governor to be sworn in three days early. It had never occurred before, but they had to make that decision. They were uncomfortable, but they had to do what they thought was best for the people."

Leech's daughter Becca, who was a young teenager at the time, remembers her father talking about the Blanton episode then and later, sometimes using elements of the story to illustrate points he made "about corruption and integrity."

"I was thirteen, and at school it came up in current events, and my teachers knew he was involved," she remembered. "A lot of times he would talk about the politics of the situation. I remember him explaining to me what was going on. He didn't tell any details about himself and his own involvement beyond what was publicly known. He was always confidential about things—he was that kind of person—but he used everything as a learning opportunity. For me, it was a civics lesson."

Mike McWherter, the speaker's son and businessman who ran for governor himself in 2010, said the Blanton ouster was the act of a group of principled leaders who rose above partisanship. Their example of bipartisan cooperation, he suggested, could benefit elected officials in the present day, when many run away from the center and even condemn acts of compromise and cooperation.

"It was a situation where Democrats and Republicans came together and did the right thing—and a lesson that both parties could benefit from today."

THERE WAS ONE LONGER-TERM BENEFIT, relating to the new governor and the speakers, and it lasted eight years.

Alexander, McWherter, and Wilder would all hold their leadership positions throughout the new governor's two four-year terms, but until the day of the coup, Alexander did not know Wilder and McWherter well at all. As Fred Thompson observed later, in 2012, "we knew each other by reputation" but not personally. Alexander suggested later that during the rapid decision making on the afternoon of the coup, he and the speakers unexpectedly developed an essentially positive regard for each other. This, he suggested, helped make it possible for them to transact state business—and to overcome the occasional dispute—with a basic mutual respect.

"We had no previous relationship," Alexander explained. "I barely knew them. But in about three hours of discussion, we came up with a grand compromise. I wanted to show them I respected their prerogatives, that I wasn't going to be a 'rookie' governor and say 'I'm going to be inaugurated on such-and-such a date.' I was going to great pains to show respect to them.

"What happened, in those two or three hours, was that it started out with us being presented with the most difficult problem we would have to deal with in the next eight years. We found a way to deal with it, and we did it together. So we ended up with a compromise, and that formed a relationship that lasted eight years. We were able to have bipartisan legislative meetings every Tuesday morning, in the governor's office, and were able to work out our problems. I'm not sure I would have been able to forge the kind of relationship I had with them—for schools and roads and the auto industry and many other things—if I hadn't had that experience. At least, it gave me a leg up in terms of dealing with the Democratic world that was Nashville that otherwise wouldn't have been."

In the weeks following the coup, and apparently at McWherter's insistence, the Tennessee legislature passed new rules governing when a new governor should properly take office.

Two Nashville legislators—Representative Steve Cobb and Senator Douglas Henry—sponsored a simply worded bill stating that a new governor "shall take the oath of office on the first Saturday" after January 14 following his election.

Henry told me it was not his own idea. He said he did not remember it coming from Wilder either; he said the lieutenant governor, his senate speaker, never mentioned the coup to him afterward. Henry said it was more likely that Cobb had brought the measure to him, asking him simply to be the senate sponsor, as was customary since Henry was Cobb's senator.

Cobb said he also did not remember anyone requesting that he offer the new amending language, but he did not dispute my suggestion that it was probably Speaker McWherter who recommended the fix. He agreed that McWherter had felt that his party, the legislature, and the entire state had been embarrassed by the Blanton affair.

In any event, this corrective and clarifying measure for the future advanced very quickly in the 1979 legislative session. It was adopted by both houses of the general assembly without a single dissenting vote.

It seemed the powers that be were in agreement—wanting to put the difficult matter behind them, with finality, and wanting it never to happen again in their lifetimes.

EIGHT YEARS LATER, McWherter succeeded Alexander as governor, winning 54 percent of the vote over his Republican opponent, the former governor Winfield Dunn. This was the same landslide margin by which Alexander had defeated Butcher in 1978. This result for McWherter, however, masked a silent legacy of discontent among die-hard Blanton supporters in parts of rural West Tennessee. If not for the coup, these particular Democrats by 1986 might have been among McWherter's most ardent voters.

J. W. Luna, an attorney in Coffee County, was McWherter's field director in the 1986 campaign. He told me their private polling "showed 6 percent of the likely Democratic voters in the August primary 'strongly believe' that Governor Blanton should not have been removed from office." The McWherter campaign "systematically approached those people," Luna said.

"When Ned McWherter did what he did in 1979, it wouldn't have taken a rocket scientist to know some Democrats would be greatly disappointed in him," Luna said. "It was not an all-positive political maneuver. This was not an easy thing for a Democratic speaker of the house to do to a governor of his own party. It did have repercussions."

In a 2005 interview, McWherter, then in his seventy-fourth year, said: "I'm comfortable with what I did."

WILDER ENCOUNTERED SOME POLITICAL consequences much sooner.

He faced reelection to his senate seat the following year. Paul G. Summers, his campaign manager in 1980, recalled hearing some comments as he traveled with Wilder through his rural southwest Tennessee district, which included Blanton's hometown.

"There were some who were resentful, and there was no explaining it to them. I can remember, periodically on the campaign trail, driving up to a store, and we'd go in and get a polite reception—but it wasn't warm. That person probably wouldn't vote for a Republican, but he probably just wouldn't go to the polls and vote at all."

Soon after the coup, Blanton and his wife, Betty, divorced.

Eight years later, concerned about her welfare, Governor McWherter arranged for the former Mrs. Blanton to be hired in the Department of Labor. Luna had become the new commissioner of personnel, and he recalled a brief phone call from McWherter, asking him to make the arrangements.

"As long as I'm governor of this state," Luna quoted McWherter as saying, "no first lady is going to be destitute."

For all the participants, the coup was a task of way finding, of reluctance, and of each minding his own role, his own constituency. All except McWherter were attorneys by training; all understood the importance of the rule of law. They laid aside politics and partisanship, in the narrow meanings of those words, and took care of business.

And all were shaped by the experience, as were the lives of many other men and women who had even a brief role upon this stage.

Lamar Alexander left office as governor in January 1987, and, at Honey Alexander's suggestion, the couple and their four children moved to Australia for six months. Later that year, after their return, Alexander was appointed president of the University of Tennessee. He was named secretary of education by President George H. W. Bush in 1991 and ran for president twice himself, in 1996 and 2000. He was elected to the US Senate in 2002, and again in 2008, and served as chairman of the Senate Republican Conference. Like Kefauver's storied coonskin cap, Alexander's red-and-black plaid shirt became iconic in Tennessee's political history. At this writing, there are five Alexander grandchildren.

Victor Ashe served in the state senate until 1984, when he ran for the US Senate, losing to Albert Gore Jr. He was elected mayor of Knoxville in 1987 and served until 2003. The following year, he was appointed, by his former college roommate, to be the US ambassador to Poland.

Doug Bailey continued to consult with Alexander throughout his eight years as governor and also advised his later campaigns, as well as those of New Jersey governor Thomas Kean and Pennsylvania governor Richard Thornburgh. He and Deardourff closed their storied firm in 1987, and Bailey cofounded the *Hotline*, a bipartisan newsletter on politics and campaigns.

Howard Baker was the senior US senator from Tennessee until 1984, was strongly considered a presidential contender, and remains a towering figure in Tennessee political history. He was chief of staff to President Ronald Reagan from 1987 to 1988, and later ambassador to Japan. He is senior counsel to the law firm Baker, Donelson, Bearman, Caldwell, and Berkowitz. With his wife, the former Kansas senator Nancy Landon Kassebaum, Baker resides in tiny Huntsville, Tennessee, which he often called "the center of the known universe."

NELSON BIDDLE was Lieutenant Governor Wilder's top assistant for another year after the coup. Following his state government service, he worked as a lobbyist for a number of clients, including the Tennessee Municipal League. He lives in Maryville.

GENE BLANTON was convicted of two counts of highway construction bid rigging and also income tax evasion and served time in federal prisons in Texarkana, Arkansas, and Leavenworth, Kansas. On the tax count, the government claimed he had underpaid approximately $7,000. He claims that after his release he received a notice from the IRS stating he had subsequently *overpaid* (and was owed by the government) approximately $14,000. He currently lives in Middle Tennessee.

RAY BLANTON became the first governor of Tennessee ever convicted of a felony—specifically, extortion relating to the sale of liquor store licenses and mail fraud—and served twenty-two months in prison at Maxwell Air Force Base, in Alabama. (The verdict on the mail fraud counts was later reversed by an appeals court.) It was never determined what, if anything, Blanton might have personally known about the money that changed hands for clemencies he granted. He ran for public office one more time, following the death of Congressman Ed Jones in 1988, hoping to regain the seat in Congress he had relinquished in 1972, but he received only 7 percent of the votes cast, losing to John Tanner. Blanton was sixty-six years old when he died in 1996 of liver failure.

TOMMY BRAGG III, the young man who drove his father's boat on the afternoon in 1972 when Ned McWherter agreed to run for speaker of the house, was elected mayor of Murfreesboro, Tennessee, in 2002.

JAKE BUTCHER had been expected to run for governor again in 1982, but by then his East Tennessee banking empire was under a cloud of regulatory scrutiny. On November 1, 1982, as the Knoxville World's Fair he championed was closing its successful six-month run, which drew eleven million to his hometown, state and federal bank examiners raided the offices and twenty-nine branches of United American Bank and City and County Bank. Butcher was convicted on federal bank fraud charges in 1985 and was sentenced to twenty years in prison. He was paroled in 1992 and moved to Georgia.

CHRIS CLARK remained the news anchor of Nashville's CBS affiliate, WTVF-TV, until 2007, when he retired. He had become the longest-serving news anchor in the South. The following year, he joined the journalism faculty at Middle Tennessee State University.

LEW CONNER was appointed by Alexander in 1980 to a judgeship on the state court of appeals. He served until 1984 and left the bench contemplating a run for governor himself in 1986. He yielded instead to Dunn, who was defeated that year by McWherter.

GENTRY CROWELL continued to serve as Tennessee's secretary of state until his death. He was later implicated in another corruption scandal relating to state regulation of bingo games, a probe called Operation Rocky Top by the FBI. He committed suicide in 1989.

LEE WADDELL (LUCAS) CURTIS not only survived the transition from Blanton to Alexander but remained a state employee for thirty-three years. In her scrapbook at home, she keeps an unlikely pair of souvenirs from her time in Blanton's front office: a commemorative photo she received of the former governor with her family at the 1978 staff Christmas party, and the federal grand jury subpoena she received two months later.

LARRY DAUGHTREY continued as the senior political writer for the *Tennessean* until his semiretirement from the newspaper in 1997, and he continued to write a weekly column on politics and other topics for another ten years. He has a home in Nashville and a cabin on Center Hill Lake.

LEWIS DONELSON served in the Alexander cabinet through the first two years of the new governor's first term, as he had promised, and then returned to his Memphis-based international law firm. He has been an advocate for tax reform and continues to be involved in Republican politics.

AMON C. EVANS and his family sold the *Nashville Tennessean* to the Gannett Corporation in 1986 for a reported $52 million. He moved to Columbia, Tennessee, where he bought and rehabilitated Rattle and Snap, the historic home of a relative of President James K. Polk. Evans served as chairman of the committee overseeing the 1980s renovation of Tennessee's state capitol building. His final home was in Henry County, Tennessee, where he died in 2011.

DAVID FOX left the *Nashville Banner* staff in 1980 and joined Howard Baker's presidential campaign. He assisted Hank Hillin with his 1985 memoir of the Blanton Tennessee pardons case, *FBI Codename TENN-PAR: Tennessee's Ray Blanton Years*. In 1990, he joined with two other former journalists who had covered Blanton and the 1979 coup—former *Knoxville News-Sentinel* bureau chief Mark McNeely and the *Banner* political writer Mike Pigott—in the Nashville public relations firm called McNeely Pigott & Fox.

JIM FREE left McWherter's legislative staff in Nashville in January 1977 to join the White House congressional liaison team of President Jimmy Carter, but he remained an adviser, close friend, and trusted confidant throughout McWherter's life. After Carter's one term ended, Free founded an influential government relations firm in Washington DC. When McWherter died in 2011, Free and former congressman John Tanner were the only non–family members to serve as active pallbearers.

SHORTY FREELAND returned to Adamsville. He continued to insist that all charges against Blanton, including those for which he went to prison, were false. He blamed, instead, unnamed associates and overzealous investigators. In 2011, he published a personal memoir of his lifelong association with the late governor, titled *Ray Blanton and I*.

JOHN GISLER was transferred by the FBI to a post in Florida at the conclusion of the Blanton investigation in Tennessee. Now retired, he lives in the mountains of western North Carolina. For his work in Tennessee, he received a commendation from the bureau and a bonus check for $150.

DOUG HALL left the *Tennessean* in 1979 and joined the staff of the *Detroit Free Press*. He later was press secretary to US senator Jim Sasser, served in the Carter administration, and worked in private industry. He lives in North Carolina.

HAL HARDIN left the US attorney's office in 1981, and US Attorney General Griffin Bell praised him as "one of the best." Hardin told a reporter he never believed in the idea of a "career prosecutor" and that he was glad to be leaving. He returned to his private practice in civil and criminal law and held leadership posts in the legal profession—general counsel to the Tennessee Bar Association, board member of the National Association of Former US Attorneys—and never entered politics as a candidate. He also served on the board of the National Peace Corps Association and the national board of the American Board of Trial Advocates. Senator Alexander invited the Democrat Hardin to be his guest at President Obama's first State of the Union Address in 2009 and also to Obama's second inauguration, in 2013. Hardin continues to practice law in Nashville.

JOE HENRY served as chief justice of the Tennessee Supreme Court until his death, of a heart attack while jogging, in 1980. He was sixty-two years old when he died. In his hometown of Pulaski, Tennessee, Martin College hosts the annual Chief Justice Joe W. Henry Law Lecture. When the local National Guard armory was named in his honor, his son Joe Henry Jr. spoke at the dedication.

HANK HILLIN retired from the FBI in November 1980, two weeks after Blanton was indicted for conspiracy to solicit kickbacks and for income tax fraud. He continued to work for the bureau, as a consultant, as the government wrapped up the complex case dubbed "TENNPAR" (the agency's code name for its Tennessee pardons investigation), which he had lead during his active service. Hillin started a private investigative agency and, in 1985, published *FBI Codename TENNPAR: Tennessee's Ray Blanton Years*, his memoir of the bureau's Blanton investigation. He was elected sheriff of Davidson County in 1990, serving until 1994.

ROGER HUMPHREYS has not been seen since January 15, 1979, the night Blanton released him.

TRIPP HUNT left the attorney general's office to join the staff of the state's Board of Professional Responsibility, from which he retired in 2008. He had once considered becoming an Episcopal priest. In his fifties, he earned a PhD with a focus on ethics at the Vanderbilt divinity school. He was later the executive director of Common Cause in Tennessee.

TOM INGRAM served as deputy to the governor through Alexander's re-election in 1982, then moved to Knoxville as an executive with Whittle Communications and later was president of the Knoxville Chamber of Commerce. Involved in all of Alexander's subsequent campaigns, Ingram was the senator's chief of staff until 2009, when he returned to his political consulting business. He was the general consultant to the successful campaigns of US senators Fred Thompson and Bob Corker and of Tennessee governor Bill Haslam.

JOEL KAPLAN left the *Tennessean* in 1986 for the *Chicago Tribune*, where he covered city hall and was part of the *Tribune* investigative team that won the Pulitzer Prize in 1987. With master's degrees in journalism and law, he joined the faculty at Syracuse University in 1991 and is the associate dean of the S. I. Newhouse School of Public Communications. In 2011, he was appointed to a three-year term as ombudsman for the Corporation for Public Broadcasting.

JIM KENNEDY continued to serve as McWherter's top adviser until his own death, during a tennis match, in 1998. A competitive Democratic Party operative, he was a favorite of the capitol hill press corps for his accessibility, affable sense of humor, and deep knowledge of how who got to be where.

JOHN K. KING was sworn in on January 20, 1979, as commissioner of revenue for the state of Tennessee. Alexander later appointed him chairman of the Tennessee Housing Development Agency. In 1989 he returned to his law practice in Knoxville, and in 2009, Governor Phil Bredesen, a Democrat, appointed him to the Tennessee Ethics Commission. He still has season tickets to University of Tennessee football.

BILL KOCH was appointed commissioner of personnel in the new Alexander administration and was later counsel to the governor. In 1984, Alexander appointed Koch to the Tennessee court of appeals. In 2007,

Governor Phil Bredesen, a Democrat, appointed Koch to the Tennessee Supreme Court.

BILL LEECH served as Tennessee's attorney general for another five years and then returned to private law practice in Columbia and Nashville. He died of a stroke, at his home in Santa Fe, in 1996. On the day he was buried, St. Peter's Episcopal Church in Columbia was filled to capacity, and at the cemetery in Charlotte, a bagpiper played "Amazing Grace." The funeral procession was a mile long. Along the way, a farmer stopped his tractor and removed his cap, holding it over his heart respectfully as the line of cars moved solemnly down Highway 7 in Santa Fe. The state later named this road the Bill Leech Memorial Highway.

DONNA LEECH BROWN still lives in Santa Fe, Tennessee. Their son **WILL LEECH III** is a graduate of the University of Memphis School of Law. Bill's daughters **BECCA LEECH** and **KATIE LEECH** became teachers.

JACK LOWERY testified in 1981 in the clemency-for-cash trials of Blanton and Sisk, telling about the visit of "Bob Roundtree" five years earlier. He continues to practice law in Lebanon, Tennessee.

CAROL MARIN continued her work as a reporter and anchor at WSMV-TV but was not in Nashville when the coup occurred. In June 1978, she was hired by NBC News to report in Chicago and has had a celebrated career as a journalist. She writes a regular column for the Chicago *Sun-Times*.

HARLAN MATHEWS continued to serve as the state treasurer until 1987, when he was appointed deputy to Governor Ned McWherter. Five years later, when Senator Al Gore Jr. became Bill Clinton's vice-presidential running mate, McWherter appointed Mathews to serve the two years remaining in Gore's Senate term. In 1995, when the term expired, Mathews joined a Nashville law firm.

MARK MCNEELY, the Knoxville *News-Sentinel* capitol bureau chief, left the newspaper in 1980 to join US Senator Jim Sasser's staff. In 1982, he managed both Sasser's and the state supreme court's reelection campaigns. He became Senator Al Gore's first state director in 1983. He established a new public relations firm in 1987 in Nashville and was later joined by Mike Pigott and David Fox, two other reporters who had covered the 1979 coup.

NED MCWHERTER remained speaker of the house until 1986, when he was elected governor, succeeding Alexander, and he served the maximum two terms. He was a trusted adviser to President Bill Clinton, who appointed him to the board of the US Postal Service—some say as a way to get him to Washington more often for his advice. McWherter remained a popular public figure in Tennessee until his death, of cancer, in 2011. His memorial service in Nashville was attended by former senator Howard Baker and all the surviving participants in the 1979 coup. Clinton, Al Gore, and Billy Stair delivered the eulogies.

John M. Parish was the governor's press secretary through Alexander's two terms and remained in Nashville in retirement. He died in 2010.

Debby Patterson Koch became Alexander's deputy press secretary in the new administration. She later was an executive with Baptist Hospital in Nashville, chaired the Tennessee Arts Commission, and served on the Tennessee Higher Education Commission. She and Bill Koch married in 1985.

Mike Pigott left the *Nashville Banner* in 1988 to join McNeely in his public relations business. In 1994, Pigott took a leave of absence from the firm to serve as communications director in the gubernatorial campaign of Nashville Mayor Phil Bredesen.

Howell Raines became executive editor of the *New York Times* in 2001 and left the newspaper in 2003.

Peggy Reisser Winburne was a reporter at the *Nashville Banner* for another four years, covering the governor's office and the state senate. She left the *Banner* in 1983 for the Memphis *Commercial Appeal*.

Gene Roberts was Alexander's commissioner of the Department of Safety, overseeing the Tennessee Highway Patrol, until 1982. He returned to Chattanooga to run for mayor of his hometown and served four terms, leaving office in 1997. He was honored as "Mayor of the Year" in 1989 by the Tennessee Municipal League. He died in 2013.

John Seigenthaler was editor-in-chief of the *Tennessean* until 1986, when the Evans family sold the newspaper to the Gannett Corporation, whereupon Seigenthaler was named chairman, editor, and publisher. In 1982, he also became the first editorial page editor of Gannett's *USA Today* and served there for ten years. In 1986, at Middle Tennessee State University, an endowed chair in First Amendment studies was established in his name. Five years later, the Freedom Forum foundation established the John Seigenthaler Center at Vanderbilt University, housing the First Amendment Center.

Eddie Sisk was convicted of violating federal racketeering statutes for his role in the clemency-for-cash scandal. After serving time in the federal prison at Marion, Illinois, he returned to Nashville, where he was employed at a mattress store.

Lee Smith continued to publish the *Tennessee Journal* until 2005, when he sold his company, M. Lee Smith Publishers. He lives in Ponte Vedre, Florida, and Brentwood, Tennessee.

Fred Thompson completed the review of the Blanton clemencies four months after the coup and resumed his law practice in Nashville and

Washington, DC. In the 1985 MGM/United Artists film *Marie: A True Story* (based on the Peter Maas biography of Marie Ragghianti), Thompson played himself, launching his acting career in movies and television. He was elected to the US Senate in 1994, succeeding Harlan Mathews, and served until 2003. Thompson ran for president in 2008.

JIM TRAVIS left the ABC affiliate in Nashville the year following the coup and joined the staff of the NBC affiliate, WSM-TV, until he retired in 2001. He lives in Hickman County, west of Nashville, by the Piney River. He kept his reporter's notes from the Blanton years in the basement for more than thirty years. The notes were lost in the flood of 2010.

JOHN WILDER continued to serve as Tennessee's lieutenant governor until 2007, holding that post longer than any other in the state's history. As a licensed private pilot, he also continued to fly his twin-engine plane countless times between his home in Somerville, Tennessee, and Nashville. He left the state senate in January 2009 and died one year later.

TOM WISEMAN continued to serve as a judge of the US district court in Nashville and from 1984 to 1991 was chief judge for the Middle Tennessee District. He took senior judge status in 1995.

ED YARBROUGH, one of the attorneys who sued Alexander for stopping the release of prisoners commuted by Blanton, served as US attorney for the Middle District of Tennessee from 2007 to 2010. He was recommended for the position by Senator Lamar Alexander.

Timeline

November 1964	Ray Blanton elected to the Tennessee House of Representatives.
May 1965	Roger Humphreys marries Susan Garrett in Johnson City, Tennessee.
November 1966	Howard H. Baker elected to US Senate.
	Blanton elected to Congress.
January 1967	Lamar Alexander joins Baker's Senate staff.
November 1968	Richard Nixon elected President.
	John Wilder elected to the Tennessee Senate.
	Ned Ray McWherter elected to Tennessee House of Representatives.
January 1969	Alexander joins Nixon's congressional liaison staff.
August 1970	Alexander resigns his White House position and moves to Nashville to manage Winfield Dunn's general election campaign for governor.
November 1970	Winfield Dunn elected Governor.
	McWherter reelected to House.
January 1971	Wilder becomes Speaker of the Senate.
November 1972	Blanton loses Senate race to Baker.
January 1973	McWherter becomes Speaker of the House.
	Blanton leaves Congress.
April 1973	Roger and Susan Humphreys divorce.
May 1973	Humphreys kills Susan and also John Roger Scholl. Humphreys is soon arrested, charged with two counts of first-degree murder, and convicted. Begins serving a sentence of twenty to forty years.
April, 1974	Alexander announces his campaign for Governor.

AUGUST 1974	Nixon resigns.
	Joe Henry elected to Tennessee Supreme Court.
SEPTEMBER 1974	President Ford pardons Nixon.
NOVEMBER 1974	Blanton elected Governor, defeating Alexander.
JANUARY 1975	Blanton inaugurated. Appoints Eddie Sisk to be his legal counsel.
AUGUST 1975	State's Court of Criminal Appeals affirms Humphreys' murder conviction.
MAY 1976	"Bob Roundtree" visits lawyer Jack Lowery in Lebanon, Tennessee, and offers to help obtain the release of Lowery's client Will Midgett from state prison. The stranger states his services will cost $20,000.
	Lowery reports the encounter to the district attorney and also to Marie Ragghianti, state extradition officer. Lowery receives a call from Sisk, asking him to cooperate with the Tennessee Bureau of Investigation. Lowery writes a report and gives it to Ragghianti.
JUNE 1976	Blanton appoints Ragghianti chairman of the state Board of Pardons and Paroles.
AUGUST 1976	Jimmy Carter of Georgia receives nomination for President at Democratic National Convention in New York City.
OCTOBER 1976	Agents of the Federal Bureau of Investigation raid Sisk's office at the Tennessee state capitol. They confiscate records including 165 files from the state's Department of Correction, which runs Tennessee's prisons.
NOVEMBER 1976	Jimmy Carter elected President
	Al Gore Jr. and Jim Sasser elected to Congress from Tennessee.
	Sisk and members of the state Board of Pardons and Paroles receive subpoenas to testify before a federal grand jury in Nashville. They are questioned about possible corruption in commutation decisions.
JANUARY 1977	Baker, now the Senate Republican Leader, invites Alexander to organize his new office. The Alexanders move back to Washington.
FEBRUARY 1977	Second grand jury convenes in Chattanooga.
JUNE 1977	James Earl Ray and six other prisoners escape from Tennessee's Brushy Mountain Prison. All are captured within three days.

JULY, 1977	Hal Hardin appointed US Attorney for Middle Tennessee by President Carter.
AUGUST 1977	Blanton fires Ragghianti from her post as chairman of the Board of Pardons and Paroles.
SEPTEMBER 1, 1977	Lee Smith discovers Roger Humphreys in downtown Nashville, working as a photographer for the state tourism office. Smith reports this fact, and other newspaper and TV journalists report Humphreys' work-release status.
SEPTEMBER 15, 1977	Blanton, in a live-broadcast TV interview, tells reporter Carol Marin that he intends to pardon Humphreys.
JANUARY 1978	Alexander announces he will run again for governor.
FEBRUARY 1978	State legislature's House of Representatives passes resolution urging Blanton to recant his pledge to pardon Humphreys.
AUGUST 1978	Jake Butcher wins Democratic nomination for governor. Alexander wins Republican nomination.
	William M. Leech Jr. appointed Attorney General by Tennessee Supreme Court.
SEPTEMBER 1978	Alexander announces creation of "The Committee to be Heard" to collect a million signatures statewide opposing the Humphreys pardon.
OCTOBER 1978	Blanton announces he has reconsidered and will not pardon Humphreys. Alexander campaign responds that the petition campaign will be stopped.
NOVEMBER 7, 1978	Alexander defeats Butcher.
NOVEMBER 17, 1978	Blanton tells reporters he has decided to pardon Humphreys after all.
DECEMBER 15, 1978	FBI agents arrest three Blanton aides, including Sisk at his state capitol office, and seize cash and documents relating to clemency cases.
DECEMBER 18, 1978	Blanton served with subpoena to testify before the federal grand jury investigating the clemency scandal.
	State Senator Victor Ashe sends a letter to Attorney General requesting opinion on whether a governor-elect can be sworn in before the formal inauguration.
JANUARY 3, 1979	Attorney General's office sends letter to Ashe opining that a governor-elect may be sworn in as early as 12:01 a.m. January 16.
JANUARY 5, 1979	Blanton confirms he has been informed he is now a target of a federal investigation.

JANUARY 11, 1979	Blanton family moves out of the official residence.
JANUARY 13, 1979	Attorney General's January 3 letter is made public. News coverage of the possibility Blanton's successor might be sworn in early.
JANUARY 15, 1979	Blanton signs commutations for fifty-two state prisoners, including Roger Humphreys.
	Correction Commissioner Murray Henderson delivers the Humphreys paperwork to the Tennessee State Prison. Humphreys departs the prison.
JANUARY 16, 1979	Second opinion letter issued by Attorney General.
JANUARY 17, 1979	FBI agent informs US Attorney Hal Hardin that more commutations are being prepared for Blanton's signature before he leaves office on January 20.
	Hardin phones Alexander, asking him to take office early.
	Afternoon of secret deliberations involving McWherter, Wilder, Leech, Hayes Cooney and Bill Koch, Hardin, and Alexander.
	Agreement is reached. Koch visits Chief Justice Joe Henry at home, asks him to administer the oath of office to Alexander.
	News media are alerted.
	Henry administers the oath to Alexander at 5:55 p.m., with McWherter, Wilder, and Leech present.
	Alexander's men secure the capitol building. Donelson tells Blanton he cannot return to the capitol.
	Koch instructs Correction Department officials they should not deliver Blanton clemency documents to prisons until further notice.
	Fred Thompson begins duty as Special Counsel to the Governor, sorting out which of the Blanton-issued clemencies are valid.
JANUARY 20, 1979	Alexander takes oath the second time, also administered by Henry.

POSTSCRIPT

A Note on Sources

The people we meet in our lives come to us at different moments, often by chance, and yet each unexpected one helps to shape the larger narrative. Had any of them not come along when they did, your own story and mine might have worked out very differently. Had we chosen to walk through that door and not this one, turned down this street and not that, the journey would surely have led to another place.

If not for my father, Sherman McKeel Hunt Jr., who was an elected official in Nashville in my teen years, I may never have known the congressman Dick Fulton, the lawyer George Barrett, or the editor John Seigenthaler. It was later Seigenthaler who led me to Bill Willis, Bill Kovach, Larry Daughtrey, John Hemphill, and Tom Ingram—who connected me with Lamar Alexander—who then linked me to Lew Conner, Lewis Donelson, Ted Welch, Lewis Lavine, and Fred Thompson—and, in due course, to Ned McWherter and John Wilder and their circles.

Had I not taken that summer job after high school, working in the 1966 Hooker campaign for governor (to the deep consternation of my father, a Clement man) I may never have met Hal Hardin, Larry Woods, Frank Woods, Charles Bone, and thence Sam Hatcher or J. Houston Gordon.

It happens to us all, these small serendipities that in time become large.

If Alexander had become a Rhodes Scholar in 1962, as he had hoped, and not gone instead to New York University law school, he surely would not have been in the registration line that day when he met a tall Georgetown graduate standing next to him named Paul Tagliabue. If Hal Hardin had not attended law school in Knoxville when he did, in 1966, he would not have had a housemate named Eddie Sisk.

What if Tom Ingram had not climbed onto that Howard Baker campaign bus in 1968, the day he met Alexander? If Jim Free of Columbia had gone anywhere to college but Middle Tennessee State University, an hour up the road, would he ever have known Representative John Bragg of Murfreesboro and the political science professor David Grubbs? It was Grubbs who recommended that Free apply, with Bragg's sponsorship, for a legislative internship in Nashville—and that's where he met McWherter and, through him, would come to know Jimmy Carter.

Had I not gone to work as a cub reporter at the *Nashville Tennessean* in 1967—learning about writing and politics under Seigenthaler's editorship—I might not have covered the governor's race three years later, nor the one four years after that. That's how it happened, one evening in Memphis in 1974, that Ingram introduced me to Alexander for an interview. Later that same summer, had I not gone to graduate school in Washington—and, coincidentally, if Elaine Shannon had not left our bureau there to take a job with *Newsweek*—I could not have been my newspaper's Washington correspondent that year. That's when I met Senator Howard Baker and his staff members A. B. Culvahouse, Bill Hamby, and Ron McMahan.

In even deeper time, what if Congressman "Fats" Everett had never met a young man named Ned McWherter and not hired him to be his driver? What if Ray Blanton had never known Jim Allen or Frank Humphreys, Roger's father? What if President Gerald Ford, when they asked him to pardon Nixon, had just said no? These alternate futures we cannot know.

But I do know this: Had it not been for my ten years at the *Tennessean*—as reporter, editorial writer, Washington correspondent, city editor—I doubt I would have gotten that phone call from my friend Tom Ingram, on a summer afternoon in 1977, saying Alexander wanted to have dinner with me. He wanted to talk about joining his team for a new campaign the next year, and if it were OK by me he next would phone Seigenthaler and clear it with him. It was OK by me, and he did, and I went.

Because of all this, there are places in the pages of this book where I cannot help but appear.

There are uses of the expression " . . . told me" in the text, because in those instances a participant made his or her observations in a personal interview with me. In many of these cases, I knew the interviewee as a colleague or friend during the period of this story.

In Chapter 7, I tell about the *Tennessean* and its behavior in the late 1960s and 1970s because I grew up there in those tumultuous years, starting when I was eighteen years old. In Chapter 2, with its description of how the newspaper staffed its coverage of so many candidates in the 1974 primary, I was part of that statewide team, assigned to Memphis. Likewise, in Chapter 3, when the ideas of the walk across Tennessee and the red-and-black plaid shirt were first discussed in Alexander's den, I was present. In the months that followed, I was involved in the detailed planning of the walk, the rest of the 1978 campaign, and the subsequent transition process that preceded the January coup. When Speaker McWherter later made a rare derisive comment about Alexander having "a bunch of essay writers" on his governor's staff, I was proudly one of them.

I should report here that on the day of the coup, I was not only caught unawares like most of the Alexander people, but I was also not present at the supreme court building when this high drama reached its climax that evening. This is because I was on the Vanderbilt campus every Wednesday during this period helping teach a 4:00 p.m. public policy seminar about the Tennessee Valley Authority, with my former *Tennessean* colleague and friend Nat Caldwell. I learned that the coup had happened only when I stopped by the Crestmoor Road transition office on my way home. Tom Beasley, one of Alexander's state campaign cochairs, was sitting there alone in front of a television set. He looked a little stunned at whatever was on the screen. When I walked in, he looked up at me and said, "Do you know what's happened?" I did not.

I was, however, part of the scramble that unfolded over the next few days. I attended the Alexander inauguration on Saturday morning, and I went to the capitol on Sunday evening to learn where my new office would be.

I tell you all this because it leads to the question of "objectivity" and how I have studied the coup and told the story.

I am neither an academic nor a trained historian. Rather, I was an eyewitness to some things and have had extraordinary access to other individuals who saw and heard even more. It is helpful to remember that the coup occurred in the time between letters and email, and hence there is little documentary record of what was said in the weeks leading up to coup, in the fast-moving events of the fateful day, and in the days and weeks that followed. We must rely therefore on memory, the recollections of what the principals did and what they and others remember. This is why the personal interviews with 163 individuals proved to be so valuable.

I have tried in these pages to be both honest and fair, and I acknowledge my own subjectivity. I have been shaped by the people I have known and learned from. I admit, in particular, to both fondness and awe of my old bosses John Seigenthaler and Lamar Alexander. It has been a quarter century since I was last employed by Alexander, and thirty-five years since I worked in Seigenthaler's newsroom. This passage of time has, I hope, given me perspective on them, their records, and the meaning of the coup.

IN THE PROCESS OF conducting 163 interviews, beginning in 1997, I have been struck by the strength and resilience of central shared memories among the principals, some now in their eighties and nineties. As rapidly as things had to happen on that long ago Wednesday, the event itself was a frightful, nerve-wracking one, the decision fraught with anxiety and uncertainty, powered by adrenaline, burdened by fatigue, accompanied by fear and trepidation. All this seems to have combined to sear the "swift and secret coup" in their memories. Whether they were Democrats or Republicans, elected officials or staff members, politicians or journalists, their common recollections dovetailed to a surprising degree. In only a few cases did I encounter an interviewee with a point of view significantly at variance with the shared memory of the event that happened so long ago.

But some of the limits of memory are self-imposed. I was disappointed that I was unable to persuade more of the original Blanton family members and partisans to come forward, though there were important exceptions. Perhaps most surprising was the willingness of Gene Blanton, brother of the late governor, and of Eddie Sisk, the former legal counsel, to talk with me. Both were understandably apprehensive at first but then generous with their time and candid though guarded in their recollections. Both had served their respective prison sentences, yet both were still of strong opinion that their governor's early ouster had been unnecessary. I also enjoyed one long conversation with Shorty Freeland, who had been the coordinator of Governor Blanton's infamous patronage apparatus during the time of its power.

I also spoke with Tom Benson, who as Blanton's cabinet member in charge of the Department of Economic and Community Development, managed the administration's unquestionable successes in agricultural exports and international business recruiting; with Brooks Parker, the former press secretary; and with Betty Chiles Nixon, who had been the deputy press secretary at the end. Commissioner Benson and Ms. Nixon were especially generous with their time and helpful in recalling the accomplishments of the Blanton administration, as well as their personal perspectives on its unraveling at the end.

But others would not talk to me. For these, as with Gene, Eddie, and Shorty, my intention was truly not to dredge up painful old memories—especially for Gene, now the important elder of the family. It did not interest me to rehash the old arguments and defenses, but instead I was interested in knowing simply what was going on in their private lives, and in the lives of the other Blanton intimates, as their public world turned upside down on that cold January night.

Two participants in the events told me they were working on their own books. One was former FBI agent Hank Hillin.

Early in his retirement, Hillin had put down his version of the larger Blanton story in a book that I list in the bibliography. But now, when I asked him about additional details, he was dismissive of anyone else trying to tell the story that he seems to consider his alone. His evasiveness did not seem to be tied to his duty to confidentiality as a retired agent of the FBI (which I expected) but rather to a preference to hold back additional details for a second book.

In my one phone interview with Shorty Freeland, he shared with me that he was in the process of compiling his own memoir of the Blanton governorship. He told me he had been working occasionally with a journalist from the *Jackson Sun* who assisted him by tape-recording his statements for transcription, but that he had come to an obstacle in his project: he told me he was torn over "how much to tell" about what happened "in those last three days." Shorty then suggested that I come to Adamsville to talk, and I accepted his invitation. In the end he never returned my calls to set up a time.

Shorty did finish his book, *Ray Blanton and I*. Its chief purpose, he explains in its pages, was to raise money for a memorial to Governor Blanton in Adamsville, the town they both came from. As for any of those secrets he alluded to in our phone conversation, from his memory of their last week in office, Shorty's book is unfortunately silent.

My aim in writing this story has not been to glorify or disparage any person, nor to make any participant seem evil or heroic. Even toward Ray Blanton, I think of the concluding lines from *The Great Gatsby*, when Fitzgerald's Nick says of Tom Buchanan: "I couldn't forgive him or like him, but I saw that what he had done was, to him, entirely justified. It was all very careless and confused. They were careless people."

My purpose in the preceding pages has been to tell how the coup itself unfolded, with enough context so that a reader three decades later might appreciate why it happened in the way that it did—and how the unprecedented decision was shaped by personality, history, politics, selflessness, and courage. These fundamental elements of humanity are central to an understanding of this tale.

Over the course of this project, I have been most absorbed by what had previously shaped the lives and characters of the men involved in the coup. The elements of their respective biographies—where they came from, by what diverse paths they had traveled to be in their positions of power, what traditions and fears and sense of duty they each brought to the day of decision, from very different backgrounds—all of this formed their thinking in the decisive final moments.

Some might say the coup was un-American. It has happened only once, this one time in Tennessee, and nowhere else in the United States. There was no road map to guide the men who participated in it. In truth, none of them wanted to go there. Yet they worked through their long day in a very American way, with a deep regard for democratic traditions and the law, and with a way of cooperating across party lines that is so atypical of many politicians in our present day.

Sources

The Interviews

Honey Alexander
Senator Lamar Alexander
Sue Allison
Ambassador Victor Ashe
Doug Bailey
J. B. Baker
George E. Barrett
Trooper Ed Beckman
Commissioner Tom Benson
Nelson Biddle
Gene Blanton
Charles W. Bone
Leonard Bradley
Chancellor Robert S. Brandt
Governor Phil Bredesen
Donna Leech Brown
Judge John P. Brown
Richard Chapman
Chris Clark
Judge Frank G. Clement Jr.
Representative Steve Cobb
Judge Lew Conner
Chief Deputy Attorney General
   C. Hayes Cooney
Justice Robert E. Cooper
Attorney General Robert E.
   Cooper Jr.
Ed Cromer
Brooks Crowell
A. B. Culvahouse Jr.
Lee Waddell (Lucas) Curtis
Larry Daughtrey

Mayor Karl Dean
Representative Lois DeBerry
Randall Dickerson
Bruce Dobie
Mike Donegan
Commissioner Lewis R. Donelson
Governor Winfield Dunn
Ron Eberhardt
Commissioner Jane G. Eskind
Jack Faris
Mike Fitts, FAIA
David B. Fox
Jim Free
O. H. (Shorty) Freeland
Senator Tom Garland
Commissioner Bill Gibbons
Frank Gibson
Agent John Gisler
Commissioner Dave Goetz
Congressman Bart Gordon
J. Houston Gordon
Vice President Al Gore
Commissioner Francis S. Guess
Doug Hall
James E. Hall
Mary Hance
William L. Harbison
US Attorney Hal Hardin
Estie Harris
Aubrey B. Harwell Jr.
Speaker Beth Harwell
Sam Hatcher

Betty Haynes
Faye Head
Senator Douglas Henry
Commissioner Jim Henry
Joseph W. Henry Jr.
Judy Hill
Agent Henderson (Hank) Hillin
John Jay Hooker Jr.
Tom Humphrey
Assistant Attorney General
    William W. (Tripp) Hunt III
Martha R. Ingram
Tom Ingram
Commissioner Billy L. Jones
Joel Kaplan
Trooper David Keck
Sam Kennedy
Trooper Denny King
Commissioner John K. King
Commissioner Matt Kisber
Debby Patterson Koch
Justice William C. Koch
Judge Walter C. Kurtz
C. Lewis Lavine
Marc F. Lavine
Becca Leech
Katie Leech
William M. Leech III
Rick Locker
Mayor B. F. (Jack) Lowery Sr.
Commissioner J. W. Luna
Judge John Jared Maddux Jr.
Commissioner David Manning
Carol Marin
Janice Mashburn
Senator Harlan Mathews
Bruce McCarty
Doug McCarty
Mark McNeely
Mike McWherter
Governor Ned McWherter

Senator Carl Moore
Bob Mueller
Ben Murphy
Speaker Jimmy Naifeh
Roy Neel
Betty Chiles Nixon
James A. O'Hara III
Charles L. Overby
Ann Marie Deer Owens
Brooks Parker
Virginia Parker
Courtney N. Pearre
Carl A. Pierce
Mike Pigott
Wendell Potter
Molly Leach Pratt
Madelyn B. Pritchett
Mayor Bill Purcell
Howell H. Raines
Ken Renner
Kenneth L. Roberts
S. H. (Bo) Roberts
Senator Bob Rochelle
Representative J. Stanley Rogers
Karl Schledwitz
Fred Sedahl
John L. Seigenthaler
John Michael Seigenthaler
Carole Sergent
T. Edward Sisk
Cleve Smith
M. Lee Smith
Billy Stair
Tom Sterritt
Attorney General Paul G. Summers
Frank Sutherland
Congressman John S. Tanner
Assistant Attorney General
    Michael E. Terry
Senator Fred Thompson
Jim Travis

Commissioner Charles A. Trost

Karl VanDevender, MD

James M. Weaver

Judge David Welles

E. W. (Bud) Wendell

Ken Whitehouse

Sharon Sinclair Wiggs

David Wilder

J. Shelton Wilder

Allen Williams

Susan Richardson Williams

Carole Martin Willis

Peggy Reisser Winburne

Trooper Herchel Winstead

Judge Tom Wiseman

Frank A. Woods

Larry D. Woods

Edward M. Yarbrough

Acknowledgments

Beyond the interviews, the following individuals were of particular help to me in compiling the available information to tell the larger story of the coup. These, in sundry ways, provided me with essential support by connecting me to colleagues, relatives (or memories of their relatives), family photographs, journals, and other documents and private records.

I am especially grateful to the principals in this story who have survived, and to the relatives of the larger number who have not, for sharing their recollections, keepsake records, and remembered comments that have helped me to tell and also illustrate this tale. Hal Hardin produced many enlightening documents, contemporary notes, and pictures from his home and office files. Bill Koch has been an especially helpful and patient guide through the legal context of decisions made during the week of January 15, 1979. Honey and Lamar Alexander walked with me through the collected photographs, memoranda, and memorabilia from their storied journey. Mike McWherter graciously invited me to visit his late father's homes in Dresden and Paris, Tennessee. Donna Leech Brown entrusted me with treasured snapshots of Bill Leech's private life on his beloved farm in Santa Fe and introduced me to his children. David Wilder drove halfway across the state to bring me the tattered old family scrapbook that his mother faithfully kept of photos and news clippings from her husband's long career in public life. The brothers Joe Henry Jr. and Bob Henry in Pulaski proudly shared memories and photos of their distinguished father.

In the list below, I acknowledge the help of all these gracious women and men for their good assistance. Of course, any error in interpretation of all this data that might appear in the preceding pages is mine alone.

Darrell Akins, Akins Crisp Public Strategies, Oak Ridge
Robert Allison, Bell Buckle, Tennessee
Sue Allison, Smithville, Tennessee
Barbara Baier, Tennessee Tech University, Cookeville
Karen Barnes, Law Office of Hal Hardin, Nashville

Charles W. Bone, Bone McAllester Norton PLLC, Nashville and
  Hendersonville
Beverly Burnett, *Tennessean* Library, Nashville
Gay Campbell, First Amendment Center, Freedom Forum, Nashville
Lew Conner, Nashville
Ed Cromer, M. Lee Smith Publishers LLC, Brentwood, Tennessee
Brooks Crowell, Lebanon, Tennessee
Frank Daniels III, Nashville
David Dickey, Adamsville, Tennessee
Susan Dulin, Office of Justice William C. Koch, Tennessee Supreme Court,
  Nashville
Kay Durham, Office of Senator Lamar Alexander, Nashville
Marcille Durham, Ingram Group, Nashville
John Egerton, Nashville
Karen Gatewood, Buchanan, Tennessee
Van Grafton, Perspective Films, Nashville
Tom Griscom, Chattanooga
Sam Hatcher, Lebanon, Tennessee
Faye Head, Office of Senator Lamar Alexander, Nashville
Joseph W. Henry, Jr. Henry, Henry, and Underwood, Pulaski, Tennessee
Robert C. Henry, Henry, Henry, and Underwood, Pulaski, Tennessee
Kem Hinton, FAIA, Tuck-Hinton Architects, Nashville
Shawn H. Hunt, AIA, Glenview, Illinois
Tom Kanon, Tennessee State Library and Archives, Nashville
Debby Patterson Koch, Nashville
Justice William C. Koch, Nashville
Bill Kovach, former Washington bureau chief, *New York Times*, and former
  editor, *Atlanta Journal-Constitution*.
Fred Marcum, Baker, Donelson, Bearman, Caldwell, and Berkowitz,
  Huntsville, Tennessee
Harlan Mathews, Farris Mathews Bobango, Nashville and Memphis
Candy McAdams, director, Ned R. McWherter Weakley County Library,
  Dresden, Tennessee
Doug McCarty, McCarty Holsaple McCarty, Knoxville
Mike McWherter, Jackson, Tennessee
William P. Morelli, Ingram Industries, and past president, Tennessee Historical
  Society, Nashville
Bobbie Murphy, Office of Fred Thompson, Nashville
Beth Odle, Special Collections Division, Nashville Public Library
James A. O'Hara III, Washington, DC
Ann Marie Deer Owens, Vanderbilt University, Nashville
Courtney N. Pearre, Amerigroup Tennessee, Nashville

Carl A. Pierce, Howard H. Baker Jr. Center for Public Policy, University of
     Tennessee, Knoxville
Mike Pigott, McNeely Pigott & Fox, Nashville
James Pratt, Pratt Government Strategies, Nashville
Molly Leach Pratt, Pratt Government Strategies, Nashville
Madelyn B. Pritchett, Dresden, Tennessee
Jay Richiuso, Tennessee State Library and Archives, Nashville
Mrs. Gene Roberts, Chattanooga
Ricky Rogers, *Tennessean* Library, Nashville
Nancy Russell, Office of Senator Douglas Henry, Nashville
Gray Sasser, Nashville
Robin L. Satyshur, Nashville
John L. Seigenthaler, Nashville
Tammy Shonting, Law Office of Hal Hardin, Nashville
Billy Stair, Stair Public Affairs, Knoxville
Frank Sutherland, Brentwood, Tennessee
Stephanie R. Taylor, Bone McAllester Norton PLLC, Nashville
Carol Tippins, assistant director, Ned R. McWherter Weakley County Library,
     Dresden, Tennessee
Troy Tomlinson, Sony/ATV Music Publishing, Nashville
Katy Varney, McNeely Pigott & Fox, Nashville
Celia S. Walker, Vanderbilt University Libraries, Nashville
Beth Welch, Office of the Chancery Court Clerk and Master, Metropolitan
     Nashville–Davidson County
James W. White, Jones, Hawkins, and Farmer PLC, Nashville
David Wilder, Somerville, Tennessee
Saralee Terry Woods, BookManBookWoman, Nashville
Edward M. Yarbrough, Walker, Tipps, and Malone PLC, Nashville

Bibliography

Abramson, Rudy, and Jean Haskell, editors. *Encyclopedia of Appalachia*. University of Tennessee Press, 2006.

Alexander, Lamar. *Six Months Off: An American Family's Australian Adventure*. William Morrow, 1988.

Alexander, Lamar. *Steps Along the Way: A Governor's Scrapbook*. Thomas Nelson, 1986.

Annis, James Lee, Jr. *Howard Baker: Conciliator in an Age of Crisis*. University of Tennessee Press, 2007.

"An Award for Gov. Blanton" (editorial). *Time*, January 22, 1979.

Baker, Jackson. "John Wilder's Fellow Citizens Bid Him Adieu." *Memphis Flyer* (Contemporary Media), January 4, 2010.

Berkow, Ira. *Red: A Biography of Red Smith*. University of Nebraska Press, 2007.

Bennett, Andy D. "Building Justice," *Tennessee Bar Journal*, November 2012, Tennessee Bar Association.

Carey, Bill. *Fortunes, Fiddles, and Fried Chicken: A Nashville Business History*. Tennessee Heritage Library. Hillsboro Press (Providence House), 2000.

Clement, Judge Frank G., Jr. "Chief Justice Joe W. Henry Law Lecture." April 8, 2010, Martin Methodist College, Pulaski, Tennessee.

Congressional Record—Senate, vol. 153, pt. 6 (March 26, 2007) pp. 3742–44.

Cooper, Robert E., Jr. "Remarks to the Tennessee Supreme Court Historical Society Annual Dinner, October 20, 2009." *Chronicle, Newsletter of the Tennessee Supreme Court Historical Society*, Fall 2010, pp. 2, 11.

Council of State Governments. "Impeachments and Removals of Governors," *State Government News*, February 2004, p. 7.

Crockett, David, and Richard Penn Smith. *Col. Crockett's Exploits and Adventures in Texas*. T. K. and P. G. Collins (Philadelphia), 1837.

Dobie, Bruce. "Stop the Presses, 1876–1998." *Nashville Scene* (City Press), February 19, 1998.

Dobie, Bruce. "With Ned Ray McWherter's Death, the Chapter Closes on the Age of the Rural Southern Democrat—The Last Common Man." *Nashville Scene* (City Press), April 7, 2001.

Donelson, Lewis R., III. *Lewie*. Rhodes College, 2012.

Dunn, Winfield. *From a Standing Start: My Tennessee Political Odyssey*. Magellan Press, 2007.

Ebert, Roger. "Marie: A True Story." *Chicago Sun-Times*, October 18, 1985.

Freeland, Shorty. *Ray Blanton and I*. Ottis H. "Shorty" Freeland and the HillHelen Group, 2011

"Going Free in Tennessee" (editorial). *Time*, January 29, 1979.

Gore, Albert. *The Eye of the Storm*. Herder and Herder, 1970.

Gorman, Joseph Bruce. *Kefauver: A Political Biography.* Oxford University Press, 1971.

Halberstam, David. *The Children.* Ballantine (Random House), 1999.

"The Halting and Fitful Battle for Integration," *Life,* vol. 41, no. 12 (September 17, 1956).

Hardin, Hal. "A Day in the Life of a Country Lawyer." *Tennessee Law Review* (special issue: *In Memoriam, William M. Leech, Jr.*), vol. 64, no. 1 (Fall 1996), pp. xi–xxiv.

Hatcher, Sam. "Lebanon's Gentry Crowell Explains His Pardon Role." *Lebanon Democrat,* January 16, 1979.

Higgins, Thomas A. "Our Friend of Happy Memory." *Tennessee Law Review* (special issue: *In Memoriam, William M. Leech, Jr.*), vol. 64, no. 1 (Fall 1996), pp. xiii–xiv.

Hillin, Henderson, with David B. Fox, editor. *FBI Codename TENNPAR: Tennessee's Ray Blanton Years.* Pine Hall Press, 1985.

Hinton, Kem G. *A Long Path: The Search for a Tennessee Bicentennial Landmark.* Hillsboro Press, 1997.

Ingram, Martha Rivers, with D. B. Kellogg. *Apollo's Struggle: A Performing Arts Odyssey in the Athens of the South, Nashville, Tennessee.* Hillsboro Press (Providence Publishing), 2004.

Key, V. O., Jr. *Southern Politics.* Vintage Books (Alfred A. Knopf and Random House), 1949.

King, Colbert I. "Origins of a Vitriolic Keynote Speaker." *Washington Post,* September 11, 2004.

Koch, Bill, et al., editors. "Three Days Early—The Role of Lawyers in the Early Swearing-In of Governor Lamar Alexander on January 17, 1979" (Harry Phillips American Inn of Court, program presented on January 18, 2005).

Koch, William C., Jr. "They Were Tennesseans First." *Nashville Bar Journal,* vol. 7, no. 2 (March 2007), pp. 8–14.

Locker, Rick, and Stephen G. Tompkins. "From Plow to State Pinnacle: The Ascent of Ned McWherter." *Commercial Appeal* (Scripps-Howard Newspaper Group), October 21, 1980.

Maas, Peter. *Marie: A True Story.* Random House, 1985.

"Pardon Me, Ray." *Newsweek,* January 29, 1979.

Parish, John. *You Should Write a Book.* Unpublished manuscript.

Peebles, Thomas H., III. "Personal Insights into Bill Leech." *Tennessee Law Review* (special issue: *In Memoriam, William M. Leech, Jr.*), vol. 64, no. 1 (Fall 1996), pp. xx–xxii.

Pierce, Carl A. "The Tennessee Supreme Court and the Struggle for Independence, Accountability, and Modernization, 1974–1998." In *A History of the Tennessee Supreme Court,* ed. Theodore Brown Jr., University of Tennessee Press, 2002.

Pigott, Mike. "Controversy Doesn't Faze Leech." *Nashville Banner,* March 10, 1981.

"The Press: The Fighting Tennessean." *Time,* September 14, 1962.

Rayburn, Ted, and Steven S. Harman. "Visionaries and Vanguards: Lamar Alexander." Videotape interview. *Tennessean* (Gannett), April 9, 2012.

Rawlins, Bill. *Tennessee's Blanton Years: A Political Biography.* Red Desert Publishers, 2001.

Rawlins, Bill. *The McWherter Years: Tennessee Comes of Age.* Red Desert Publishers, 2001.

Reedy, George E. *The Twilight of the Presidency.* Signet, 1970.

Robins, Lisa. "Deep Roots, Strong Tree." *Vanderbilt Magazine,* Spring 2010.

Senate Joint Resolution 62, "A Resolution to Reflect on the Life and Accomplishments of Former Tennessee Attorney General and Reporter William M. Leech, Jr., and Honor His Memory," filed for introduction on February 20, 1997, by Keith Jordan.

Senate Joint Resolution 688, "A Resolution to Honor the Memory of Judge Paul Reeves Summers," filed for introduction on January 22, 2004, by John Wilder.

Squires, James D. *The Secrets of the Hopewell Box: Stolen Elections, Southern Politics, and a City's Coming of Age.* Times Books (Random House), 1996.

Stair, Billy. *McWherter: The Life and Career of Ned McWherter.* Stair Public Affairs, 2011.

Tardiff, Justin. "Q&A with Sen. Lamar Alexander." *InsideVandy.com*, October 17, 2009.

Tennessee Blue Book, 1971–1972. Secretary of State, State of Tennessee.

Tennessee Blue Book, 1979–1980. Secretary of State, State of Tennessee.

The Tennessee Encyclopedia of History and Culture. Carroll Van West, editor-in-chief, Tennessee Historical Society. Rutledge Hill Press, 1998.

Tennessee Journal. M. Lee Smith and Associates, September 5, 1977.

Tennessee State Library and Archives. "Governor (Leonard) Ray Blanton Papers 1975–1979"

Trost, Charles A. "Ten Lessons on Life and the Law I Learned from Bill Leech." *Tennessee Law Review* (special issue: *In Memoriam, William M. Leech, Jr.*), vol. 64, no. 1 (Fall 1996), pp. xxii–xxiv.

Van der Linden, F. Robert. *Airlines and Air Mail: The Post Office and the Birth of the Commercial Aviation Industry.* University Press of Kentucky, 2002.

York, Max. "Where Hal Hardin Got Off the Boat." *Nashville Tennessean*, March 7, 1965.

Index

Page numbers in **bold** refer to photographs.